8.61

Essay I

P9-CKL-922

GP8-27-69

MAR 22 '68

# INVITATION TO

# *Learning*

# INVITATION TO

# *Learning*

HUNTINGTON CAIRNS

ALLEN TATE

MARK VAN DOREN

THE NEW HOME LIBRARY

*New York*

COPYRIGHT, 1941, BY THE COLUMBIA BROADCASTING SYSTEM, INC.
COPYRIGHT IN CANADA, 1941, BY THE COLUMBIA BROADCASTING SYSTEM, INC.

THE NEW HOME LIBRARY EDITION PUBLISHED SEPTEMBER, 1942

THE NEW HOME LIBRARY, 14 West Forty-ninth Street
New York, N. Y.

CL

MANUFACTURED IN THE UNITED STATES OF AMERICA

# Contents

*Contents*

# PREFACE

GENERATION after generation has found pleasure in discussing the books that form the subject of this volume. They are the books that have nourished Western thought—some of them for more than two thousand years. It is scarcely necessary to say that their vitality lies in their pertinency: the problems they treat are the problems that confront every individual, whatever his century may be.

The dialogues contained in this volume are transcripts from direct recordings of unrehearsed conversations broadcast weekly by the Columbia Broadcasting System on a coast-to-coast network. Our method is simple: We first agree upon the several aspects of the subject that should be discussed and choose, in advance, the passage that is to be read at the close of the broadcast. We do, however, not prearrange the detailed development of the discussion.

It appears advisable to emphasize that the participants in these discussions will feel that their purposes are defeated if the dialogues are taken by the reader as substitutes for a reading of the books themselves.

Our obligations are numerous: to CBS and its Adult Education Board for undertaking an experiment new in radio; to Lyman Bryson, chairman of the CBS Adult Education Board, and Sterling Fisher, Director of the CBS Department of Education, for encouragement and counsel; to Douglas Coulter, Assistant Director of the CBS Program Division, for the organization and initiation of the series; to Leon Levine, Assistant Director of the CBS Department of Education, for his able direction and helpful criticisms; and to Mrs. Corinne Poole for valuable editorial assistance.

The notes printed in italics which preface the dialogues were written by Mr. Mark Van Doren.

H. C.

*Washington, April 1, 1941.*

# Introduction

*THE twenty-seven books discussed on the following pages are books which the world has not been willing or able to let die. They are classics in the special sense that the ideas and visions which they contain are present in our thought even when we have not read them. For they are present in all discussion, and determine in some measure the character of every person's thought. But if we have not read them they come to us imperfectly; through textbooks which repeat them, through historians who quote them for a special purpose, through amateurs who misquote them. It is better to read them ourselves and return to the sources of our wisdom such as it is. They are more alive than many contemporary books because they are true; and the fact of their survival through centuries is a guarantee of their form. If they have been read so long, then they are readable. And if they have been remembered so well, then they are wise.*

*The great books are surprisingly few; but those few can be read again and again. They take the place of multitudes, and they can be discussed forever. The pleasure of reading such a book is only greater than the pleasure of talking about it or hearing it talked about by those who have practiced the art of doing so. To argue with the author, or to approve of what he has done, is to keep good company; and is to be occupied with the uncontaminated springs of what we know, believe, and feel.*

*(Scene: Mr. Cairns' Library in Washington)*

*Cairns:* I have been thinking about the twenty-seven dialogues we are publishing as a book. Isn't it interesting that of all the art forms the Greeks used, only the dialogue has not survived?

*Van Doren:* I wonder if the dialogue has not actually survived in Plato alone. We still read him and even hear him, and I do not doubt that the dialogue has survived in him to the same extent that tragedy has survived in Sophocles, because there has never been an equivalent of Sophocles either.

*Tate:* No exact equivalent. But Shakespeare and Racine are great tragic poets. We have nothing like Plato after his time.

*Cairns:* Plato showed us the wonderful possibilities of the dialogue, but it has been largely ignored by our men of letters. Walter Savage Landor and George Moore used it and so have Santayana, Valéry and G. Lowes Dickinson, but they, with a few others, have been the exceptions. Why has the dialogue as an art form been neglected? Is it because the dialogue is essentially a form in which to analyze ideas, and our age is not interested in ideas?

*Tate:* I was going to say that both of you gentlemen are overlooking one great fact, and that is that the dialogue as a literary form has never been as widespread or as popular as other literary forms. It is a highly sophisticated medium for the conveyance of ideas. I agree with Mr. Van Doren that the Platonic dialogues, in the sense that they are still read, survive. Nevertheless, if I am not committing myself to a merely polite impartiality, it seems to me that Mr. Cairns is also right in that the modern dialogue is much more limited in scope than the Platonic. I think of

Bishop Berkeley's *Dialogues* in the eighteenth century. They are comparatively limited in scope, and so are *Dialogues in Limbo* by George Santayana.

*Van Doren:* Perhaps the limitation you have in mind is an absence of drama.

*Tate:* Very much so. In Santayana the dramatic element almost ceases to exist.

*Van Doren:* And, as Plato is a great dramatist—some say a comic genius—perhaps we should remember that great dramatists are very rare, and that such a one as he cannot be expected to occur more than once in a thousand years.

*Cairns:* I agree that the dialogue has, of course, survived in Plato. But the point I am thinking about now is: Why is the dialogue as an art form not utilized to a greater extent by contemporary men of letters? I have suggested that it may be due to a contemporary lack of interest in ideas. By that I mean, in other periods ideas were handled and explored as such. Today ideas predominantly are means to ends. Their truth or falsity is of little moment.

*Tate:* Very true. We are pragmatists interested in getting things done, not in *what* should be done. So we are all specialists in one field or another, with the result that direct speech, conversation, the vocabulary of the educated man, are no longer equal to the abstruse developments in the different departments of knowledge. In the case of Plato, philosophy had not developed technically very much beyond conversation, so that Plato can set forth his philosophy as drama, as it is being discussed by human beings. For this reason the Platonic Dialogue was a natural form of expression. The dialogues of Santayana are conscious and artificial and not based upon a living style of conversation.

*Van Doren:* Can philosophy, however, be said to have any possible and fruitful development beyond conversation? Plato undoubtedly thought of himself as coming at the end of an old philosophical tradition. I should say that our contemporary practice of writing philosophy in the form of treatises shows that we are immature.

*Tate:* That seems to me to be perfectly right. Certain departments of philosophy are ingenious exercises for the adept, but they are far removed from immediate human experience. It is the immaturity of decadence.

*Cairns:* When you ask if philosophy can have any fruitful development beyond conversation, I assume you mean that in philosophy we cannot bring our ideas to conclusive tests as by the experimental method. When we get beyond the range of the exact sciences, conversation is our most powerful weapon of analysis. Our educational system, however, emphasizes facts and neglects almost entirely one of the most valuable heritages the Greeks passed on to us—conversation.

*Van Doren:* I was assuming that philosophy at its best is conversation at its best.

*Tate:* I doubt that "education" can create the art of conversation, which depends upon the kind of social life we have. In the great periods of history the arts and sciences have been available to men in their social intercourse. Specialization of knowledge and interest in "practicality" make for the decline of conversation—which is also the decline of the dialogue as a natural form.

*Cairns:* Plato thought that "conversation" or "dialectic" could be taught. In the *Republic* he provided an instruction period of five years for it. I am not thinking so much of conversation as an "art" but as an instrument of analysis—the best instrument we have in philosophy. I am concerned, however, with another question. Do you think that the dialogue has been replaced by the novel? It seems historically that the dialogue was used by men of letters as their medium of expression until the novel began to develop in its modern form. It was used, for example, before the rise of the novel in France, by Fontenelle and Fenelon. It was similarly used by Dryden and Berkeley in England, by Wieland in Germany, and by Galileo and Leopardi in Italy.

*Tate:* Perhaps some of H. G. Wells's "problem" novels are an example of what Mr. Cairns means. But there are two things to say about novels of that sort—first, they are likely to be bad novels and, second, they are likely to give us dialogues which are dramatically unconvincing.

*Cairns:* What do you think of Santayana's *The Last Puritan* as falling in that classification?

*Tate:* It is a good example: the dialogue in *The Last Puritan* is fluent and sensitive, but the characters are not speaking in it, and it is not dramatic. It is always Mr. Santayana's voice.

*Van Doren:* The thing we call the philosophical novel is certainly pertinent here. But when a really good example occurs, as for instance, *The Root and the Flower,* by L. H. Myers, the effect is what it should be in fiction, an effect of action rather than of reflection.

*Cairns:* Myers viewed the novel as a description of persons, and philosophy as a description of the universe. He thought that there was a natural connection between the two fields. He was concerned with what he called "the deep-seated spiritual vulgarity that lies at the heart of our civilization." And he attempted to show that the distinction between the beautiful and the unbeautiful in character is not simply one of individual likes and dislikes. The total effect of his attempt, however, is, as you say, fictional rather than philosophical.

*Tate:* Didn't Dostoyevsky write the kind of philosophical novels that Mr. Cairns has in mind? I am thinking particularly of *The Possessed,* in which "ideas" are so powerful that they lead to direct action, as in the suicide of Stavrogin.

*Cairns:* Are you taking the position that the modern novel in some of its forms is the true equivalent of the Platonic Dialogue? I don't think so, myself.

*Van Doren:* Perhaps we should say that some modern novels contain something like an equivalent of it as one ingredient, and I mean Dostoyevsky much more than Wells.

*Tate:* The Platonic Dialogue has no exact equivalent today. It represents a certain harmony of materials which our modern literary forms tend to exaggerate in one direction or another. For example, the modern novel would greatly exaggerate the social setting of the dialogue. The modern drama, as in Shaw's plays, would represent a crude philosophical interest—crude because restricted, and directed toward a narrow thesis.

*Van Doren:* Whereas ideas have their own drama, and the Platonic Dialogue is something like a pure drama of ideas.

*Cairns:* Are our weekly discussions, then, dialectical ones on the Platonic model, or are they descriptions of a given book? Is the dialectical method in its Platonic form a method available to us in our radio dialogues?

*Van Doren:* I have assumed each week that our job was to describe a book—nothing very easy, if description implies understanding of the whole thing which is there. I take it that you mean by "dialectic" the investigation of ideas with a view to estimating their truth by eliminating their contradictory elements.

*Cairns:* The dialectical method has acquired so many meanings since the time of Socrates that perhaps the term ought to be discarded altogether. However, I think we can assume it means what you say; although, for our purposes, I would prefer to define it more generally as a process of critical reflection intended to clarify assertions. When Matthew Arnold, for example, states that "Poetry is a criticism of life" dialectic requires us to ascertain what the phrase means and whether it corresponds to what is the case. Our first inquiry might be: Is it a definition or an epigram? The great advantage of the method, of course, is that it is not concerned with utility, or current wishes and opinions. In Plato's hands its only object was the truth.

*Tate:* Pure dialectic could not be based upon any single book, since rigorous pursuit of an "idea" would include all books. So isn't dialectic one feature of our dialogues, but only one? In our discussion of Plato's *Symposium,* we undertook to get at the fundamental idea, but, as I remember that discussion, we were particularly interested in showing that the metaphysical ideas could not be separated from the social occasion of the *Sym-*

*posium.* (In that sense, our own conversations are Platonic, but not wholly dialectical.) We are not only discussing ideas; we are trying to give a picture of the imaginative experience out of which those ideas come. In other words, we are trying to honor the whole book.

*Cairns:* We are concerned to an extent, but only to an extent, with the truth or falsity of the ideas in the books we discuss. Those books have many additional aspects—among others their dramatic, aesthetic and poetic sides—to which we may be attracted as much as to the ideas they contain. No single method is comprehensive enough to handle all the aspects of a book. Dialectic will not do the work of description and description will not do the work of dialectic. There is a further point, however, about the method of dialogue itself. Do you think that the dialogue method we employ is more advantageous than the method of a lecture by a single individual?

*Van Doren:* Certainly I do. One man speaking does not correct himself as readily as any one of us is corrected by the others.

*Tate:* Isn't another advantage of the dialogue a certain measure and proportion in presenting a book? If you have three minds working on the same ideas, there is not likely to be much exaggeration in the total effect; hence perhaps a sense of proportion will be conveyed to the listener.

*Van Doren:* And the very fact that a sense of proportion sometimes keeps us from exploring the full possibilities of a theme stimulates the listener to do so for himself.

*Cairns:* I take it that the method we employ is a combination of the dialectical method and the descriptive method and that it possesses the advantages we have enumerated. I wonder if it does not also possess some disadvantages. If we compare our dialogues with the Platonic Dialogues . . .

*Van Doren:* Oh! Oh!

*Tate:* Please don't do it!

*Cairns:* . . . merely as a matter of form—there is at least one conspicuous difference: We participate in our dialogues but Plato participated in none of his. Is that a disadvantage?

*Van Doren:* That is to say, Agathon, we have not the leisure to correct ourselves completely. Because Plato is not a participant, he is free to manipulate a dialogue and make it go where he wants it to go. We cannot polish our own performances.

*Tate:* The Platonic Dialogues are artfully written works of the imagination; ours are real conversations. Have there ever been any real conversations recorded as ours are, in a book?

*Cairns:* Not so far as I am aware. I think the fact that our dialogue is a real, unprepared, conversation gives it an advantage over the written dialogue. In the traditional form of the written dialogue, the author must use dummies which he constantly knocks down. I know of only one exception to that which is Schopenhauer's *Dialogue on Religion.* Schopenhauer's mind was evenly balanced on the question he was discussing, and he was therefore able to give both sides their due. We need no artificial devices, no imaginary opponent, for, in general, we represent three distinct points of view.

*Van Doren:* The books we have discussed are great books—that is to say, endlessly interesting ones—and, although we are bound to be incomplete, there is no aspect of them which is not somehow interesting.

*Tate:* A half hour on *War and Peace* is as good as two hours, because anything short of a month would be inadequate.

*Van Doren:* It is better to be embarrassed by riches than appalled by poverty.

# POLITICS

(384-322 B.C.)

# ARISTOTLE

# *Politics*

*THE* POLITICS *of Aristotle is one of his excursions into practical philosophy. The great speculator upon universal principles turns his attention to human affairs, considering now, as he did in the* ETHICS, *the good of man as man. But whereas in the* ETHICS *he studied the good of man as an individual and found it to be happiness, or an activity of soul according to virtue, in the* POLITICS *he finds it to be the general good of the citizen. This also is happiness, but the search is for conditions in the state which will permit the citizen to govern and be governed for the sake of the good life. The most important and famous distinction made by Aristotle in this book is the distinction between governments which aim at the general good and those which aim at their own good. Of those which aim at the general good, monarchy is the best, being government by one who excels in virtue; aristocracy, or the rule of a virtuous class, comes second; and commonwealth, or the rule of a virtuous majority, comes third. Of those which aim at their own good, the worst is tyranny, aiming at the good of one, and the best is democracy, aiming at the good of the majority; oligarchy, aiming at the good of the few, occupies the middle position. The distinction was and is of the greatest profundity. In a day when democracy seems difficult to define, Aristotle's* POLITICS *can be read again with immense profit.*

*Cairns:* In *The Republic* Plato attempted to describe how an ideal state should be organized. In Aristotle we have the opposite approach. He asks: What are the actual forms states take from time to time? And which of these types of states is the most stable and therefore the most desirable? The emphasis that Aristotle puts on stability in government, even the most corrupt governments, is the basis of much that Machiavelli has to say in *The Prince.* Aristotle thinks the state takes six forms: three of these he holds are good and three are bad. The three good states are monarchy, aristocracy and the commonwealth. The bad varieties are tyranny, oligarchy and democracy.

Mr. Van Doren, do you think that the types of states listed by Aristotle cover the situation today? In other words, have we in two thousand years discovered anything new in political organization?

*Van Doren:* I should say no, Mr. Cairns—substantially no—in spite of the fact that one would want to qualify the statement.

*Cairns:* Don't you think that the representative form of government is a form that was not contemplated by Aristotle?

*Van Doren:* The idea of representative government is an idea that fits, however, into his picture of the commonwealth.

*Tate:* Mr. Van Doren, don't you think—going back to Mr. Cairns' question—that if he did contemplate representative government, that it was probably a qualified sort of representation? His notion of a citizen is not merely that of a man who lives in a certain state; it's a man who actually participates in the government and who may hold office.

*Van Doren:* Yes, but he excludes certain classes of citizens from participation.

*Tate:* That's very true—mechanics and . . .

*Cairns:* . . . Laborers, husbandmen . . .

*Tate:* Laborers, yes. Probably in the history of European states, the property qualification for the vote is at least a semi-Aristotelian principle.

*Cairns:* Perhaps I ought to state what I understand Aristotle means by the six forms.

*Tate:* Yes, won't you point out to us how they are connected?

*Cairns:* As I read the *Politics,* by a kingdom or a monarchy he means one person exercising power in the state for the benefit of all members of the state. Now the perversion of that is tyranny, in which the supreme ruler exercises power for his own benefit. In the aristocracy you have a few rich people—wealthy people, aristocrats—acting for the benefit of the community. In the oligarchy they act for their own benefit. In the commonwealth you have many people exercising power for the benefit of everyone, and in a pure democracy in Aristotle's sense the poor people are in control but exercise their power for their own interest.

*Tate:* And not through law.

*Cairns:* Yes.

*Tate:* Tyranny and democracy, extreme tyranny and extreme democracy, as I understand it, Mr. Cairns, from Aristotle's view are the worst forms we could have.

*Van Doren:* Yes, the distinction always in his case is between those states in which the good is considered and those states in which the individual or class is considered. I should think it would be interesting to anyone today—when we are being called upon to define and defend democracy—to remember that Aristotle lists the sort of state which he, at any rate, calls a democracy among the perversions. Is that painful to any of us?

*Tate:* Not to me at all. It seems to me that the American state at its best could possibly realize Aristotle's conception of the commonwealth, which I believe he says combines the best features of oligarchy and democracy. Doesn't it seem to you curious that he should use the word oligarchy there rather than aristocracy? And isn't that because, looking at it as a realist, he says that in any state you will find a great number of rich men, but you will find very few noble men who are worthy of being a ruling class?

*Cairns:* Yes.

*Tate:* You still have to be realistic about it and do the best you can with the rich men.

*Cairns:* Do you think, Mr. Tate, that each of these three pure types can serve the welfare of all?

*Tate:* You mean, the best . . . ?

*Cairns:* Yes.

*Van Doren:* Do you mean, any of them, Mr. Cairns?

*Cairns:* Do you think any of the three of them?

*Tate:* I don't know, Mr. Cairns. Aristotle himself in the course of his *Politics* cites so many exceptions and so many different forms of all these states that it's almost impossible to answer your question.

*Cairns:* We might be able to answer the question if we could get the pure type; but the pure type never exists, or rarely so. Marcus Aurelius and Louis IX are among the most model rulers in history, and even they had their limitations.

*Van Doren:* Aristotle is very well aware of original sin. Don't you think so? He doesn't expect to find many good men on earth.

*Tate:* Yes, he, in fact, says that everybody, outside of the law, is motivated by one of two things, either insolence or malice. Insolence from the rich; malice from the mob.

*Cairns:* I think the book really is intended as a statesman's manual, and while it does discuss ideal states, Aristotle is more concerned with the practical states, the states that actually exist. He wants to educate statesmen.

*Van Doren:* I don't agree with you if you mean—perhaps you don't—that Aristotle is not interested in the ideal state. I should say that his interest began there and perhaps ended there, and I for one wouldn't expect a statesman to be practical who wasn't capable of entertaining conceptions of the ideal state always as a background of his thought.

*Cairns:* I agree with you that he is interested in the ideal state, but at the same time he says he doubts that it can be realized on this earth.

*Van Doren:* Which doesn't prevent us from remembering it.

*Cairns:* No, as an ideal type toward which we should aspire.

*Tate:* Mr. Cairns, shouldn't we distinguish now between the utopian state such as Plato was interested in and the Aristotelian perfect state? They seem to me to be very different things. If we can draw out those differences it would be useful.

*Cairns:* I think we ought to distinguish, and in that respect Aristotle marks a real advance over Plato in political thinking, in the sense that Aristotle is much more practical.

*Tate:* Yes, he's interested in what actually exists, and Plato is interested in what ought to be. Don't you think, Mr. Cairns, that his criticism of Plato is germane to our discussion? He says that a state so highly organized as Plato's *Republic* could not possibly exist, that all the citizens would be extinguished. And he also says that Plato ignores actual existing classes, like the agricultural people and mechanics.

*Van Doren:* May I interrupt?

*Cairns:* Yes, indeed, Mr. Van Doren.

*Van Doren:* It's only fair to Plato to remember that Socrates's description of an ideal state did not end that dialogue. Plato, I think, was just as well aware as Aristotle could be, or as anyone could be, that the ideal state was not to be found on earth. The book is probably not an erection of an ideal state, but a discussion of justice, and in the course of demonstrating how difficult justice is to attain, out of desperation if nothing else, the picture of an ideal state is painted. But the dialogue goes on far beyond that point.

*Cairns:* But you would agree, Mr. Van Doren, that Aristotle does mark an advance over Plato in the two respects I've mentioned, namely, that he's more practical; secondly, that his analytical method reveals facts that have proved of use to subsequent investigators in the sense that Plato's thoughts have not.

*Tate:* What do you mean there by "practical," Mr. Cairns? Do you mean that Aristotle actually observed a great many existing states—I think some hundred and fifty he's supposed to have looked at in the Greek world, including some of the Asiatic tyrannies. Now, does that mean he's more practical, or does it mean that he was actually observing the politics of his time?

*Cairns:* I mean both. First, he observed the politics of his time and made an analytical study of the constitutions of the various states; secondly, he suggested courses of action. The course of action he suggested was one that could be, he thought, realized in an actual existing state.

*Tate:* Yes, that's the point I was trying to get at, that although he's examining the political organizations in Ancient Greece, what he was actually doing in the long run was to find out what it was possible for men to do, their moral natures being what they were. All these different states were limited by the moral nature of man.

*Cairns:* I think that's where the great virtue of this book lies. Now I'm curious to know why—you raised the point a minute ago—why he ignored the existing empires and leagues.

*Tate:* He probably ignored them because he felt that they were largely trade organizations, and he says explicitly somewhere in the *Politics* that a nation or a group of city states organized solely for purposes of trade is not a real state. On that level, they are not states—you have to have in view some moral purpose for a society, or you don't have a real state.

*Cairns:* You mean he is suggesting the principle that size doesn't go to the essence of a good organization?

*Tate:* In fact, he says that a very large nation is not necessarily any better than a very small nation.

*Van Doren:* And an organization of nations chiefly interested in trade would, after all, take care only of that activity of man which engages in trade.

*Tate:* Which probably would turn to an oligarchical form of government, because the rich merchants would be interested primarily in that trade.

*Van Doren:* Or, if you wanted to take it in larger units, the rich nations would be running the group.

*Tate:* But doesn't he also say that smallness may be a disadvantage on occasion, because you've got to consider not only the internal welfare of the state, but the enemies abroad, and your size will protect you.

*Van Doren:* I don't want to hold the conversation back, but I'm still a little bothered by the fact that we seem to be saying that Plato is not practical. It seems to me he is one of the most practical of all thinkers. For instance, doesn't Aristotle owe to him here his conception of the ideal state? What Aristotle means by law—that thing which a monarch or an aristocracy or the citizens of a commonwealth should love more than themselves—I should say that that was justice.

*Cairns:* I think that Plato's thought is impressed on every page of Aristotle. There is no doubt about that; but I do feel . . .

*Van Doren:* . . . Therefore, a very practical author, I should say.

*Cairns:* I don't think you could say that Plato has written a statesman's manual, but I think you can make that assertion of the *Politics*. Now to come back to this other point, Aristotle insists that the smaller community really contributes to the better life. Do you agree with that, Mr. Van Doren?

*Van Doren:* You mean that a community can be too large?

*Cairns:* It is Aristotle's position that there is more chance of realizing the good life, or the better life, in a smaller community than in a large community.

*Van Doren:* Yes, to me that is clearly true.

*Tate:* And it is obviously true that Aristotle is using his common sense there, because the less a state is dependent upon remote relations, political or economic, the more independent it's going to be and the less trouble it's going to have.

*Van Doren:* And the more it is possible to know what is going on within the state.

*Cairns:* Exactly. Furthermore, he defines the state as a collective body of citizens, sufficient in themselves to all the purposes of life. I am wondering if that definition is adequate today.

*Tate:* It seems to be inadequate, because the specialization of certain industries in different countries has tended to break the idea down. The self-sufficient countries are practically gone.

*Van Doren:* Well, wouldn't his definition nevertheless hold good?

*Tate:* Exactly. . . .

*Van Doren:* I mean, if we could have citizens of that sort, shouldn't we be better off?

*Tate:* Much better off; and probably a great deal of trouble in modern international politics is due to the fact that we've become so specialized.

*Van Doren:* And specialization prevents a person from being a good citizen, prevents him from being wise in addition to being expert.

*Tate:* Now, Mr. Van Doren, can't we trip you up there on your advocacy of Plato? Everyone in the Platonic state was so highly specialized that he almost ceased to exist.

*Van Doren:* Yes, but it seems to me the drift of the whole book is in the direction of saying that all members of that state—I'm not talking now merely about the section of the *Republic* which gives us the ideal state—should be interested in the truth and love it.

*Tate:* I think that's true, but how does that differ from Aristotle?

*Van Doren:* I think it doesn't differ at all. That is what Aristotle is saying, too, when he is considering what states should be. Aristotle does not expect any state to be what a state can be. Neither, incidentally, does Plato.

*Tate:* There's a question I'd like to bring up at this point, Mr. Van Doren. Mr. Cairns was talking about it a minute ago. Although Aristotle sets forth six types of states—three good and three bad, the bad being perversions of the good types—it seems that at bottom he's saying that there are just two types, really, that appear frequently—in fact, almost invariably—democracy and oligarchy. And that his chief discussion is concerned with just those two types and the combination of the two.

*Van Doren:* Yes, and for him history would doubtless be what it is for us, namely, the story of the alternate attempts of the few and the many, the rich and the poor, to seize power from one another, regardless,I should say, of the question of a third alternative, namely, the worship of the good.

*Tate:* The worship of the good, yes. And do you think Aristotle's conception of the middle class as the defenders of the good is sound and applies to the history of our society, beginning, say, at the end of the Reformation on down to the present time? What of the middle-of-the-roader—the middle class? Had it been what Aristotle said it should be, would life be something different today?

*Cairns:* I think it has been what he predicted it would be; at the same time, I think his outlook was quite pessimistic. As I read the *Politics,* he saw nothing ahead but mob rule, and that contrasts curiously with the nineteenth-century view of progress. The nineteenth-century political thinkers were optimistic; but Aristotle, for some reason, was pessimistic.

*Van Doren:* But who do you think was right?

*Cairns:* I think Aristotle was right, at least in viewing things pessimistically, since I see no basis for the nineteenth-century notion of progress.

*Van Doren:* He seems to have thought that tyrannies were pretty well put behind, doesn't he? Remember, there's a passage in which he says that tyrannies are less likely to occur in the future than democracies are, chiefly because the man who could most easily become a tyrant was the general who could seize military power. I don't know what Aristotle would have said about our tyrants of today, if the dictators are the tyrants of today. Are they, by the way, Mr. Cairns? Does it seem to you that he is describing the men whom we call dictators?

*Cairns:* I think in large part he certainly is.

*Tate:* But our modern dictators don't rise through military power. Primarily, they come up through politics.

*Cairns:* Politics coupled with force.

*Tate:* It isn't so much force, though. Mussolini's march on Rome was not backed by tremendous force.

*Cairns:* He gave the impression of force, which was what counted; it is true that the historians have now shown that the amount of force behind him was small.

*Van Doren:* There's another passage in which Aristotle says that in these days, when warfare is so much a matter of the past, a man is more likely to rise to power through his eloquence. He addresses the public in such a way that the public cannot resist him.

*Cairns:* He is full of acute observations of that sort; that is what makes the book so interesting.

*Tate:* There is a point, I think, we've left behind. I'd like to bring it up again, just to see what you gentlemen think of it. Isn't it curious that Aristotle's conception of the practical-ideal state should be a combination of the two worst forms of the state, taken in their extremes and alone? You have oligarchy, which is unbridled rule by the rich; you have democracy, which is unbridled rule by the poor—mob rule. But the combination and the balance of those two things gives you something like the government of the commonwealth, which he says in the long run is the best form man can hope to achieve over a great many years.

*Van Doren:* Well, I should say that he was very practical just at that point. A democracy is, to him, an undesirable thing, but it may become desirable by being modified in the direction of a commonwealth. It can never be modified very far in that direction; he doesn't expect, I think, to find a commonwealth. So is an oligarchy undesirable, and yet one can be made less undesirable if it is modified in the direction of an aristocracy.

*Cairns:* I think it's merely an expression of his pessimism. All that he had actually seen was oligarchy and democracy, and he hoped by a combination through a mean or a middle course to get a commonwealth. He would like to obtain a commonwealth from a good combination, rather than from a bad combination, but he was being quite practical and merely applying what he thought he could realize.

*Tate:* Yes, but now can't we ask this question: if the best practicable state is the commonwealth, what becomes of the people in such a state who are noble, on the one hand, and what becomes of the people who represent the democratic phase of that state, that is, the people who are interested in freedom? He says that democracy at its best is interested in freedom.

*Cairns:* He says you should make allowances for those people, but he doesn't imply that allowances will be made.

*Van Doren:* But he doesn't say how they're going to be made, either, does he?

*Tate:* Well, don't we find a little difficulty in Aristotle's conception?

*Cairns:* We find there are very many difficulties, because there are quite a few gaps in his thoughts.

*Tate:* I want to bring that out because we should not assume that Aristotle thought of everything.

*Van Doren:* You may remember there is a rather frightening section in which he tells us how in the old days a commonwealth, or a democracy, got rid of its superior citizens; it cut their heads off or sent them away. It ostracized them.

*Tate:* If a man got too much power or was too prominent.

*Van Doren:* If a man got too much power or if a man seemed so attractive to a great many people that there was danger power would be offered him. Now, he goes on to say—of course, he's always shifting back and forth between the ideal and the practical levels—that if this man had been superior in virtue there would have been no sense in sending him out, because a man cannot be too virtuous. A man can be too rich, but he cannot be too virtuous.

*Cairns:* That brings up the point that I think he insists upon throughout the book that the common objective of citizens living together is the safety of the commonwealth. By which, I take it, he means the general acceptance of the main principles of the community, and therefore that leads him to the conclusion that the good citizen is a different being in an oligarchy, a democracy and an aristocracy. In other words, a good citizen—that is, a man who follows the constitutional principle of his community—may, nevertheless, be a bad man. He may be a good citizen and yet a bad man.

*Tate:* But doesn't he also, Mr. Cairns, say that there's a certain kind of state in which the good citizen and the good man tend to be the same man?

*Cairns:* But that would be the ideal state.

*Tate:* Certainly.

*Cairns:* Which he doesn't hope for.

*Tate:* But doesn't he say, though, that the commonwealth most closely approximates that of all the practicable states?

*Cairns:* Oh, yes.

*Tate:* I should say he did.

*Cairns:* There is no dispute about that. I think, however, we ought to see if we agree on Aristotle's meaning of citizenship. As I read him, he says a citizen is one who holds or is capable of holding an administrative or judicial office.

*Van Doren:* And, furthermore, is willing to hold it.

*Cairns:* Well, in order to be a good citizen, he ought to be willing to hold it, because he can't learn to rule unless he first obeys and then rules.

*Tate:* But doesn't he say then the best citizen is the man in the middle—neither the oligarch nor the democrat—because he neither covets office nor refuses to hold office? He does his duty; he is not ambitious.

*Cairns:* Are you by any chance suggesting that it is desirable to raise our standards to the Greek standards?

*Tate:* I think it very desirable.

*Van Doren:* I think it is always desirable to raise them.

*Cairns:* Do you think his reasons are valid for denying citizenship to certain groups, such as servants and mechanics?

*Van Doren:* Mechanics and husbandmen. Does that mean farmers?

*Cairns:* Husbandmen must be farmers.

*Tate:* I would say that probably the farmers ought to vote more than anyone else.

*Van Doren:* As an old agrarian, so should I.

*Tate:* The landowners—the landowners who are not too great.

*Van Doren:* It is clear to me that Aristotle means by a citizen a man capable of deliberating, capable of being disinterested, capable of considering a question not merely in terms of how it affects him.

*Cairns:* Do you think there is an inconsistency in Aristotle at this point? He seems to assert that those should rule who are most fit to rule. At the same time he says all citizens should rule by turn.

*Tate:* I don't know whether that's true, but I think perhaps when he says all citizens should rule by turn, he means only those who are qualified to rule under that constitution. Certain persons are excluded from suffrage; they don't get their turn.

*Van Doren:* Only those who are considered citizens, who deserve it.

*Cairns:* Who are fit and, in his word, virtuous.

*Tate:* Now we're back at this question as to whether the servants and mechanics should have the suffrage and participate in the state. We have to go back to Aristotle's definition of a slave. This is the definition: The slave is a live tool. We can't possibly entertain such a conception today; that's something so foreign to us that it shocks us.

*Van Doren:* Unless we put the machine in that position.

*Tate:* Yes.

*Van Doren:* We should not make a dynamo a citizen, and possibly that analogy takes care of what was in Aristotle's imagination.

*Cairns:* I think so. He said that the mechanic ought not to participate because he didn't have the leisure to reflect, but now the machine gives the mechanic leisure to reflect, and he therefore can participate in government.

*Van Doren:* But the dynamo does not.

*Cairns:* No, the dynamo does not.

*Van Doren:* Or the pick and the axe do not, but the men who hold them.

*Cairns:* Aren't we becoming a little utopian right now? Is there anything in prospect that is going to bring that about: that the dynamo will become a citizen?

*Tate:* I don't think so. Aristotle uses the word "virtuous." Don't you think Aristotle's observation was a shrewd one, to the effect that even in the Greek states people were granted certain political privileges, but the oligarchs in power kept those privileges from ever amounting to anything, as the old device of using a prevailing form of government for some private purpose or class interest.

*Cairns:* What do you think he means by virtuous, Mr. Van Doren?

*Van Doren:* Well, he defines that more carefully in his *Ethics*. I should say that he gives us a clue to what he means by it in this book, when he says that the law is the mean—the law is a mean. That is to say, it is only through a study of the law that a man is encouraged, at least in political terms, to approach the truth.

*Cairns:* Do you think this is a fair statement, that those who contribute to the well-being of the community are the virtuous people and not those who excel in some particular line, such as flute-playing?

*Tate:* Perhaps so, but, Mr. Cairns, couldn't you say this: that the virtuous people are not merely those who contribute to the well-being of the community, but they have to have a community in which they can contribute their well-being? You see, they have to have the commonwealth or that middle state that he's talking about.

*Van Doren:* And your use of the word "commonwealth" once more interests me a great deal. I wonder whether in these days when we are being asked to define democracy we shouldn't try defining commonwealth.

*Tate:* It's just on that point, gentlemen, we have a passage in the *Politics*. Aristotle is talking about those people who will be happiest. "For if it has been rightly said in the *Ethics* that the happy life is the life lived without impediment in accordance with virtue, and that virtue is the middle course, it necessarily follows that the middle course of life is the best, such a middle course as it is possible for each class of men to attain. And these same criteria must also necessarily apply to the goodness and badness of the state and of a constitution. In all states, therefore, there exist three divisions of the state: the very rich, the very poor, and thirdly, those who are between the two. Since then it is admitted that what is moderate, or in the middle, is best, it is manifest that the middle amount of all the good things of fortune is the best amount to possess."

(1469-1527)

# NICCOLO MACHIAVELLI

# *The Prince*

*THE extent of Machiavelli's fame is best indicated by the fact that his name has become an adjective; and the quality of his repute is signified by the popular meaning of "machiavellian." The word as commonly spoken suggests devilish craft, unscrupulous guile and indeed all that is inhuman in an intelligence misused for purposes of self-aggrandizement. The origin of such a reputation is the little treatise on politics called* THE PRINCE. *To read it is to understand at once why the impression made by its author upon the world should have been so powerful. For it is a masterpiece of merciless brevity, and the persistence with which it sticks to its subject is something almost unique in literature. But the subject of* THE PRINCE *is not politics in general, nor was the work intended as a moral treatise. Machiavelli, like the Italian prince for whom it was written, confined his interest to a single set of questions having to do with the one large question of how a ruler can keep his power. By being honest? By doing kindnesses? By trusting human nature? By forgiving his enemies? The answers are not edifying. But neither perhaps is power, and the millions who have abused the book have not paused to consider that Machiavelli was aiming, above all things, to be realistic in his account of human behavior. That he succeeded is clear from the fact that his little book now reads like a primer for dictators: a primer, furthermore, which their enemies should know as well as they do.*

*Cairns:* Machiavelli's little book — it is less than a hundred pages—is so explicit and pointed with anecdotes that it has sent chills along our spines for four centuries. The strong state maintains order and is best for everyone in the long run. Therefore there should be no sentimentality or nonsense about it. That is his thesis. He describes how orderly states in the past have been built and maintained, how weak states have been built and why they disintegrated. He has been denounced as infamous because he argued that the value obtained through unity and order was worth any price. He asserts that the powerful and stable state is founded on the love and respect of the people for their ruler and on a strong army to protect them from other states. This, he says, is the highest good, the morality to which all other morality is secondary. I think that much that is explicit in Machiavelli is implied in Aristotle's *Politics,* exactly as Aristotle made explicit much that was only implied by Plato.

Mr. Tate, do you agree with Machiavelli's thesis that a strong and stable state based on the love and respect of the people is the highest good to be attained in any community? This may seem a bit obvious.

*Tate:* Yes, Mr. Cairns, I do agree. But don't you think that we ought to point out first of all that Machiavelli is not the cynic that he has been made out to be, that he is interested in something like Aristotle's Commonwealth, or certainly the political virtues that come from such a state?

*Cairns:* Mr. Van Doren, do you think that Machiavelli's state is Aristotle's ideal state, or do you agree with Mr. Tate that it is comparable to Aristotle's idea of a commonwealth?

*Van Doren:* Machiavelli is interested in what Aristotle calls the commonwealth, yes, although he spends precious little time talking about it in this particular book. He assumes its existence and its importance, but his concern is not with the defense of it or with an analysis of it.

*Tate:* But don't you believe that Machiavelli is quite Aristotelian in another sense, that perhaps one reason why he doesn't discuss the commonwealth very much is that, like Aristotle, he is interested in observing what is actually around him—the Italian city-states of his time?

*Van Doren:* I should say that there is no conflict between him and either Aristotle or Plato. You remember, I was insisting that there was not too much conflict between Aristotle and Plato. That is to say, Machiavelli is grounded upon the same vision of society, except that the actual area which he cultivates here is rather small.

*Cairns:* Don't you agree that they both have the same ideal conception, namely, one man ruling for the good of all? Isn't that the basis both of Machiavelli and Aristotle?

*Tate:* I think it is, Mr. Cairns. Machiavelli is not so much interested in classifying the different kinds of states and their theoretical possibilities as Aristotle. It must have appeared to Machiavelli that the most recurrent type of state was a state ruled by a prince. Then the problem arose: How could you rule the state well, and did a prince's personal virtue mean that he would also have political virtue, or vice versa?

*Van Doren:* You may remember, toward the beginning of one of his chapters he seems to remember Aristotle but he departs from him. He says that the incessant rivalry between the populace and the nobility of any state can end in any one of three forms of government. Whereas those three forms, for Aristotle, were monarchy, commonwealth and something in between—aristocracy or, if perverted, oligarchy—that third form in Machiavelli's classification drops out altogether, and he gives you merely anarchy. He seems not to have supposed that there would ever be stability with a ruling group in power. Either the prince at one extreme or the people at the other.

*Tate:* But does he really say that the people themselves can rule?

*Van Doren:* I think he doesn't mean that. He means that the prince is ruling with the people's consent.

*Tate:* Yes. And for their benefit.

*Cairns:* I do think that Machiavelli believed that the most important thing, whether it was a republic or a tyranny, was that the government should be powerful and stable.

*Van Doren:* That would be true for any government, wouldn't it?

*Cairns:* He insisted upon strength in government whether the government itself was good or bad, and I think Aristotle took the same point of view.

*Van Doren:* And it is only fair to Machiavelli to remember that perhaps his first sentence is: "I am not writing about republics."

*Tate:* In which book?

*Van Doren:* In the second chapter of *The Prince.*

*Tate:* What, Mr. Van Doren, would Machiavelli mean by a republic? Of course he doesn't actually define that. If he meant the *res publica* of the Romans — that is, the public thing — it wouldn't mean democracy in our sense, would it?

*Van Doren:* In our sense, no. I think again it would be a prince, or possibly a consul, or at any rate some individual with great power ruling the people with their consent.

*Cairns:* I wonder, Mr. Tate, if you agree with the point that Aristotle and Machiavelli both make, that the morals or the virtue of the ruler must be different from the morals or virtues of the ordinary citizen.

*Tate:* Mr. Cairns, I believe that neither Aristotle nor Machiavelli is conclusive on that point. Machiavelli is inclined to believe that the ruler's personal virtue has very little to do with it. That is, a virtuous fool would make a worse ruler than a knavish intelligent man.

*Van Doren:* Yes. He has nothing but contempt for the virtuous fool, if you mean by that a man who does not know the world.

*Tate:* And doesn't know how men actually behave.

*Van Doren:* Probably his greatest respect would be for the man who knew the world and was virtuous.

*Cairns:* But he does insist that the virtues that we admire in the ordinary man, such as good faith and square dealing, must not be present in the ruler, that the ruler is beyond such virtues, because the stability of the state and the good of all are the objects of the ruler and they are not the objects of the ordinary citizen.

*Tate:* Mr. Cairns, don't you think that there Machiavelli has a conception of kingship which ended in England only with the Stuart kings? For example, the king is not a person and you don't judge him by standards of personal morality.

*Cairns:* You mean that he is an institution?

*Tate:* Yes, if the king makes a personal promise it is potentially void in the beginning.

*Van Doren:* I can't help remembering, though, that he says, in defense of the proposition that the ruler does not need always to keep faith, that people themselves do not keep faith, implying that, after all, the ruler perhaps should be very much like the people. No better and no worse.

*Cairns:* As I read *The Prince,* it appears that Machiavelli's principal aim is to tell the prince what he must do if he wants a strong government. He does not attempt to answer the question: Is it good for the ruler to do this or are these methods bad? He merely says that if the ruler wants to accomplish such and such an objective, then he must do these things.

*Van Doren:* Stability perhaps is the first virtue of a government.

*Tate:* Gentlemen, there's a point I'd like to raise right there, as to the nature of Machiavelli's advice to the prince. How are we to understand this advice? If Machiavelli is not chiefly interested in sheer power, as Hobbes later on was, are we to understand him as being a little ironical in the advice he gives the prince? He says you can do these things in order to get power. If you go beyond certain extremes you will lose power. Was he thinking of it primarily in terms of power or not? It seems to me it's just a convention, perhaps a sort of literary convention in which he is addressing his patron, the prince, but what he is actually interested in is the good life, a state in which people could live the good life.

*Cairns:* I can't agree with that. I look upon this book as a textbook for a prince. For example, Machiavelli tells the prince: "When you have conquered a people who are accustomed to live at liberty under their own laws, there are three ways to hold them. The first is to despoil them. The second is to go there and live in person. The third is to allow them to live under their own laws, taking tribute of them and creating within the country a government composed of a few who will keep it friendly to you."

*Tate:* That is certainly very true. I agree with you, Mr. Cairns, about the practical phase of his observations.

*Cairns:* I don't see any satire in it.

*Tate:* No, I don't mean there was satire. He had to convey his ideas in terms that would flatter the prince—the terms of power. His own views had to be inserted slyly, ironically. The powerful and stable commonwealth or something like that is the thing desired by Machiavelli.

*Cairns:* I think that is his aim, but he says, "You must do these things this way if you want to achieve the stable state." Now some of those things are bad morally. At least we regard them as bad.

*Tate:* Yes, but do you think he is exhorting the prince to do these things for their own sake, or is he merely saying that power is a means to an end and that the prince will conduct himself along these lines inevitably?

*Van Doren:* There is a very nice line, apparently, that one would have to draw between a cruel prince whom he seems to respect, Cesare Borgia, and two cruel princes whom he did not respect. Both of them, all three of them, for that matter, fair, but he respects Cesare more than he does the two others, in spite of the fact that all three are cruel. And that fine line of distinction, it seems to me, is a line drawn along Cesare's general purpose, which was not purely his own aggrandizement but the peace of his state.

*Cairns:* Don't you agree that he is really in the position of an engineer? He says if you want to put a bridge across this stream you can do it this way or this way or this way?

*Tate:* Yes, but I think at the same time he has some conception of the purpose of the bridges.

*Van Doren:* And, I should say, of your reason for wanting to cross the bridge.

*Cairns:* No, he's an engineer. He doesn't say whether the bridge is good or bad to put across the stream. He merely says if you want a bridge, build it this way; whether it is good or bad is for somebody else to determine.

*Van Doren:* If you want to keep in power, this is the way to do it. Is that what you mean?

*Cairns:* Yes.

*Van Doren:* But by the very subtlety of the problem as he presents it, it seems to me, he betrays that he has a vision of what government might be. After all, he isn't giving just a few simple rules. It is a very wise man, actually, who keeps his power.

*Cairns:* He has a very interesting paragraph on a subject that is of great importance today, the subject of neutrality.

*Tate:* I have it right here, Mr. Cairns, and I'll read it. "And it will always happen that the one who is not your friend will want you to remain neutral and the one who is your friend will require you to declare yourself by taking arms. Irresolute princes, to avoid present dangers, usually follow the way of neutrality and are mostly ruined by it. But when the prince declares himself frankly in favor of one side, if the one to whom you adhere conquers, even if he is powerful and you remain at his discretion, he is under an obligation to you and friendship has been established."

*Cairns:* Don't you think in that paragraph he is merely attempting to describe things as they exist, and that there is no satire, although he may be cynical because things are the way they are?

*Tate:* Yes, I agree with you there, but at the same time, I would like to bring up another passage in the book. I don't think it's necessary to quote it. He says that in history it seems that kingdoms have been governed in two ways. First, either by a prince and his servants—and there you have an absolute government; you have satraps or appointed governors. Secondly, you have another state where the prince rules with his barons, men of the titled nobility who are semi-independent of the ruler. Now he goes on to point out that if you conquer either one of those states, say, the first one, that is, the state ruled by a king or a single ruler of some kind who delegates power to mere servants, that state is easy to hold because the people have no spirit. There is no diffusion of power. It seems to me what he is interested in there is some kind of diffusion of power throughout the state. Something like a commonwealth.

*Van Doren:* Yes. And it seems to me that he never is in a position of saying cynically to his prince: "Follow my instructions and you will succeed." It is clear, at any rate, that the instructions are going to be hard to follow. For instance, his advice about flatterers. He says: "A prince of course must surround himself with persons who can give him advice." A prince who is foolish surrounds himself with sycophants who tell him what he wants to hear. That is one extreme to be avoided, but the opposite extreme is the extreme of listening to everybody. He says one must find a mean there—a very difficult thing to do. You must have a group of counselors who are known to have liberty of tongue and then listen to no one else. I should say that to follow this prescription is difficult, for the danger of any ruler consists chiefly in not knowing how to take advice.

*Cairns:* And to discourage unsolicited advice. You will remember that Lord Palmerston told Victoria that if any of her counselors offered her unsolicited advice she should change the subject at once. That would embarrass them and save her from things she didn't want to hear.

*Van Doren:* Yes. But to follow that prescription wisely, it seems to me, would take a man himself so wise that he would understand that the business of ruling was more than the business of getting what he personally wanted.

*Cairns:* That may be why states generally are badly governed. The men possessing that amount of wisdom are so rare in number. Machiavelli makes a distinction, however, between achieving power and achieving glory. You will recall he said that it cannot be called virtue to kill one's fellow citizens, to betray one's friends, to be without faith, without pity and without religion. By these methods one may indeed gain power but not glory.

*Van Doren:* Machiavelli is very much interested in glory, and at this point the reader is likely to remember Cesare Borgia who had done all those things. And yet there was a difference, because Cesare was interested in power, and I should say that the hypothetical man he is here talking about was interested in no one but himself.

*Cairns:* He used Cesare as a model for deducing the necessary virtues in a ruler, and you will recall that he summed up those virtues by two phrases: the lion and the fox. I was wondering if you agreed with him that both those virtues are necessary: the virtue of the lion—courage—and the virtue of the fox—cunning.

*Tate:* I think so, Mr. Cairns, and I think the fact that those virtues are necessary, points to Machiavelli's belief in some kind of good political order. Either of those virtues alone would certainly ruin a state, and I admit that it looks bad to say that the ruler can have only the two virtues that arise from the nature of beasts. But at the same time courage is balanced by intelligence. Aren't the beasts used ironically? At first sight it looks as if Machiavelli is saying men are mere animals; then we suddenly realize that men are often actually more brutal than either lion or fox.

*Van Doren:* Yes, but at the beginning of the chapter in which he discusses the lion and the fox, he says: "A good ruler must be both a human being and a beast." The two kinds of beast that he can be are the lion and the fox. But there once more Machiavelli, I think, has paid as much tribute as we need for the moment to hear paid to humanity. After which he says: "Since I am talking here about the beastly virtues I shall talk about nothing else."

*Cairns:* He makes two points in discussing the virtues of the fox—among many others he makes these two explicitly—that it is necessary for the ruler to have virtues which are dangerous. He must appear to have them, but not have them actually. That is, his subjects must think that the prince keeps his word when in fact he doesn't. He also makes the point that the prince must never keep faith if it is harmful to the state. Do you agree with Machiavelli that this is necessary?

*Tate:* American history itself would show that they have been. Some of our very greatest statesmen have had to do that.

*Van Doren:* Have had to go back on their word; have had to break a plank in their platform, for instance.

*Tate:* Yes. Abraham Lincoln is a beautiful example of that.

*Van Doren:* Woodrow Wilson would be another.

*Tate:* And George Washington a third.

*Van Doren:* And although the question may be discussed for a long time whether they should have done so, it would finally be answered in the light of the further question whether the state had benefited.

*Cairns:* Do you think Machiavelli is deducing these qualities of the ruler from a position merely of cold observation or was he himself personally a scoundrel?

*Van Doren:* Certainly not a scoundrel, I should say. He was a very interesting, humane person, and very learned. He wrote, of course, many books besides this one.

*Cairns:* He says that the ruler must not be despised, and in order to avoid being despised he must avoid appearing feminine, frivolous, irresolute and timid. On the other hand, he had to cultivate the qualities of the lion—fortitude, decision, gravity and spirit.

*Van Doren:* He knew the truth of the commonplace that there is never respect without fear, some form of fear.

*Tate:* Mr. Cairns, don't you think that Machiavelli was interested in the virtue of courage chiefly insofar as the prince had to wage war?

*Cairns:* He said that the sole duty of the prince was to wage war. That was his whole occupation.

*Tate:* What do you think of his maxims for the conduct of the prince in conquering other states? Do you think that they apply to history generally or only to Machiavelli's own time?

*Cairns:* Which particular maxims are you referring to?

*Tate:* The way to hold states . . .

*Cairns:* The ones I read, you mean?

*Tate:* Yes, for example, he says in one place, outside the passage that you read, that if you conquer a people you should either annihilate them or caress them; that the middle ground is . . .

*Cairns:* . . . leads to disaster.

*Tate:* How does that apply? I wonder if it applies to our immediate history.

*Van Doren:* Yes. Two countries that we are thinking about a great deal these days have been ruled by "princes" who had to consider whether they should do their injury swiftly or seriatim, so to speak. Haven't you in mind the passage, Mr. Tate, in which he says that if you are going to have to do injuries to rivals or citizens, you must do them all at once, so that they can be forgotten as soon as possible?

*Tate:* Yes.

*Cairns:* Are you thinking of something in contemporary history, Mr. Van Doren?

*Van Doren:* I'm thinking of purges. Of the two "princes" we happen to be talking about today, Hitler did his purging more sensibly, since he did it all at once, in one day.

*Cairns:* He followed Machiavelli's prescription.

*Van Doren:* Yes. Whereas Stalin did not—allowing his trials to go on month after month and become a series of trials. I should say he lost the respect of a great many more millions of persons than ceased to give their respect to Hitler. I'm not defending either course, by the way.

*Cairns:* Would you say that *The Prince,* like Aristotle's book on politics, is a handbook for statesmen?

*Van Doren:* Yes. I should say a handbook for statesmen which has not been very well read.

*Cairns:* You wouldn't say, as Rousseau said, that *The Prince* is merely satire? You would say that Machiavelli is in earnest.

*Tate:* I think he is in earnest. What I was saying a while ago about possible irony in *The Prince* doesn't mean that it is at all satirical. I think that he started with actual observation.

*Van Doren:* He certainly is not cynical. Or at least it is a vulgar error always to confound cynicism with realism. There can be a very great deal of difference.

*Cairns:* Do you regard him as an Italian patriot?

*Van Doren:* Yes, surely. His last chapter, if no other, would make that clear.

*Cairns:* I was going to ask if you felt that the last chapter was an afterthought. In that chapter he pleads for Italy to free herself from the barbarians. The barbarians, I take it, being the French.

*Van Doren:* The French chiefly. The Northern nations.

*Cairns:* You don't say that that is an afterthought?

*Van Doren:* I shouldn't think so. It seems to me it might come very easily under the head of a prince's obligation to preserve his commonwealth. I should like to read a passage, not from *The Prince* itself, but from a letter of Machiavelli written about the time he was composing *The Prince*. It will make clear that he was an interesting and richly endowed man. This helps to answer your earlier question. "I am at my farm," he says. "I rise with the sun and go into a wood of mine that is being cut, where I remain two hours inspecting the work of the previous day and conversing with the woodcutters who have always some trouble on hand among themselves or with their neighbors. When I leave the wood I proceed to a well and thence to the place which I use for snaring birds, with a book under my arm, Dante or Plutarch or one of the minor poets. I read the story of their passions and let their loves remind me of my own, which is a pleasant pastime for a while. Next I take the road, enter the inn door, talk with the passersby, inquire the news of the neighborhood, listen to a variety of matters and make note of the different tastes and humors of men.

This brings me to dinnertime, when I join my family and eat the poor produce of my farm. After dinner I go back to the inn, where I generally find the host, a butcher, a miller and a pair of bakers. With these companions I play the fool all day at cards or backgammon. A thousand squabbles, a thousand insults and abusive dialogues take place while we haggle over a farthing, shouting loud enough to be heard from San Cacciano. But when evening falls I go home and enter my writing room. On the threshold I put off my country habit, filthy with mud and mire, and array myself in royal, courtly garments. Thus worthily attired, I make my entrance into the ancient courts of the men of old, where they receive me with love and where I feed upon that food which only is my own and for which I was born. I feel no shame in conversing with them and asking them a reason for their actions. They, moved by their humanity, make answer. For a four-hour space I feel no annoyance, forget all care. Poverty cannot frighten me nor death appal me."

# ETHICS

(c. 428-348 B.C.)

# PLATO

## *Symposium*

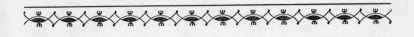

*PLATO'S* SYMPOSIUM *or* BANQUET *is the most illustrious of all discourses upon love. Into a relatively short dialogue between Socrates and his convivial friends, the philosopher has packed so many ideas that new ones are still being discovered there, and old ones are constantly being redefined. The influence of the* SYMPOSIUM *has been immense not only upon philosophy, but upon poetry and upon the behavior of men. It is here, if anywhere, that we shall discover the full meaning of that frequently ill-used phrase, "Platonic love." For Plato's love was neither pale nor negative. He understood all the kinds of love, and he gave them their frankest due in language of the greatest power and realism; but he reserved his final praise for the kind of love which has for its object not a woman or a man, not a country or an idea, but truth itself —existence in its pure and permanent form. The truth is always Plato's subject, whatever may be the ostensible theme of the con-*

*versation he is reporting. Here, after permitting Socrates to remind us of what is most worthy of human worship, he concludes with a panegyric by Alcibiades upon the character of Socrates. This interrupts the discussion but it tells us what we should love in man—namely, his virtue. Then it is morning, and those who can walk after so much wine and eloquence go home to their ordinary lives.*

*Cairns:* In *The Prince* we discussed Machiavelli's idea of how a ruler should act in order to produce the greatest happiness for all concerned. The four books we shall discuss under the classification of Ethics approach more directly than fiction or drama or politics the problem of how to live in order to get the greatest happiness from life. In about forty-five pages Plato asserts, or so I read him, that through love man reaches the fullest happiness. He argues that a man's love for a beautiful person stimulates him to strive for immortality through creative activities, through the performance of noble deeds and through the acquisition of knowledge which he calls virtue. He thinks, however, that the noblest utilization of the creative impulse is in governing states and in educating young men of ability in wisdom and virtue. He adds, however, that a still higher stage is reached when the love object which inspires a man is no longer one beautiful person but universal, absolute beauty. Now that phrase, absolute beauty, is ambiguous. I wonder, Mr. Van Doren, what your theory of its meaning is.

*Van Doren:* You may remember that he adds to the adjective "absolute" the adjectives "separate," "simple" and "everlasting." Those three, I should say, assist us in understanding the word "absolute." This absolute beauty of which Socrates speaks—because you meant, I daresay, Socrates . . .

*Cairns:* Socrates if you like, although, of course, it is Plato who is writing.

*Van Doren:* . . . this absolute beauty, which is often called, by those who comment on the dialogue or who report it, the highest beauty, is highest only in the sense that it is the most abstract.

We can mislead ourselves and others if we use the word "high" or "higher" in connection with Plato with any other notion than that it indicates abstraction as a direction. Do you agree, Mr. Tate?

*Tate:* Yes, I do, but I think in the case of this particular dialogue, the *Symposium,* that in Plato's conception of the abstract good or abstract beauty—and the terms seem to be interchangeable—he gives you a little different background for it. He says that the lover is characterized by not merely loving something, but he has a privation of something that he is trying to compensate for. He says that the lover is parellel to the poet in certain ways. He says that artisans are first creators: they are making things; and the poet is a maker also, but he is a maker in a more specific sense; he has a more specific aim in view and therefore the true lover has a more specific aim in view than mere perfection; that his aim is the highest good.

*Van Doren:* The object of love is not love.

*Tate:* No.

*Cairns:* What does Plato mean by love in this sense?

*Tate:* Are you asking me, Mr. Cairns?

*Cairns:* Either one of you. Difficult words like "absolute beauty" and "love" demand some statement of their meaning.

*Van Doren:* Perhaps you don't mean Plato, Mr. Cairns, because Plato ostensibly is not talking anywhere in this dialogue. He is writing the dialogue as a report of what other men have said.

*Cairns:* But he was a child when they said it. The *Symposium* is too characteristically Platonic for me to say that Plato is not in it.

*Tate:* Mr. Van Doren, aren't you bringing up the question of the historical Socrates—whether he is Plato's mouthpiece or whether he is Socrates'?

*Van Doren:* No. I simply find the man Socrates here and I find some others—Agathon and the rest. They are talking about love, and I assume that Plato finds all of them necessary for the statement about love which he wants to make.

*Cairns:* The theme of the dinner party, of course, is to celebrate love.

*Tate:* Yes. It seems to me, then, that we've got to ask this question: Do you think what Socrates says about love in this dialogue represents all that can be said in the entire work, or is what the other guests say important? For example, you remember Aristophanes' speech. He says that love is due to the fact that our natures are split; that we once were unitary beings and that the gods in anger divided us so that we are always trying to come back together again. Doesn't Socrates really develop a phase of that idea? He doesn't do it in quite the same way. He says that we are not trying to be reunited; we are trying to be united with the good, and the love of the good object, the good person, is a medium through which we reach that highest good.

*Van Doren:* That is one of the things we still say about love—lovers are seeking to be one—and this myth of Aristophanes, or this poem of Aristophanes if you like, took care of it 2,000 years ago. Almost anything that is said about love, it seems to me, or that can ever be said about love, is said here. That is why I am sure we ought always to make it clear that we are not talking about what "Plato says" love is, because the whole dialogue is engaged in doing that.

*Cairns:* In this dialogue there are a half dozen speakers, each one giving his own interpretation of love. The peak of the dialogue to me is Socrates' explanation of the highest utilization of our creative energies. There are many other things, great things, in the *Symposium,* of course; but the peak to me is Socrates' explanation.

*Tate:* But don't you think that the difference between what Socrates says and what the others say lies in two things: first, he says it dialectically; that is, he builds up every step in terms of reason, one step after another, while the previous speakers have been rather orators than philosophers? Each of them has delivered his eulogy of love, without supporting it rationally. Secondly, Socrates takes the different ideas of love that they have praised and puts them together with a deeper insight.

*Cairns:* But he takes it a step further than any other speaker.

*Tate:* Very much so, yes. What you are asking us, then, is what that step is.

*Cairns:* Yes. Is that a mystical step?

*Van Doren:* It is the "peak" if you like of the statement about love which the dialogue is making, but the word "peak" suggests a cone or triangle, and I should say that Plato's interest was in the whole of that triangle quite as much as in any angle of it. That is, the higher love—I should say the so-called higher love—is not necessarily any more important to him than the lower.

*Cairns:* Important in what sense? As a moralist, don't you think he would like men to strive to reach the peak of the triangle?

*Van Doren:* As a moralist he was interested in all that could be said about love, including the things that Aristophanes and the doctor say. Those are parts of it. The irony of Socrates, it seems to me, consists in his understanding that what a philosopher says about love or about anything else isn't all that can be said about it.

*Tate:* Don't you think that when Socrates begins to speak and says something very complimentary to Agathon, he really means it? While he says that Agathon is right in trying to discuss the nature of love, it's obvious he doesn't think Agathon has completed the discussion, but he is quite sincere in that tribute to Agathon.

*Van Doren:* Yes. This peak, after all, upon which we find Socrates is a peak where he is contemplating an abstraction. I mean the most abstract form of the thing which is lovable. But abstraction is important in his mind, in Plato's mind, only because all the preliminary stages have been lived also. Plato and Socrates did not live in a merely rarefied atmosphere.

*Tate:* You should consider a difference between Aristotle and Plato in the statement of any idea. Aristotle gives you a treatise; Plato gives you dramatically all the steps by which he reached the idea in terms of experience. Plato expresses himself, in other words, through figures of speech, metaphors of all kinds, even myths; Aristotle, in observation and reason.

*Cairns:* Are you asserting that he did not mean something definite and concrete in his idea of absolute beauty?

*Van Doren:* You mean he intended Socrates to mean something definite?

*Cairns:* Yes, if you want to make that point. I do not think it is important in the present connection.

*Van Doren:* But the ladder of love which Socrates describes us as ascending if we are going to be completely happy, from fair forms to fair practices to fair notions to the notions of absolute beauty and the knowledge of the excellence of beauty—I take that ladder to be a ladder which is standing on top of a building. The building also is important. This dialogue has seldom been read to the fullest advantage because people have looked in it only for two or three pages on which the right sort of thing has been said by somebody.

*Cairns:* Do you think that the metaphor of the ladder that you have mentioned is comparable to the mystic's path, the upward path of Plotinus, Mr. Van Doren? You used the phrase, "ladder of love."

*Van Doren:* It seems to me that it is not.

*Cairns:* How would you differentiate it?

*Van Doren:* I should say that although Socrates at this point is not being explicit and not elaborating his theme at all, he is speaking of an intellectual operation, the operation of abstraction.

*Tate:* I think so, too, Mr. Cairns, because in the case of Plotinus the mystical achievement of the highest good, the highest good being God, is not an intellectual operation. It's a mystical, immediate experience and is a leap. You reach the object of that experience without any mediation, but Socrates' exposition of the highest good is something quite different. It's dialectical and rational. If we want to introduce another idea here, we can show that. Doesn't Socrates say something about a kind of good or beauty which is a little lower than his abstract good? You might call it the second-highest good, if that's not a contradiction.

*Cairns:* You mean what Plato calls the longing for immortality?

*Tate:* Yes. He said that even among men who are not philosophically rational there is evidence that humanity is blindly searching for this highest good in pursuing honorable things, doing honorable deeds, achieving an honorable reputation to pass on to posterity. On that level men are trying to achieve this separate, unique good. Honor approximates the eternal. Doesn't he say that the lover is the person who is pursuing a good which is everlastingly possessed, and honor and great deeds—

*Cairns:* I think it is essentially the Greek idea of *arete,* virtue, or longing to excel. Perhaps it is also comparable to medieval romantic chivalry.

*Tate:* I should think it only vaguely comparable. Perhaps there was some influence due to the development of Christian ideas which were based to some extent on Plato.

*Cairns:* I was thinking of the inspiration for noble deeds which he found in love.

*Van Doren:* But to what extent is the reward of this second-highest love reputation and honor among men? Did you use the word "honor" only in the sense of that reward which we receive through applause, through respect and admiration?

*Tate:* Yes, and I think for that reason honor is not quite as selfless as the highest love. It's not as disinterested as the pursuit of the abstract.

*Van Doren:* You don't find that form of lover, for instance, loving beauty or the good for its own self.

*Tate:* As Plato would say, it is somewhat contaminated by material considerations.

*Van Doren:* Yes, but the lover in both cases is aware of the lack of something in himself.

*Tate:* Yes. He is trying to reach the good.

*Van Doren:* A bit of dialectic, perhaps a third of the way through the dialogue, demonstrates pretty well that this thing which is being called "love" is hardly a thing in itself at all. It is almost formless, colorless. It is merely a state which exists between one who wants something and the thing he wants.

*Tate:* Doesn't it seem to you that Plato's great skill in the writing of dialogues comes out in that bit of dialectic that you are referring to? He says—Socrates in substance says: All you gentlemen have been very interesting, but you've forgotten to say that love must be the love of something. It's not just love. A father must have some relation to somebody else, that is, to his son; love must have a relation to something else. The highest relation is to the good.

*Cairns:* Perhaps this second kind of love, this longing for immortality, the thing which is stimulated by the second kind of love, we would regard today as a higher form than the form that Socrates puts first.

*Tate:* Why should we do that?

*Cairns:* Because it perhaps is more socially useful. Today we are quite utilitarian and that second form of love is a socially useful form of love.

*Tate:* But wouldn't Socrates ask how we can tell whether it is socially useful unless that kind of love is directed toward objects which can be defined in terms of the highest good? How do you know whether the secondary love is right unless it has a relation to the primary love, the highest love?

*Van Doren:* You must have a standard for measurement.

*Cairns:* I think it was Socrates who pointed out that the warriors in Homer went to war stimulated by love. This was a manifestation of the second love of which he was speaking, an evidence of its social usefulness.

*Tate:* We might refer to Plato again to put this in another perspective. In the *Republic,* you know, he is talking about the timocracy, that is, the state of society in which men pursue honor, but today we would call that a kind of careerism—this trying to be conspicuous or have careers or be prominent—which is a very different idea from the Socratic conception of it in the *Symposium.*

*Van Doren:* Yes, and if the conception of absolute or separate or single or perfectly abstract love were lacking from this picture, pretty soon we should have statesmen longing for inferior forms of immortality—longing for fame upon an undistinguished level.

*Cairns:* Did not Socrates say that rulers and educators were the highest examples of this second form of love?

*Tate:* They are, if their conduct is in the light of justice and temperance. He says, of course, that this second-highest love leads to justice and temperance in social conduct.

*Cairns:* And did not Athens extend special privileges to lovers of this second class?

*Tate:* Yes, the honorable men were greatly cherished in Athens.

*Van Doren:* Nevertheless, according to Socrates, if we remember the *Republic* again, would these statesmen learn what temperance or justice was? What would have been their education? There would have been no contact with philosophers. The philosopher is the lover always, I should say, in Plato.

*Cairns:* You mean to say they would learn it from the contemplation of absolute beauty?

*Van Doren:* Yes, if you like.

*Tate:* Doesn't Socrates end up by maintaining that the ordinary sense of the word "lover" is meaningless, that the lover is the same man as the philosopher—that is, etymologically, doesn't the word "philosopher" mean a lover of wisdom? Well, that is the only kind of lover that Socrates admits in the long run.

*Van Doren:* In the long run it is the kind of love that interests him most, that seems to him the pure thing, the real thing.

*Tate:* Yes. Every other form is incomplete.

*Van Doren:* Although interesting to him.

*Tate:* Interesting and necessary. The reason why I would be inclined to argue with Mr. Cairns on that point is this: that with Socrates you can't omit the intermediate stages.

*Van Doren:* That is why it seems to me important, when we are discussing this dialogue about love, to remember that it is a dialogue, that a number of persons are talking in it, and that almost every possible point of view toward love, including Socrates', is somehow taken into account.

*Tate:* Can you think of any point of view toward love that is not touched upon, perhaps briefly, in this dialogue?

*Van Doren:* I know of none. For instance, one way of talking about love is being funny about it, and this dialogue is from time to time funny.

*Tate:* Aristophanes, the comic poet, is funny. That is one of the remarkable things about this dialogue—the people seem to speak in character. Aristophanes gives us the myth of the origin of love and it is grotesque and at the same time it is very moving.

*Cairns:* Why don't you state that myth? You touched briefly upon it before.

*Tate:* I think it is very interesting. Aristophanes begins by saying that originally human beings had two heads, four arms and four legs, and that they were completely round. They were monsters. They rolled over the earth and they became so powerful that they decided that they would be insolent toward the gods. The gods to punish them took them and split them in two and that's what we are today. That is, we have two arms, two legs and one head, and ever since we've been trying to get back together, to get into unity again.

*Cairns:* Do you read that purely as comic relief or do you see anything serious in it?

*Tate:* I think it's very serious.

*Cairns:* What is the serious element?

*Tate:* The permanent truth that is expressed in it. It's a truth that Socrates himself recognizes and builds upon when his turn comes.

*Van Doren:* It is as if any profound and highly imaginative person, hearing an ordinary person say, "In love we are attempting to join ourselves with our double, from whom we have been separated," recognized the truth of such a statement and went on: "Well, let me put it in the form of a myth. Let me write you a poem about that or make you a speech about it, and of course

I will not be more serious than the conception deserves, but I will give it all its due."

*Tate:* Don't you think that we might do an Aristophanes here ourselves and say: Doesn't it strike you as funny that some biologists who have read this dialogue say there is a profound biological truth expressed in it; that is, more forms of life are reproduced by division than by fertilization. To suppose that Plato must have had some intuition of that scientific fact—well, that seems to me to be funny.

*Van Doren:* You are supporting our statement made a moment ago that every conceivable sort of thing is either said or suggested here.

*Tate:* Yes. On practically every level.

*Cairns:* I don't see anything more serious in it than Mr. Van Doren has mentioned.

*Tate:* Don't you think the myth of unity is a permanent thing and a serious thing? That the myth of unity of being runs through all literature at all times?

*Cairns:* That was what I understood Mr. Van Doren's point to be.

*Van Doren:* And if you like, to come back to this business of the high and the absolute and so forth, Socrates, of course, was serious in saying that the man who wants to love an object which will not elude his grasp, which will not die on him, which will not disappear from him, and which will not cease to be satisfactory, had better cultivate his powers of abstraction.

*Cairns:* If he wants happiness.

*Van Doren:* Because to love a single beautiful person, to love a single beautiful thing, is not to love enough, since that thing may disappear. You must learn to love the beauty in that thing which is like the beauty in any other thing. Finally, there is the contemplation of beauty—if you like, with a capital B. But my point would be that although this is a very important idea to Socrates and inspires the passage of the dialogue most people remember, yet he has not lost his sense of perspective; he sees that sort of statement in proper perspective among many other statements which are being made. There is the doctor, for instance, who is very amusing and casual and very personal about his friend who has the hiccoughs.

*Cairns:* Aristophanes had the hiccoughs.

*Tate:* The physician recommends an old remedy, doesn't he?

*Van Doren:* He says to tickle yourself and make yourself sneeze, and they have a little kidding back and forth about that. To me it is very important to say that for Plato this was just as necessary a part of a good discussion of love as the moment when Socrates climbs to the top of his ladder. He belongs there, but he doesn't lose contact with the ground either.

*Tate:* Aren't you saying, Mr. Van Doren, that this is a great work of literature which is whole, complete, and no part of it may be ignored?

*Van Doren:* I think it is one of the greatest of all works of literature, one of the most consistently brilliant, one of the books which you can read over and over again, always discovering it to be more delightful than it was before. I used to think of it as a dialogue at the center of which was a ladder of love, but now I find all of it necessary.

*Tate:* The ladder of love reminds me of Mr. Cairns' point. I would like to hear what he has to say about that.

*Cairns:* I was wondering whether the top of the ladder of love isn't something more than a transcendental metaphysics. Or do you take it seriously? I think we can take it seriously and explain his point in general terms. Through self-control—the complete physical repose of prayer or contemplation—the physical energy is directed into intellectual or imaginative effort. This freedom from conflict gives the mind or imagination a sense of spaceless, timeless exhilaration; this concentration of energy produces a creative power, a clearness of perception, a sensuous awareness. The creative power generated through this concentration of energy is genius, intuition, ecstasy. That is what happened to Socrates, Plotinus, Plato and many others. Socrates considered it the highest form of love, since it is the highest expression of creative energy. To him it was the realization of absolute beauty.

It is the method by which we are alive to the fullest extent of our power; sometimes that intense aliveness is called mystical insight, sometimes awareness of beauty, sometimes other things. But it should, I feel, be taken seriously when it is genuine.

*Tate:* Yes, I think we've got to take the *Symposium* seriously. We've got to take this insight seriously to understand the other things that are said in the dialogue. Otherwise they are incomprehensible. That is the informing idea of the dialogue.

*Van Doren:* We can assume that Socrates assumed that the men with whom he was talking knew how important he thought abstraction was and knew that he didn't have to defend the process.

*Cairns:* You thought that the speech of Aristophanes had both serious elements and comic relief. No doubt it has. I wonder if you feel the same way about Alcibiades' interruption. You will remember that after Socrates reaches the top of the ladder of love, ordinarily one would suppose that the dialogue would end at that point; but it is here that Plato's great art manifests itself. Socrates finishes on the very peak of the ladder. Alcibiades comes in; he is quite drunk and very witty. His speech is grossly material, spiritually a million miles below that of Socrates. But altogether it is wonderful. A lesser artist would have been afraid to risk it as an anticlimax. In Plato's hands it comes off perfectly.

*Van Doren:* That is precisely what I had in mind; to distinguish between the literary part of this dialogue and the philosophical part seems to me to be vicious, because the literary part is also philosophical. It is all philosophical, if you like, or all literary. To begin with, we learn that the dialogue recorded here did not take place yesterday. It took place a long time ago and men have remembered it, indeed have not been able to forget it. It comes to us in the dialogue itself through a chain of memory, so to speak, until finally here is one man who can say it all. Then there is the preliminary business of Socrates coming late to the dinner, having stood outside in the street, lost in thought through half of the meal. The entrance of Socrates is very skilfully delayed, I should say. Then you have the dialogue, which as you say at the end—and this is extremely important, it seems to me, because it shows how in Plato's mind the lighter side is not . . .

*Cairns:* Is not absolute beauty?

*Van Doren:* Oh, he's talking about absolute beauty, but that is not the only thing to talk about. He is more than willing to let Alcibiades rush in with the sound of the girl playing the flute and break up the formal gathering; then go on to describe Socrates as a person worthy of being loved.

*Cairns:* But I think that his artistry is even deeper there. I think that Alcibiades' anecdotes about Socrates paint for us a picture of Socrates as a living example of the philosopher who has actually achieved the highest stage of love.

*Van Doren:* Quite.

*Tate:* Gentlemen, we were talking at the beginning of this conversation about the origin of love. We said that love was neutral. Socrates denies that he is a god at all. I would like to read to you the passage in which the origin of love is described. Socrates gives us a little myth. He says that love is the child of Poverty and of Plenty. Poverty and Plenty attended a feast, and from their marriage they had the child Love. But only for the reason that it was a feast of Aphrodite is Love an attendant upon her. And as his parentage is, says Socrates, so also are his fortunes. In the first place, "He is always poor, and anything but tender and fair, and he is rough and squalid and has no shoes nor a house to dwell in. On the very earth exposed he lies under the open heaven, in the streets or at the doors of houses taking his rest, and like his mother, he is always in distress. Like his father, too, whom he also partly resembles, he is always plotting against the fair and the good. He is bold, enterprising, strong, a mighty hunter, always weaving some intrigue or other, keen in the pursuit of wisdom, fertile in resources; a philosopher at all times, terrible as an enchanter, sorcerer, sophist. He is by nature neither mortal nor immortal, but alive and flourishing at one moment when he is in plenty, and dead at another moment; and again alive by reason of his father's nature. But that which is always flowing in is always flowing out, and so he is never in want and never in wealth. And further, he is in a mean between ignorance and knowledge. Wisdom is a most beautiful thing, and love is of the beautiful, and therefore Love is also a philosopher or lover of wisdom. And being a lover of wisdom, he is in a mean between wise and ignorant. And of this too his birth is because his father is wealthy and wise and his mother, poor and foolish."

(384-322 B. C.)

# ARISTOTLE

# *Ethics*

*THE* ETHICS *of Aristotle is the wisest work of its kind. It was written by one whom Dante called "the master of them who know," and a sign of its mastery is the warning it gives on an early page to readers who suppose that the attainment of happiness through virtue is quick or easy. Aristotle does not pretend that he is writing for children or that he can prescribe to them. Virtue—or rather the virtues, for the author very sensibly admits the existence of more than one form which the good life must take, at least if it is to be lived in the world of men—is the result of taking thought, and the act of taking thought must be a long-established habit before excellence can be expected. Excellence will never be wholly achieved in a world of accident and imperfection, yet the study of it is something which the human mind cannot evade—and remain human. Aristotle proceeds as a human being to discuss the problems which all men recognize as central to conduct. In the course of doing so he develops his famous theory of the golden mean. He can be misunderstood about this only by those who do not read him. But it must be true that many have not read him, since the golden mean is commonly set forth as a compromise easily and quickly arrived at by measuring the distance between extremes and dividing it in half. The* ETHICS *is worth reading if only for its demonstration that the mean is in fact the ideal and, like any other ideal, unattainable.*

*Cairns:* We shall find a close correlation between the thought of Plato and that of Aristotle as formulated in the *Ethics*. Ideas which are characteristically Greek underlie both works. The Greeks were interested in this life, not in some future life. They asked themselves how a man should conduct himself to derive the greatest happiness from life. They observed that activity was the source of pleasure. They concluded that mental activity was the source of greater pleasure than physical activity. An activity which is a voluntary, rational choice of a middle course between extremes is the activity of the virtuous and therefore of the happy man. At this point Aristotle takes a step beyond Socrates. Aristotle argues that it is not enough to know what action is best, but men must be trained by the state to control their appetites and their fears, so that they will be able to do what they know is good. There is a curious sentence in Aristotle, near the beginning of the book, which reads, "It is hard to be good." I wonder, Mr. Tate, if that sentence had any special meaning to you.

*Tate:* Mr. Cairns, I believe that the sentence means to me just about what it does to you and Mr. Van Doren—that it is hard to be good! Aristotle, I think, is saying that it is very difficult to find the mean behavior—that is, behavior which is between excess and defect. The mean is not to be taken as a general average; you can't say that you're a little good and a little bad and that the average will be the mean. It is something more difficult than that. For example, suppose you have the virtue of courage, which Aristotle discusses. The excess of that is rashness; the defect is cowardice. Now let us see if we can take that a little further.

*Cairns:* They are both defects.

*Tate:* Both are departures from true courage. The rash man is no more courageous than the coward. Suppose you have a young man who is indignant at some other country, and his country goes to war. He joins the army. We say that he is doing that for patriotic reasons, and he is a brave man. But suppose also he has a wife and several children whom his bravery compels him to neglect. Now is he a brave man without any qualification? In other words, Aristotle is not saying that you can derive this mean mechanically. Probably the virtuous man is he who confronts all these situations simultaneously and who somehow has the moral sense to mediate among them and to carry them all forward at once. It takes moral insight to do justice to all the different virtues at the same time, and therefore it is hard to be good.

*Van Doren:* And neither, Mr. Tate, does he seem to be saying that it is easy to arrive at the mean, as it were, arithmetically. We do not discover what the mean is by dividing in half the line which extends from one extreme to the other, because there is no such line, I take it.

*Tate:* No, there is no such line because the defect or the excess of any virtue is not a substance in our minds or a substance of the world. We have appetites and passions that are driving us in one direction or the other all the time.

*Van Doren:* Virtue, the mean state in other words, is the positive thing for Aristotle. It is the thing which we as human beings, presumably, are capable of. The defect and the excess are fallings-off from that, in the one direction or the other, so that the ordinary notion—I think it would be the ordinary notion—that the golden mean is a kind of compromise arrived at negatively through our not being defective or excessive is incorrect.

*Tate:* No, it is not correct. Virtue is certainly a positive thing.

*Van Doren:* The only negative things are the excess and the defect.

*Cairns:* I think it's possible to state the doctrine in another way in Aristotle's own terms. He makes the point that the natural impulses are not good and not bad in themselves, that there is a right amount of each and a right time and a right manner and right objects for each.

*Tate:* Do you think that Aristotle has any puritanism in his doctrine of the mean?

*Cairns:* No. Aristotle's doctrine is one of moderation. He is opposed to asceticism. I think, for example, that he anticipated the criticism of Manichaeism in its ascetic aspects; I think at the other extreme—I wonder if you agree with me—that he would reject Rousseau's doctrine of naturalism.

*Tate:* I agree. Doesn't he say that of the two sensations, pleasure and pain, we should avoid pleasure more than pain because we are not impartial judges of pleasure? We can easily be seduced by it. But pain acts as its own corrective since we recoil from it.

*Van Doren:* And of course it is well to remember that the whole reason for man's being good is that it is the only way in which he can be happy. This is not puritanism in the ordinary sense of that term. Temperance or moderation or meanness, to play upon the word, is what gives us pleasure because it is what makes us human.

*Cairns:* Aristotle's successors had difficulty with this notion of the mean and they severely criticized it—first, on the ground that it is a quantitative notion and that as such it is impossible to apply it to elements in an ethical situation.

*Van Doren:* I thought I was disposing of that, Mr. Cairns, when I denied that the solution was arithmetical.

*Cairns:* Aristotle himself denies that the solution is arithmetical, but we must not forget that the notion remains quantitative, not qualitative. While the solution is not arithmetical it is quantitative; the difficulty is, however, that the elements we have to estimate in an ethical situation are only too frequently qualitative.

*Tate:* I agree with you there, Mr. Cairns, because every abstract scheme of ideas is quantitative; when you reduce it to experience, then it becomes qualitative in being an experience. Aristotle says that the moral sense alone will give us the details of right behavior in the mean, the details being the concrete situations that we find ourselves in.

*Van Doren:* Now take that virtue—in my translation at any rate; you may not be using the same one—which he called "easy pleasantry." I might translate it as good humor, as the quality of the good-natured or the good-humored man. Aristotle considers that one thing a man is when he is a man is good-natured, good-humored, witty. He says that the excess of this virtue—that is, the falling away into excess—is buffoonery, foolishness, silliness, and the defect of it is clownishness: that is to say, witlessness, stupidity or denseness. Now it seems to me that in our discussion of our fellow beings we are always being Aristotelian; we are using his ideas, whether we know it or not, when we say of a given person that he doesn't know where to draw the line between wit and buffoonery, or we say he doesn't know how to draw the line between wit and stupidity. Of course, no one assumes that there is a line to be drawn as if by a geometer. No one assumes that there are any numbers, any quantities involved. We perceive these things to be qualities.

*Cairns:* I think that is right in large part. But suppose you have a young man who is motivated by the impulse of love. Is he going to put at one extreme brunettes and at the other extreme platinum blondes and try to find a mean between them for his love object?

*Van Doren:* That isn't an ethical matter at all, Mr. Cairns.

*Tate:* That's a matter of taste.

*Cairns:* No, that is a course of action which leads to happiness; and Aristotle asserts that the end of human life is happiness or well-being, and actions directed toward that end are ethical actions.

*Tate:* Perhaps Aristotle might have an answer to that, although he doesn't explicitly discuss the question. Wouldn't he say that the young man who chose his wife on the basis of the blondeness or the brunetteness would be just a fool? That wouldn't be a sufficient basis for any moral choice.

*Van Doren:* It would be a defect or an excess of that impulse which makes us consider taste in the matter. But I don't see that the question as you put it has any ethical weight at all.

*Cairns:* I am only applying the Aristotelian system. In other systems it may be a matter of taste. There is another point I am worried about in connection with the mean. Do you think the right action is always in a mean? Isn't it true that particular feelings should be encouraged to the uttermost and that particular feelings should be suppressed altogether apart from the mean?

*Tate:* I don't quite follow you there. Say that again.

*Cairns:* I am asking you if the right action is always in a mean.

*Tate:* In other words, that it is between the two extremes; that is, the excess or the defect.

*Cairns:* Yes. Aren't there occasions on which a particular feeling should be entirely suppressed?

*Tate:* For example, if I have an impulse to murder someone or to steal something, I think it ought to be suppressed, and Aristotle, I believe, agrees.

*Van Doren:* Or to tell a flat lie.

*Tate:* There is no possible mediation between extremes involved there. They are absolutely bad.

*Cairns:* On the other hand, if you were in the Japanese army and it was necessary to reduce a Chinese fort, you might strap a torpedo on your back and run into the wall of the fort, blowing yourself up and the fort as well. Now that is a feeling of courage or perhaps you would say rashness, but from the point of view of the Japanese that is a feeling which should be completely encouraged. No mean can be found there.

*Tate:* I think probably in that situation, from the point of view of the Japanese moral code, whatever that may be, especially the military code, that it would not be rashness; that it would be bravery. It would be rashness for me as a citizen in a country which is at present at peace to strap a torpedo to me and run into a building. It would be an act of foolhardiness. It depends. Doesn't Aristotle say that the mean depends on the situation? What is a mean at one time is an extreme at another time.

*Cairns:* I am saying there is no mean in that situation.

*Van Doren:* In that situation, no, because the mean has disappeared there, along with all morality. Morality is not relevant to such a situation.

*Cairns:* What do you do with the other case, when you have an impulse to murder and you suppress that feeling completely? Has morality disappeared?

*Van Doren:* Yes, I should say so. Aristotle is not writing this book for people who are trying to decide whether or not they should commit murder. He takes it for granted that murder is beyond the realm in which you discuss morals, using your mind in order to do so.

*Cairns:* But don't you think that Aristotle's real point is that the average human being does not calculate his course of action? He doesn't take two extremes and say, "I will follow this course." Aristotle says that we directly perceive right and wrong. We don't calculate our courses of action as a rule. We perceive a situation and act more or less impulsively.

*Tate:* He brings in the idea of intuition, but that comes at a further stage of our moral development. Aren't we really getting around to the point where Aristotle says that our moral education is the process of what he calls "habituation"?

*Van Doren:* Habits, of course, are very important.

*Tate:* Aristotle explicitly says many times that you can understand intellectually all the ethics in the world, but that you will not know how to behave, that you have to be trained in it. I recall a quotation from *Hamlet,* when Hamlet is talking to the gravediggers. He is watching the gravediggers handle the skulls, and Horatio says, "Custom hath made it in them a property of easiness." Their moral natures, their sensibilities, are blunted. They can handle those objects with ease because they are trained for it. Well, you are trained for good in the same way.

*Van Doren:* You are trained for good by having been good all your life, or at least all of your mature life. You remember Aristotle says that he is not writing this book for children or for very young men to read—young either in years or in brains.

*Tate:* Doesn't he bring in the concept of the will as being closely related to the moral sense? By acting morally over a number of years you train your will to act morally, and you will to do the good thing after you have developed the insight to perceive the good thing.

*Cairns:* He also says that the trained legislator lays down the mean and that the trained educators mold character. Apparently he thinks the average man can't determine the mean himself, that it requires a certain capacity—intellectual capacity and moral capacity.

*Van Doren:* We may assume that Aristotle, as a matter of fact, is perfectly willing to reason circularly here, as he does several times. It is the practical world that he is discussing, and he makes no attempt to prove that what he is saying is true against our probable disbelief. As a matter of fact, he assumes our belief. He says, "I am talking as a man to other men about conduct." He says, "I assume that all men know what conduct is and what good conduct is." So whenever it is necessary he falls back upon that general assumption. You doubtless remember that he is never claiming for this work any kind of intellectual rigor. We may find it to be intellectually very able, but he is not being "technically," I should say, a philosopher at all.

*Cairns:* But he says that goodness of character is neither natural nor unnatural to man, that we start with a capacity which has to be developed by practice.

*Van Doren:* Yes, but the practice is all-important because practicing virtue is having virtue. Practicing virtue is putting yourself in that state eventually in which you will have it relatively without effort.

*Cairns:* I think that he would disagree with Socrates in thinking that it is enough to know which course of action is best.

*Van Doren:* He surely would.

*Tate:* Socrates sees virtue as an intellectual thing. You discover it with your intellect. But not so with Aristotle, because Aristotle is a little more realistic. There's a question that occurs to me at this point, since Mr. Van Doren has mentioned the fact that Aristotle reasons in a circle. What is the ultimate authority, we might ask?

*Cairns:* For Aristotle?

*Tate:* Yes.

*Cairns:* He proposes the opinions of the wise men.

*Tate:* Yes, but the wise men are those we accept as wise, you see. Is there an absolute standard of ethics or is the standard relative? I think Aristotle leans to the relative.

*Cairns:* He leans to the relative in applied ethics. I think if he were dealing with theoretical ethics, if he were determining what is the nature of "ought" and what ought we to do, then he would be quite certain.

*Tate:* But what about it in terms of the conduct of the ordinary man? The ordinary man sees a certain object as good. How does he know that it is good?

*Van Doren:* It is a curious thing, but Aristotle tells him that he will know it as good by measuring it by what he knows of some good man or of good men in general. If you ask him what a good man is, he says you already know. Or he will tell you a good man is a man who has been good all his life. But the question still remains: What is good? Aristotle prefers to leave it there.

*Cairns:* His circular reasoning occurs at many points. For example, he asserts that we become good by doing good actions. When he makes that assertion the question naturally suggests itself: How can we do good acts if we are not ourselves good?

*Van Doren:* I should say the question that that raised was: What are good actions? His answer is: The actions of a good man.

*Tate:* A bad man might accidentally do something good, but in his behavior it would have no moral significance because it would be done by a bad man.

*Van Doren:* I take it that this circularity of his reasoning—I'm willing to take his word for it—is necessary in the realm of human conduct. In some other realm, in the realm of metaphysics, such reasoning would be intolerable. In the realm of science, in the laboratory, for instance . . .

*Tate:* Mr. Van Doren, don't you think at the end of the *Ethics* Aristotle brings up a very difficult metaphysical conception? The idea of happiness as the supreme end of morals.

*Van Doren:* He assumes that the subject which the book accepts for itself when it sets out to discuss human conduct is a subject of limited interest and importance, and he goes on in the tenth book to suggest what more a man might entertain himself with. The curious thing about a man—Aristotle here is meaning by a good man a man who is completely a man—is this. We know what an animal is, perhaps. We may be able to define God. We have never been able to define man. Aristotle, I should say, predicts our incapacity in this book. When we say to a man, "Be a man," what do we mean? The answer, I suppose, is either obvious or it is impossible. Aristotle prefers to say it is obvious.

*Cairns:* I think one of the great virtues of the book is the assertion that Aristotle makes at the beginning; namely, that the subject he is discussing is not exact.

*Tate:* He says that you can get only that distinctness out of the subject which the subject will yield.

*Cairns:* You can only get the peaks. He says, for example, that men aim at four things in the general conduct of their life. They aim at honor, at pleasure, at wealth and at contemplation. No doubt you can think of other things at which they aim, but those four, for a treatise on practical ethics, seem to cover the case very well.

*Van Doren:* Aristotle lists the greatest of these as contemplation.

*Cairns:* Aristotle thinks that the main ingredient in well-being is contemplation, but he qualifies this by saying that the life of contemplation is too high for the ordinary man. We just cannot live it as men because there are too many irrational elements in us, too many defects. That is a life for the gods to lead; man himself can't live that life although he should aim at it.

*Van Doren:* The man living the contemplative life described in the tenth book would at least be a harmless man; that is, he would be stationary; he would have been rendered perfectly stationary in the act of thinking.

*Cairns:* That brings up a point that I haven't been able to satisfy myself about. By the contemplative life I take it that Aristotle meant the contemplation of truth in at least three departments, perhaps four departments, of knowledge: mathematics, metaphysics, natural philosophy and perhaps theology. But then he also says that the happy life is not one of search for truth, but one of contemplation of truth already attained. How do you reconcile such a contemplative life with his insistence upon activity?

*Tate:* Doesn't he make a distinction first? For the ordinary citizen at all times practical wisdom seems to be attainable, although again it is difficult to say what it is. But the contemplative man is a man in a sense removed from life, and I believe Aristotle discusses this question: To what extent is the contemplative man, who is supposedly removed from life, at the same time involved in life? That is, must he have practical wisdom as well as contemplative wisdom?

*Van Doren:* Aristotle has assumed practical wisdom first, don't you think? The contemplative man is the man who has passed through practical wisdom and is now able to consider those things which are true always, whether or not we make them so. The realm of ethics is the realm in which we discuss those things we can control. But Aristotle assumes that we cannot control the physical elements which make up the universe, that we cannot control the will of the gods.

*Tate:* Doesn't he say also that the contemplative man is concerned with those things that we cannot control, with those which are eternal and fixed?

*Van Doren:* Yes. For instance, the existence of God.

*Tate:* And yet those things that are eternally fixed are not the realm of ethical inquiry. There is a paradox involved there that we can't state logically, but it contains a very great deal of insight.

*Cairns:* Your introducing the point of control brings up the fact that Aristotle put ethics and politics together as one subject. After Aristotle, as you know, ethics and politics separated.

*Tate:* I didn't know they did, Mr. Cairns.

*Cairns:* I don't think that in St. Thomas or in Dante you will find ethics and politics joined in the way that they were joined by Aristotle as a single branch of inquiry. I think that early Christianity and, later on, Protestantism, separated ethics and politics. Aristotle, looking at the good life, saw its realization in the life of the whole community. Christianity emphasized the future life, not the life on this earth, which resulted in a separation of ethics and politics. I wonder if today there is not a return to a conjunction of ethics and politics in modern political theories.

*Tate:* Mr. Cairns, what do you mean by that more specifically? Do you mean that man is going in the future to live entirely for the state?

*Van Doren:* Mr. Cairns could not have meant that, for Aristotle nowhere talks of an individual living for the state. The state lives for itself, and it is made up of its government and its people.

*Tate:* It is signficant that Aristotle's ethics precedes his politics, that the individual comes first; but he doesn't live apart from the state. There is a connection but the individual is not lost in the state. You mean, Mr. Cairns, that today the individual is going to be lost in the state.

*Cairns:* Is the political theory of Communism or Fascism or Nazism returning to anything approximating Aristotle's position, or have they gone beyond Aristotle in their insistence on the state's control of the life of man? At any rate, these modern political theories seem to be putting ethics and politics together again in the sense that their ethical content embraces both the state and the individual. Of course, modern political thought may have debased Aristotle.

*Tate:* It may have debased him because I understand that some political theorists in Europe today lean on Aristotle. They attempt to use him to justify their notion of authority.

*Van Doren:* But I should say that there is very little resemblance between them and Aristotle, who, as I say, always kept firmly in mind the concept of the whole state and its good. As soon as there is a distinction between the individual and the state at all, it seems to me, something unfortunate has happened.

*Cairns:* Don't you think that it is sound to put, as Aristotle did, the individual life and the life of the whole community together from the point of view of morals?

*Tate:* It ought to be. That ought to be an ideal, but there are certain difficulties. It seems to me that in Plato's ideal state the individual would almost cease to exist.

*Cairns:* I agree with you. I think Plato is much closer to Fascism than Aristotle, if Aristotle is close at all.

*Tate:* What about medieval Christianity? Certainly the individual was identified with a secular order which was dominated by religious ideas?

*Van Doren:* I should say that if anything good is happening today it is that many individuals are beginning to remember—they are forced to remember by one disaster or another—that they are members of states. Not to be overwhelmed by those states but in order that they may understand their responsibilities to them as well as to themselves.

*Cairns:* So you think that a return to the Aristotelian concept of the unity of ethics and politics is a good thing?

*Van Doren:* Yes. I should like to read a paragraph from Aristotle which Mr. Cairns quoted in part. "Human excellence is of two kinds, intellectual and moral. Now the intellectual springs originally and is increased subsequently from teaching, for the most part that is, and needs therefore experience and time, whereas the moral comes from custom. From this fact, it is plain that not one of the moral virtues comes to be in us merely by nature, because of such things as exist by nature none can be changed by custom. A stone, for instance, by nature gravitating downwards, can never by custom be brought to ascend, not even if one were to try to accustom it by throwing it up ten thousand times, nor could fire again be brought to descend, nor in fact could anything whose nature is in one way be brought by custom to be in another. The virtues, then, come to be in us neither by nature nor in despite of nature, but we are furnished by nature with the capacity for receiving them and are perfected in them through custom."

(1533-1592)

# MONTAIGNE

## *Essays*

*MONTAIGNE'S motto, "What do I know?", is characteristically a question. For he loved questions, and as a writer of essays—the original meaning of the word was "attempts"—he enjoyed the pursuit of the answer more than he did the answer itself. He was, in other words, a skeptic, and he has been called not only the first, but easily the best of his tribe. A skeptic by his definition would not be one who believes nothing but one who believes everything or who at any rate tries to do so. Montaigne, a citizen of the Renaissance and of France, was so much at home in the realm of speculation that he preferred never to leave it. His pleasure was to play with ideas, and his delight was the differences among men. His own personality, which the* ESSAYS *richly if modestly declare, was so charming that many of his readers are devoted to it alone; but he would have preferred that their devotion be given, as his was, to the perennially vary-*

*ing spectacle which men present. His scholarship was that of one who wanted to see from books what men used to be like; and his interest in his own times was an interest in their variety. Comparative in his view, he was one of the first anthropologists; indulgent by temperament and by choice, he was a forerunner of the principle of tolerance; brilliant and unassuming, he remains one of the most engaging of all ancient or modern writers.*

## (MR. MARVIN LOWENTHAL, GUEST)

*Cairns:* Montaigne introduced a new literary form, the essay. His essays are concerned principally with problems of human conduct and with a word portrait of himself. He had been trained in classic literature and we see in his writings a reflection of the Greek ethical ideas we have been discussing. His plea is for moderation. Know thyself, he quotes from the Greeks. He argues that through self-knowledge we shall learn to doubt that we are necessarily right and that other men who disagree with us are necessarily wrong. Mr. Lowenthal, you have written a book on Montaigne called the *Autobiography of Montaigne.* Is it your thought that Montaigne's chief aim in writing was the word portrait that he has painted of himself?

*Lowenthal:* Well, I'll tell you, Mr. Cairns. I'm just enough of a skeptic that I feel I must answer that question yes and no.

*Cairns:* Do you mean you have been too much influenced by Montaigne?

*Lowenthal:* Perhaps that's true; anyway, with respect to Montaigne's purpose in writing his essays, in one sense his chief aim was to paint a portrait of himself. And his reason was a very sound one. Many people write books on what they think they know about and a lot of people write books concerning what they know nothing about. So Montaigne—he has said it somewhere in his essays—proclaimed that he was the most learned man alive in what he undertook to write about, and that was himself. He felt that he knew more about himself than anyone else could know.

*Van Doren:* Mr. Lowenthal, would you go so far as to say

that any skeptic chooses to answer a question with the three words yes and no? I rather like that definition of a skeptic.

*Lowenthal:* Sometimes they would answer that way and sometimes they would answer as Montaigne himself answered when he adopted the motto, "What do I know?"

*Tate:* But do you not think, Mr. Lowenthal, that in Montaigne there is something of the Renaissance arrogance in his assumption that he could know himself? What is this knowledge of himself that he gives us in the essays?

*Lowenthal:* There perhaps was something of the Renaissance interest in one's own personality that induced him to examine himself, but he certainly showed no arrogance in the results.

*Tate:* I think that's quite true. And don't you think, Mr. Lowenthal, that there is a great difference between Montaigne and Rousseau in that respect? They are both interested in themselves but isn't there a difference in the way in which they are interested in themselves?

*Lowenthal:* Yes. Chiefly the fact that when Montaigne's search concerning himself was over, he discovered he knew really as little about himself as he did about anything else.

*Cairns:* Wouldn't you say, Mr. Lowenthal, that that could be reversed, that actually Montaigne gives us more of himself than Rousseau gives of himself?

*Lowenthal:* Oh, I feel sure that's true.

*Tate:* Do you think it's because Montaigne attempts to conceal nothing and Rousseau is concealing a great deal?

*Lowenthal:* Yes. Rousseau painted a portrait so that the rest of the world could see what an unusual man he was. On the contrary—that was why I said yes and no—I think one of the chief aims of Montaigne's book was to paint this portrait in order that others could discover how much they resembled Montaigne.

*Van Doren:* They will discover themselves in him.

*Lowenthal:* The portrait really is a mirror in which other people can look at their own faces.

*Tate:* Mr. Lowenthal, don't you think that this sentence from Montaigne indicates his real aim: "This constant premeditation of all the life is that which makes the wonder." That is, he reflects the world, and the self tends to be subordinated to the picture of the world that he gives us.

*Lowenthal:* That's true, Mr. Tate. He put it another way once, when he said that every man, meaning not only himself but everyone, carries within himself the whole condition of humanity.

*Van Doren:* This question of whether we should or can know ourselves reminds me all at once of Socrates, to whom we credit the injunction, Know Thyself. Surely there was a modest man, for when he talked of knowing himself he seemed to be talking about knowing almost everything except himself.

*Tate:* There is a great difference, though, between Socrates and Montaigne, isn't there, Mr. Van Doren? Socrates knows himself through reason, and Montaigne through experience, don't you think?

*Lowenthal:* But also through reason.

*Van Doren:* I take it that Socrates meant, "I want to know the mind—not my mind necessarily, but the human mind."

*Cairns:* You wouldn't suggest, Mr. Van Doren, that the whole of Montaigne's philosophy can be summed up by philosophical skepticism: What do I know?

*Van Doren:* It is a very significant question. It is the sort of question that Montaigne would ask, and I think it goes a great way. But I asked Mr. Lowenthal my first question about skepticism because it seems to me that the word is frequently ill used, or, at any rate, used in a variety of meanings. For instance, I don't get the impression from Montaigne that he believes nothing. Almost the opposite would be true, don't you think—that he believes everything or that he likes every idea.

*Lowenthal:* Well, I hold that Montaigne is a representative of what I feel to be the finest school of skepticism. He merely doubted and said he didn't know and nobody could ever know ultimate dogmatic truths; but the experiences of life—that hot water burns you and that cold water freezes you, everything that life conveys to your senses—he believed in. He also believed in the use of reason so long as we do not claim, by its use, to discover final and absolute truths.

*Cairns:* But he also believed that the practice of doubt leads to certain philosophical virtues. He thought that self-knowledge, for example, led to tolerance, to moderation.

*Van Doren:* And, curiously, to courage also. He talks about courage.

*Cairns:* In addition, he had a theory of nature. Not in the sense of Wordsworth, but in a sense perhaps akin to Aristotle. I think his view of nature was part of his positive philosophy insofar as you can say he had a philosophy. He was not, of course, an abstract, systematic philosopher.

*Van Doren:* He somewhere says—I've forgotten in what essay, and perhaps it doesn't make much difference because a given thing that he says might appear in almost any essay he wrote, regardless of its title—he says somewhere that nature knows her business better than we do.

*Tate:* Doesn't he say, Mr. Van Doren, that it is better to know nature through himself than, for example, through Cicero? I believe he makes that remark; that is, know nature by introspection and observation of your own experience rather than through abstract treatises.

*Cairns:* How, Mr. Tate, do you reconcile that statement with his essay on cannibals? Of course, I know Montaigne was contradictory, but he wrote a famous essay on cannibals and he seemed to prefer cannibals to Frenchmen.

*Tate:* He felt that cannibals were living closer to nature, and his plea for cannibals is probably the beginning of the modern romantic belief in the noble savage.

*Cairns:* I think it is similar to Rousseau, but I think it commits the same error that Rousseau commits.

*Tate:* Do you think he takes it far enough to make it an error? Isn't the idea of the noble savage just something to meditate on, rather than an actual belief?

*Cairns:* I think it can be said of Montaigne that he attributed the evil existing in the world in the sixteenth century—and the sixteenth century is supposed to be the most tragic of all centuries—he attributed those evils of the sixteenth century to civilization.

*Lowenthal:* I think that Montaigne very often had hidden meanings and hidden intentions in his writings which he doesn't dare bring openly to the surface. For example, I don't know whether Montaigne really believed that the savage was leading a better life than the civilized man of France. When he painted those virtues of the savage—a painting, incidentally, which Shakespeare copied practically word for word in a scene in *The Tempest*—I think he did it for a satiric purpose. That is to say, he used the supposed virtues of the savage simply by way of contrast to the vices, the warfare and the degeneration of civilized Europe.

*Van Doren:* And one sign that he really did this might be that Shakespeare handled it in much the same way in *The Tempest.*

*Tate:* But Shakespeare doesn't say that the world of *The Tempest* was ever a historical event. It's a version of the golden age, not a historical reality.

*Van Doren:* And *The Tempest* contains in itself a great deal of criticism of this idea.

*Lowenthal:* I think the real proof of what I've been trying to urge would be one of Montaigne's keen succinct remarks. Remember the chapter is called "On Cannibals." He admitted that the noble savages used to engage in cannibal practices, and he says in that chapter: "I'm not sorry we denounce the barbarity of such acts of cannibalism. My sorrow is that we remain blind to our own. I think it is more barbarous to eat a man while he is still alive than after he is dead." And his reference is to the use of torture in criminal cases and to the outrageous punishments inflicted on heretics, practically eating them alive.

*Van Doren:* He was very fond of comparing customs.

*Cairns:* He actually met some aborigines in Rouen. I think he met two or perhaps more.

*Lowenthal:* Yes, he did.

*Tate:* On this comparison of primitive with modern civilizations, I'd like to ask Mr. Lowenthal what he thinks. It seems to me that in the essay "On Cannibals" he produces an idea just in passing; characteristically he doesn't emphasize it. He says you get truth only in terms of a particular people, under the conditions they happen to be living in at the time. That's something we get in the nineteenth-century historians, Taine, Michelet and Buckle. Isn't Montaigne the first modern man to voice that opinion?

*Cairns:* You mean the comparative method?

*Van Doren:* No, the theory.

*Tate:* The relativity of truth.

*Cairns:* Well, that is very often a product of the comparative method, particularly in the field of morals. Machiavelli used that same method and we know what his moral outlook was.

*Van Doren:* The theory that a man's ideas are conditioned by his life.

*Tate:* By climate and soil.

*Lowenthal:* That was merely extending the method he used when he was painting his own portrait. One of his famous remarks—it's not, I believe, in that chapter on cannibals—was the observation concerning that strange thing, that thing called truth, which we find is true on one side of a mountain range and false on the other side. He was constantly urging us to examine the habits and the behavior of other peoples, for we shall then discover that every people think that their habits are right.

*Van Doren:* Bernard Shaw once said: "Most Englishmen think that the customs of their native isle are the laws of nature." That is precisely the same idea.

*Cairns:* Montaigne was very much interested in custom and wrote, I think, altogether three essays on the subject. But I think the point—I'd like to know if you agree with this, Mr. Lowenthal—was that our ways are different but are not better. You will remember that he praised Alcibiades because in Sparta Alcibiades was a Spartan but at the sultan's court he had the indolence of the Persian. I think that is one of the points of his study of custom.

*Lowenthal:* Another way of putting it. It happens to be a quotation from that essay on cannibals. He says: "Everyone calls barbarism anything not in use in his own country, but in his own country *there* is always the perfect religion, the perfect government, the perfect everything."

*Van Doren:* And he is smiling as he uses the word perfect. There is one sentence I remember from Montaigne—I've forgotten what essay it was in; I think "Experience"—in which he seems to be saying something not tentatively at all, not with the notion that the opposite might be true somewhere else. He says that he loves freedom, and that he loves it so much that if he were suddenly told there was a corner of the Indies which he would be prevented from entering, he would be miserable, even though he never intended to go there, had never planned to go there. I should say that his love of freedom was a positive thing.

*Cairns:* Oh, it was. I think it is quite interesting that in the sixteenth century he felt so strongly about freedom.

*Lowenthal:* Then, Mr. Cairns, I think there is a third motive, a totally different one, which led him to paint that portrait of himself. Assume that a reader has read all about the habits and ways and appetites and ideas of this man Montaigne and discovers that Montaigne is a very contradictory creature, and then he is induced to look into his own life and his own behavior and he discovers that he too is an inconsistent, contradictory, more or less weak individual. The conclusion he will draw—and it's a conclusion that Montaigne, I think, wanted every reader to draw—is that things that so many of us hold with such fanatical faith—in his day it was faith in religion in either the Protestant or Catholic religion which was the great issue; today we hold political faiths, economic faiths, with a similar fanaticism—are only the products of our own feeble erring minds.

*Cairns:* And the virtue of Montaigne, as he saw it, was that he didn't take sides in the struggle at all. He remained aloof from it.

*Lowenthal:* He wanted to make us understand that most of our dogmas are guesses, and he put this idea in what I think is one of the great lines of all literature, in which he said that all truths are a guess and it's setting a pretty high price on a guess to burn another man alive for it.

*Van Doren:* I'm very much interested in our discussion or our description of Montaigne as a believer in tolerance. Does it seem to you to be a limitation in him? For instance, is tolerance all that we can desire?

*Lowenthal:* Oh, no.

*Van Doren:* Obviously, we should be free. But do you feel that Montaigne lacks an interest in positive things?

*Tate:* I think we should ask at that point: Do you think there's anything like positive Christianity in Montaigne, Christian morals? I should say not. But you couldn't say that Montaigne was unchristian in the sense that a Buddhist is unchristian.

*Cairns:* Oh, no. I think Montaigne was a sincere Catholic, but still at the same time a non-participant in active Catholic controversy.

*Lowenthal:* A sincere, conforming Catholic.

*Cairns:* What you might call a hickory Catholic.

*Van Doren:* But tolerance on its weaker side, its less significant side, means that everyone has the right to say what he thinks even though he thinks badly and speaks badly.

*Cairns:* I think he was tolerant because he was prudent, but he nevertheless sincerely believed in tolerance.

*Tate:* Do you think, Mr. Cairns, that he would have tolerated anything? Do you think that the principle of tolerance in Montaigne would go that far?

*Cairns:* No. He was opposed to asceticism. He wouldn't tolerate asceticism.

*Van Doren:* He was opposed to slavery in any form, I should say. He was opposed to bad manners also. Tolerance ideally would permit bad manners.

*Lowenthal:* Doesn't that come down to how far you are going to carry your intolerance? He wouldn't burn a man alive for reading the classics and therefore thinking he was a learned man, though that was an attitude toward which Montaigne was pretty intolerant.

*Tate:* Isn't the characteristic thing in Montaigne, then, a positive spirit of inquiry, rather than a negative tolerance? A humanistic balance, mediation between all excesses and extremes.

*Lowenthal:* Well, Mr. Tate, he was put to the test once. He lived, as you know, during thirty years of civil war and it raged all about his own countryside. Dozens of his own neighbors' castles and houses were burned, yet he said somewhere that when it comes to a bitter, final issue a man has got to take sides. But, he added, there is a limit to how far you should go in your defense of the cause you believe in. That is to say, what must remain uppermost in your mind is your loyalty to life and the values of life. He says you might dispute what truth is but you can't dispute what treachery is, or cruelty or death.

*Cairns:* To moderation he also added experience, and as you recall, he wrote one of his best essays on experience. I think by experience that he meant knowledge of ourselves.

*Tate:* By knowledge he meant what Aristotle, I think, would mean with the same word. It's knowledge of how other people behave. Montaigne's standard was that of the wise man.

*Van Doren:* The wise man not, however, I think, as Aristotle illuminated the term, or Plato, for that matter. I've been impressed in Montaigne's various accounts of his reading by the fact that he seems to be on the whole not very much interested in either Plato or Aristotle. What do you make, Mr. Lowenthal, of the fact that he seems to prefer to them the historians and the poets, on the one hand, and, in the line of philosophers, on the other, Plutarch and Seneca? What does it mean that the two greatest philosophers, perhaps the only two philosophers we've ever had, leave him untouched?

*Lowenthal:* I think there are two reasons. With respect to Plato, of course, neither Montaigne nor his whole age knew very much about Plato. There had been no widespread translations in Latin, which was the language everybody read. On the other hand, Aristotle was enshrined and enthroned in his day as the absolute god to decide all questions of human thought; and I think Montaigne just didn't like hearing Aristotle called the Just . . .

*Van Doren:* Or an authority. And he was sound there. When Aristotle was an authority he was perhaps less potent than he has been at times when we have read him for whatever he could say.

*Lowenthal:* I think if he had known Plato he would have liked him.

*Van Doren:* I should guess so too.

*Lowenthal:* But Aristotle was a dry old codger who never seemed to get down to the immediate realities of human life.

*Tate:* Oh, I have to dispute that with you.

*Lowenthal:* I beg your pardon. Life, I meant, in concrete terms . . .

*Van Doren:* And, of course, Montaigne was suffering a great deal from the fact that he was able to get hold of Aristotle only through commentaries upon him.

*Cairns:* And he did hate commentaries.

*Van Doren:* He preferred to have a man talking directly to him.

*Tate:* Don't you think there would be a parallel today? For example, in educational theory today Rousseau is largely in the background. Many of us are annoyed by certain modern educational excesses, but we don't really read Rousseau. Montaigne probably resented the scholastic commentaries but without going to Aristotle to see what he had to say. I would say that the Aristotelian *Ethics* was certainly one of the most practical books in the world.

*Lowenthal:* I used the wrong word. I mean that he didn't feel in Aristotle a man who was concretely interested in the details of life. You remember that he once said, "I can't recognize my most common doings when I read them in Aristotle." He said these scholars put such refinements on things that the matter completely escaped him. Whereas in Plato he would have found, with his homely illustrations of the marketplace and the people talking, more of that human touch. It's not the ideas of Aristotle that repelled him.

*Tate:* Yes, I think it is Aristotle's method.

*Van Doren:* You can almost imagine him saying: "I don't enjoy Aristotle because I don't hear a voice speaking there." It is obvious that he loved conversation, loved the human voice—although he thought his own was unattractive.

*Lowenthal:* He had a very high voice. Too loud and shrill.

*Cairns:* I cannot agree with what you have said about Aristotle and Plato. I think that Aristotle is more concrete in his discussion of ethics than Plato is, and just as, if not more, homely, but I feel that Montaigne had a real point when he says he can learn more about life from actually experiencing it than he can from reading about it. I think that is his principal objection to Aristotle.

*Tate:* But how do you account for the fact, then, Mr. Cairns, that Montaigne's *Essays* are largely a tissue of quotations?

*Cairns:* But they are quotations that have gone through his mind and have actually become a part of Montaigne. He has absorbed the ideas they express so that those ideas have really become his own. I think an interesting thing about Montaigne is that actually he doesn't add much to knowledge. The substance of his ideas had been expressed before, but what he has done is to add form.

*Tate:* But his quotations, as Mr. Van Doren was saying, are from history and poetry—concrete events—and they give the assurance of an actual happening.

*Cairns:* But you must remember that Montaigne even rejected that. He said that you can learn more from experience than from reading the life of Caesar.

*Lowenthal:* Of course you know the curious thing is that when he first wrote those essays there were very few quotations in them, and quoting, especially from Latin poets and historians, was a fad of the day. He thought it would make his book more palatable and sell better if he interlarded it with quotations, and he went back in afteryears and just stuffed them in as you stick raisins in a cake.

*Tate:* Does that apply also to the examples he uses?

*Lowenthal:* No. Those were woven right into the context. He felt where his own life perhaps wasn't sufficient to illustrate a point, he might borrow something from another man's life, and of course Plutarch is full of anecdotes of other men and he used those anecdotes just as he used anecdotes from his own experience.

*Cairns:* We all have favorite books and Plutarch was his favorite author.

*Lowenthal:* Through Montaigne I learned to love Plutarch.

*Van Doren:* He seems to mean not only the *Lives* but the *Morals* of Plutarch.

*Cairns:* But I think that Montaigne's essay on *Education* is the least discursive. It was, as you know, addressed to a friend to aid her in the training of her young son.

*Van Doren:* But of course that essay is pat to our discussion at this point because he was a progressive educator, if I may use that term—and I like him as such much better than Rousseau.

*Cairns:* You think he was a progressive educator? In what sense?

*Van Doren:* Of course. He insisted that the child should enjoy his education. I should say that that is the essence of progressive education. At least it ought to be. Many children who are given progressive educations are not enjoying them. But his point is really this: that the child should be made to understand or should be encouraged to understand what an author he is reading is talking about. He should not have to commit to memory what he does not understand. He should not be told that a book is important before he knows what its author was saying.

*Cairns:* He insisted also that the teacher become a child. Do you agree with that, Mr. Van Doren?

*Van Doren:* I don't remember his saying that.

*Cairns:* He said that the teacher in order to impart knowledge to the child must actually have the child's outlook and put himself on a level with the child.

*Van Doren:* I take that for granted in any teaching.

*Lowenthal:* I like, Mr. Van Doren, that other remark about a teacher, which ought to interest you, since you have conducted classes. Remember where he said that if he had a boy who was seeking for a teacher he'd try to find one who had a well-made and well-turned instead of a well-filled head?

*Van Doren:* But I like the well-filled head also. I should take the combination if I could find it.

*Cairns:* Do you go as far as Montaigne does in insisting that the education of the young is the most difficult and important branch of human knowledge?

*Van Doren:* Education is not a branch of knowledge.

*Cairns:* Montaigne seemed to think it was, and so, I gather, do the progressive educators of today. Montaigne treated the theory of education as a branch of knowledge capable of study and communication. That is the point as I understand it.

*Van Doren:* I agree with him that education is very important.

*Tate:* Everything else depends on education. What people do later depends on it.

*Van Doren:* Few things could be more important.

*Cairns:* Do you agree with Montaigne that the teacher's experience and character are more important than his scholarship?

*Van Doren:* No, I don't. And I think Montaigne wanted a teacher to know a great deal. He took for granted that he would.

*Tate:* Gentlemen, I'd like to read a passage here which seems to me to represent Montaigne and the humanistic point of view. It is a point of view which is balanced and just, the complete moderation that we have spoken of before. "Seeing, however, the miseries which have overwhelmed us and for what we have not done, I do not forthwith conclude that we are at the last gasp. The endurance of a state is apt to surpass our understanding. It is a puissant and mighty thing and it often persists despite tyranny, unjust laws, corrupt rulers and the license and sedition of its inhabitants. For my part, I do not despair. Meanwhile, let us follow that great teacher, Epipamondas, and boldly declare that there are some things not allowed, even in fighting an enemy; that the public interest does not require all things of all men, but all things are not permissible to a man of honor because he happens to be in the service of his king, his country and the laws. This doctrine is fitting for our times. We have no need to harden our hearts with steel armor. Enough if our shoulders are hardened. It will do to dip our pens in ink without dipping them in blood."

(1632-1662)

# PASCAL

## *Pensées*

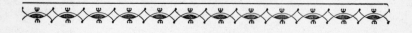

*B*LAISE PASCAL *was a devoted reader of Montaigne, with whose skepticism he is sometimes credited by those who do not feel the force of his religious nature. In his* PENSÉES, *or* THOUGHTS, *a miscellany of his opinions upon reason and revelation, the two sides of the man are clearly to be seen. No more interesting struggle with doubt has ever been witnessed in the modern world. For this seventeenth-century Frenchman was an acute mathematician and natural philosopher at the same time that he was possessed in extraordinary degree of the mystic's sensibility. Accepting revelation by instinct, he has also the compulsion to go on using his mind. Using his mind because it is a good one which will not leave him alone, he feels also the necessity of taking it with him into the realm of faith. The whole struggle between faith and reason expresses itself in this fragmentary book, whose style is one of the permanent glories of*

*French literature. It is the style of a man who in the midst of an impassioned passage can drop suddenly into prose or levity, or who can spring instantly from the ground to the dizziest heights of eloquence. The* PENSÉES *have been quoted to every purpose, and it is true that the man who speaks through them is all but baffling in the range of his fancies. But he is one man after all, and he sums up in himself a spiritual conflict which has raged in the world ever since his day.*

*Cairns:* Montaigne doubted that we could ever be certain of anything. In Pascal we find a Catholic who undertook to refute Montaigne. Pascal insists that if we will only will-to-know, truth, certainty, faith will be given to us. It is through our intuition, not through our reason, that certainty is acquired. A famous passage in Pascal states this problem of intuition and reason in the form of a wager. Pascal argued that the value of eternal happiness is infinite. Our only chance of winning such eternal happiness is by leading a religious life, and even though the probabilities of our winning are very small we should lead such a life because the expectation is infinite. Do you think, Mr. Tate, that this wager of Pascal's should be taken seriously? You will recall that at another point in the *Pensées* Pascal asks, "Is probability probable?"

*Tate:* Mr. Cairns, I despair right here at the beginning of giving a satisfactory answer to that question because Pascal is such a great writer and he covers so many problems of our experience that I can't hope to say anything illuminating. I do think emphatically that we ought to take his wager seriously. A great many critics, particularly in the eighteenth century, thought it was a very frivolous way to discuss eternal salvation.

*Van Doren:* Voltaire, for instance?

*Tate:* Yes, Voltaire. It was he who said that Pascal put the question of salvation up to a cast of the dice.

*Cairns:* He said that it was, as I recall it, unworthy of the dignity of the subject.

*Tate:* But as a matter of fact, Voltaire was a little disingenuous because he didn't think the subject had any dignity. There is another point in that connection that I think will help us to get at this problem. Pascal says: "We have an incapacity of proof insurmountable by all dogmatism. We also have an idea of truth invincible to all skepticism." And in his dilemma he frames his famous wager. You can't prove salvation by reason, but you can't disprove it by reason. It's a distinct realm of experience.

*Cairns:* I feel also, in answer to Voltaire, that Pascal was not interested in the odds as a gambler would be interested; his interest was that of a mathematician who had worked on the calculus of probability and of a passionate amateur theologian.

*Tate:* I should think that this wager is a metaphorical expression. It's a way of stating a spiritual issue in terms of something that is perfectly plain and visible to everybody.

*Van Doren:* But he does carry out all the terms of the wager. For instance, we haven't said that Pascal represents the man in question here as risking something, as offering something, as a man who is bidding a certain amount of money on the chance that he'll win either that much or more or lose that much or more. So our citizen risks something. We haven't said what that was.

*Tate:* Don't you think that from our modern point of view we can throw a little light on that question? In our age when religious experience, at least some specific kind of religious experience, does not seem inevitable to everybody, we look back upon Pascal's remark that the reason why men fear religion is that they won't undertake the responsibility of it. Our age doesn't compel us to face the religious issue, and we drift along neither religious nor irreligious.

*Van Doren:* He assumes, and as a matter of fact he says, that there is no way out of this wager. One must wager. But I'm still interested in the question of what it is that one wagers. What does one risk?

*Tate:* One risks the responsibilities of the fear of eternal punishment.

*Van Doren:* Also isn't it his independence? We have to surrender ourselves in the very act of admitting that we have no choice except the choice of making this wager. We surrender something of that independence which we might have prized.

*Cairns:* I think also that the problem can be generalized—the wager can be generalized beyond the field of religion. You will recall that William James said something similar of Voltaire. He said that if he were in the place of the Deity he would probably take particular pleasure in cutting off the believers of this pattern from the infinite reward. If he were the Deity he would disappoint the straight gamblers even if they won. But he went further and said that nevertheless our passional nature not only may but must decide an option between propositions whenever there is a genuine option that cannot from its nature be decided on intellectual grounds.

*Tate:* Now, Mr. Cairns, don't you think you're granting that the wager is a metaphor?

*Cairns:* I don't think it is a metaphor.

*Tate:* I do, but I think it breaks down at one point and that's the point that you bring up there. A gambler in casting the dice either wins or loses. Either way there is no act of will involved. He either wins or loses, so the metaphor of the wager seems to me to break down. There is something in this choice involving faith that is not involved in an event of pure chance.

*Cairns:* I am not so sure. If we carry William James' thought a step further, if you say under circumstances where you are confronted with a choice that you can't decide on intellectual grounds, if you say: "Do not decide but leave the question open," that is itself a decision just like deciding yes or no, and you run the same risk of losing the truth if you take that position.

*Van Doren:* Yes, and if he heard us using the word independence he might ask: "Was it by reason that you decided you wanted to be independent?" and his answer would definitely be no.

*Tate:* On the question of independence, Mr. Van Doren, Pascal makes a very fine statement. A man who has had a religious conversion and leads a religious life submits to certain externals, certain disciplines, and Pascal says that to expect help from these externals is superstition; to refuse to join them to the internal life is pride.

*Cairns:* But to come back to your question, in Pascal's terms what you are wagering is the Christian way of life or the life of pleasure and luxury. Don't you read Pascal that way?

*Tate:* I was going to say that for us the dilemma is not so exclusive. As we see it today, we have not merely a choice between a Christian life and a life of luxury and pride. We are probably on a neutral ground; that is, we're today neither Christians nor pagans. We make no choice.

*Van Doren:* He himself creates an interlocutor who asks him the question: Why should I have to consider this a dilemma at all?

*Tate:* What about that? It's very interesting.

*Van Doren:* He says you will find out that you are interested if you give yourself to the kind of life which produces such an interest. Like Aristotle's, his reasoning becomes circular at this point, and on several occasions in this book he admits that his reasoning must be circular. We can improve ourselves, he once says, only if we are already improved. If we have been improving ourselves we can continue to improve ourselves, but if we have never improved ourselves we are incapable of doing so now.

*Tate:* How is that connected with the wager, Mr. Cairns?

*Cairns:* I must have read Pascal in a different sense. I took it strictly as the Christian way of life against a life of pleasure and luxury.

*Van Doren:* I should say: the Christian way of life against nothing at all, against no way of life. Are men insisting upon being free from the necessity of any sort of choice at all?

*Tate:* Pascal would call that a life of custom, or inertia.

*Van Doren:* Or mere reason, perhaps. Or mere mathematics. That suggests to me that we have not asked how important this whole passage is in Pascal's mind in view of the fact that it is merely mathematical, that only the mathematics of probability, for instance, is here involved. He was a great mathematician, he is important in the history of mathematics. Yet obviously mathematics is only one of the procedures he takes here and he considers it, I should say, but secondary.

*Cairns:* I think it goes back to his fundamental position that you would soon have faith if you renounced pleasure. I think that is what he is attempting to show.

*Tate:* Before the dawn of Christianity, though, if you renounced pleasure you wouldn't necessarily get faith; you might get just asceticism or stoicism or something like that.

*Cairns:* Plato in the *Phaedo* raised this same problem. You will recall he said that if there be any risk in believing that the state of the soul will be such after death, it is a risk which it is good to run. Pascal's position is the Platonic position.

*Van Doren:* I was interested, Mr. Cairns, during your preliminary remarks, in your use of the word "refute" with respect to Montaigne. Is it clear that Pascal is refuting Montaigne? I should like to substitute the word "extend."

*Tate:* Montaigne stood by worldly experience, and Pascal simply couldn't ignore it because he is first of all a worldly man.

*Van Doren:* It's very important to realize that this man knows everything along with Montaigne. He is not so much refuting him as accepting him, I should say, as far as he goes, and then adding to him all that we mean by Christianity.

*Cairns:* He may accept Montaigne in the sense that all French intellectuals who followed Montaigne were permeated by Montaigne's thought, but Pascal says, "I hate Montaigne."

*Van Doren:* Well, yes, he says that just as one says it of an old teacher whom one may love a great deal and be greatly indebted to. When he says he hates Montaigne or that Montaigne is a fool, he means nothing other, I think, than that he is impatient with Montaigne for not knowing absolutely everything—for instance, that his skepticism was not all. I should say that Pascal has all of Montaigne's skepticism plus that tremendous thing which we think of as Christian thought and Christian feeling.

*Tate:* It seems to me, Mr. Van Doren, he has more than Montaigne's skepticism because it is more rigorous and more subtle.

*Van Doren:* More rigorous, more subtle, and much more flexible.

*Tate:* He takes one of the risks that he urges upon us. He takes the great risk of reason which Montaigne never took in any thoroughgoing way.

*Van Doren:* The reason his faith is impressive to me is that I find him going the whole way of skepticism first. Indeed he insists that that is the only way in which faith can be reached.

*Cairns:* Yes, but at the same time, I think he opposed Montaigne's form of skepticism. Pascal liked his own form but if you asked him the question: "Do you approve of Montaigne's skepticism?" he would say "no."

*Tate:* How would you phrase Montaigne's skepticism then?

*Van Doren:* It would be pretty hard to put it briefly, wouldn't it?

*Cairns:* Yes, it would, but I think Pascal's skepticism is the intellectual doubt of Descartes. It was certainly closely related to it, and it is obvious that Pascal absorbed the thought of his period. It was a century of systematic intellectual doubt in Descartes' sense, and Pascal was a child of his age, as we all are.

*Van Doren:* But in Pascal's book we find that skepticism amounts to this, his misery amounts to this: he discovers either by looking at himself or by looking at other men that man is both miserable and capable of joy, of spiritual success, and capable perhaps in like degree. But the thing he keeps coming back to all the time is that man is both bad and good, both hopeless and worthy of having hope, both great and small.

*Cairns:* But his emphasis is on the miserable side of man's nature.

*Tate:* Isn't that because he believed in the natural depravity of man?

*Van Doren:* We always can afford to be reminded of the miserable side of our nature.

*Cairns:* It may be because Pascal was an ill man.

*Van Doren:* I should doubt that.

*Cairns:* That is a possibility.

*Tate:* Merely that.

*Van Doren:* I should say it was because he was a profound man.

*Cairns:* Your remarks about Montaigne remind me of the fact that Pascal's book is regarded by French critics as the most beautiful book in the French language and the most representative of the high quality of the French people. Some of the admiration of this book strikes one who is not in the direct current of French thought as quite extraordinary, and I wondered if you shared that admiration. For example, the book is admired for its style, and it is insisted that the style is logical and ironic, eloquent, poetic, passionate, tender. Those are all words that the French critics use in describing it.

*Van Doren:* We may be reminded there of something he himself says about style. He remarks that every now and then, instead of finding what we expected to find, namely, an author, we find a man.

*Tate:* I don't think you're really aware of the style.

*Van Doren:* I think you find a man here.

*Tate:* For example, both in the *Pensées* and in the *Provincial Letters* you get the most difficult questions discussed in this lucid prose style, non-technical, perfectly direct, every word a word that somebody would know in common cultivated usage.

*Van Doren:* And he seems to be able to say literally anything, because some of the things he says here with apparent ease were of the utmost difficulty.

*Cairns:* Do you agree with the general estimate of Pascal today in modern letters?

*Tate:* I don't know about Mr. Van Doren, but I would certainly agree with it. I think he is one of the very great men.

*Van Doren:* I do. This book is surely one of the finest of all books, one of the most moving, one of the most complicated—and yet as you say, while complicated, simple.

*Tate:* It is interesting that, in addition to this French praise of Pascal, about twenty-five years ago there was a strong intellectual movement in England which amounted to a revival of Pascal's central position, which I hope we are going to talk about. T. E. Hulme, a very remarkable amateur philosopher, left some manuscripts behind him—he was killed in the last war . . .

*Van Doren:* He was a poet also.

*Tate:* Yes, and the book was edited after his death under the title *Speculations,* and it had a very profound influence on literary criticism in England and America.

*Van Doren:* Incidentally, I'm a little worried about the impression we might have left. We seemed to agree that Pascal chiefly discusses the miseries of men, or the misery of man. This is not true for me. Although he makes it clear that he knows the misery of man and is not necessarily sick in doing so, the book is also full of joy.

*Tate:* Yes, it is, and in that connection Pascal has his greatest message for the modern world. Doesn't he believe in a real distinction between the natural level of experience and the spiritual level? And isn't it true that in modern times we have confused those two realms of experience? Our wretchedness now is augmented by intellectual confusion?

*Van Doren:* Yes. When we now encounter the statement that man is vile or that man is poor or that man is lost, we read both too much and too little into it. When a Christian says that man is vile he does not necessarily mean what we should mean. He means he is vile relatively, of course.

*Cairns:* But Pascal's morality was bleak. He was quite close to the chief exponent of Jansenism, Saint-Cyran, and he was very much influenced by him. Saint-Cyran disliked the spring and its flowers. They displeased him "because they pass too quickly and in most cases die without bearing fruit. He preferred the last days of autumn, although only dry and withered leaves are seen upon the trees." That is what is recorded of him.

*Tate:* There was certainly a strong vein of puritanism in Pascal.

*Cairns:* He had no feeling for poetry and he was contemptuous of art. He suppressed his emotions and he couldn't bear to see his sister's children kiss their mother.

*Van Doren:* Of course, I should say that one reason that he had contempt for poetry was that he was a great poet. It is only little poets who think that poetry is wonderful and keep on saying so.

*Cairns:* You don't think great poets think poetry is wonderful?

*Van Doren:* Never. I've never known one who said so. They take it for granted.

*Cairns:* But they don't disapprove of it.

*Van Doren:* Shakespeare disapproved of it. He is always making fun of poetry. He has no respect for it at all.

*Cairns:* Not in Pascal's sense.

*Van Doren:* No, I really am very serious there. A person to whom poetry is his life, as Mr. Tate says, takes it so much for granted that he wouldn't praise it. To praise it would be to belittle it.

*Tate:* But he takes it seriously in the sense that he takes life seriously.

*Van Doren:* Take a man who thinks that life is important. He doesn't tell you that. The great poets when they are talking about life are not praising life. As a matter of fact, they are likely to be praising death, which is their way of suggesting that life is important. We don't find them performing songs and dances in recommendation of life.

*Cairns:* I don't think you can take the position that Pascal was a lover of life, in Aldous Huxley's phrase, "a life worshipper."

*Tate:* No, that was Montaigne—Montaigne represented that. May I raise a point that I brought up a minute ago? This distinction that runs through all of Pascal's thought, the three realms of experience—nature, mind and what he calls charity. It seems to me that they are very valuable for us to think about today.

*Van Doren:* What you say connects directly with what Mr. Cairns was saying. Life for him was lived on all those levels; it included all those three orders of experience. Now I should say that Pascal was a lover of life. I hate to be perverse here. He loved life, of course, not in the relatively simple sense in which Montaigne loved it, all the varieties of experience coming day after day. Life for Pascal included a sensation of terror which he felt when suspended between the infinities—between infinity and nothing. For him the terror that he felt—isolated in the universe, not knowing why he was born now rather than 200 years ago and in France rather than in England—the terror he felt there was a very rich and beautiful thing, and I should say that it was his way of enjoying life because life for him was not merely the life we live day by day. It was the life we lead in the universe.

*Cairns:* I have no doubt Pascal felt that terror. That is a psychological fact, but I think it is significant that he was an ill man. I don't know of any other man in the history of thought who has felt that terror and who was at the same time a strong, healthy individual.

*Van Doren:* What about Walt Whitman?

*Cairns:* Did the universe frighten him?

*Van Doren:* Absolutely.

*Cairns:* That is news to me. I always read him as the world's most ardent celebrant.

*Tate:* What about Dante? What about Charles Baudelaire? They all felt that.

*Cairns:* I think we're getting into a realm beyond the ordinary —into the abnormal, perhaps—when we mention Baudelaire.

*Tate:* Oh, I don't think so. He was perfectly healthy.

*Cairns:* As a man, yes. But I would hardly call his outlook normal.

*Van Doren:* Only a weak man praises strength. A strong man doesn't praise strength.

*Cairns:* A strong man doesn't have to.

*Van Doren:* Exactly. That's my point. A strong man is more likely to be praising weakness and misery and terror and imperfection.

*Cairns:* Would you find any praise of strength in Pascal?

*Van Doren:* No, he praises weakness.

*Cairns:* That is my point. Because he was sick. Some sick people make virtues of their infirmities.

*Tate:* But, apart from biographical considerations, don't you think that Pascal feels that the spiritual life has a supremacy and is a separate order of truth and is not to be invaded by scientific truth? It's a different order of truth altogether.

*Cairns:* That is an essential point in Pascal. He says that the heart has reasons which reason does not know.

*Tate:* But that has been interpreted sentimentally.

*Van Doren:* The word "heart" should certainly not be read sentimentally there. It is difficult to find a passage in the *Pensées* which can be said to be representative or central or to be the most representative. Any paragraph here, I should say, becomes representative because the book is well knit, even though it is a collection of disparate sayings.

*Cairns:* You get a sense of unity in the book, although it is made up of separate thoughts as you read it.

*Van Doren:* It is made up of separate thoughts, but each one of them is a member of the body. Here is one: "It is dangerous to make man see too clearly his equality with the brutes without showing him his greatness. It is also dangerous to make him see his greatness too clearly apart from his vileness. It is still more dangerous to leave him in ignorance of both, but it is very advantageous to show him both. Man must not think that he is on a level either with the brutes or with the angels, nor must he be ignorant of both sides of his nature, but he must know both. If he exalt himself I humble him. If he humble himself I exalt him, and I always contradict him until he understands that he is an incomprehensible monster."

# AUTOBIOGRAPHY

(1712-1788)

# ROUSSEAU

# *Confessions*

*ROUSSEAU claims at the beginning of his* CONFESSIONS *that he will prove himself unique among men by telling the whole truth about himself even when the truth is trivial or shameful. Such a thing is doubtless impossible, but Rousseau as an autobiographer still stands for a symbol of candor and completeness. He was a novelist as well, and a popular philosopher whose ideas about politics and education exerted an influence now almost beyond computation and still widely felt. His* CONFESSIONS *do not reveal the noble soul whom many eighteenth-century disciples worshipped. Its author seems on the contrary to have been often mean, neurotic, childish and dull. But then it is the truth about himself which he says he is telling; and the world has rewarded him for his frankness quite as generously as it once did for his sentiments. Some of the truth he tells appears between the lines and was perhaps unsuspected by himself. Most of it, however, disarms us by the simplicity with which it is offered, as well as through the prose style which Rousseau keeps always rapid, sensitive and flexible; and there are few readers who will not recognize themselves in one or another of his peccadillos. The motives behind autobiography as the modern world knows it are complex and obscure, nor is it easy to say what those of Rousseau were. There is no question, however, that his book is a classic of its kind.*

*Cairns:* More so than any other figure, Rousseau is the man who made our modern world. But hardly two people agree on what he stood for. He did not make his mark as a man of letters until middle age, with a famous essay attacking civilization and lauding the virtues of savages. What interested me on rereading the life story of this mentally, physically and morally weak man was to find some explanation of why he became and has remained a dominating influence for 150 years. If it is true that Western civilization is tottering, what has the life story of the man who—at least his enemies so assert—willed its destruction to tell us of the personality which so dominates our thoughts and actions? Mr. Van Doren, do you find in Rousseau's *Confessions* anything to account for his phenomenal influence?

*Van Doren:* Everything there, I think, accounts for this influence. The modern world, insofar as it has been made by Rousseau or insofar as it made him, is clearly a world which, if it knows a great deal about mental and moral weakness, to use your term, knows little about mental or moral strength. I take the chief fact about Rousseau, as he expresses himself here, to be that he knows little or nothing.

*Tate:* Mr. Van Doren, why do you think that? Why do you think that he lacked that kind of knowledge? Is it a personal deficiency in Rousseau or something about his time?

*Van Doren:* It is clear that he lacks the knowledge, but the fact of his reputation proves to me that his age lacked the knowledge—and our age too. Even as recently as the seventeenth century he would have been unable to get anywhere except as a curiosity.

*Tate:* I gather from something Mr. Cairns said that perhaps he thinks Rousseau created the modern age. I know we use that kind of expression in speaking historically, as a sort of shorthand.

*Cairns:* If I may answer for Mr. Van Doren, I will tell you exactly what I have in mind. He is regarded as the father of the French Revolution, romanticism, democracy, anarchism, republicanism, communism and fascism.

*Van Doren:* Well, the books we have been reading ourselves make it clear enough that he was not the inventor of democracy.

*Cairns:* But the men who work in those fields claim him as their ancestor. It is very unusual that a man should be the father of so many contradictory movements, but that is the claim made by his disciples in those fields.

*Tate:* Shouldn't we inquire a little further into the nature of this influence? In England the fashion for Rousseau, of course, was never so extreme as in France, but at the same time, a man like Byron took it up and developed it into a new phase.

*Cairns:* In the Romantic movement, and particularly in Byron and Shelley.

*Tate:* What do you think this Romantic movement consists of? Isn't it a glorification of sentiment and instinct, the expansion of the merely emotional aspect of life and a general neglect of objective truth?

*Van Doren:* Doesn't it seem clear to you, Mr. Tate, that only in an age which itself had lost wisdom such a man as Rousseau could become great?

*Tate:* Yes. It is not only a question of his writings. We know from the *Confessions* that Rousseau was a very popular person. He made a great many enemies, but he must have been exceedingly ingratiating because he found many supporters and patrons. That is a sad commentary on the age.

*Cairns:* What do you find in the *Confessions,* if anything, to account for this influence?

*Tate:* Over the Western world by the eighteenth century the decline of objective moral and religious standards had set in. The development of mere ego, reliance upon personality and a feeling for the natural rightness of one's actions—all that superseded the religious standards, and Rousseau appealed to everybody who wanted to let down the bars, so to speak.

*Van Doren:* Would you be willing to substitute the word "temperament" for "personality"?

*Tate:* Yes. Temperament.

*Cairns:* Schopenhauer said that on Rousseau alone has nature bestowed the gift to be a moralist without being a bore.

*Van Doren:* I am astonished in reading this book again to discover how ignorant Rousseau is in even the elementary matters of temperament. For instance, he is very proud of being unique and makes the claim in his first paragraph that he is telling the whole truth about himself as no man ever has done before, and he elsewhere says that he despises Montaigne because Montaigne who talked about himself seems to have talked only about those aspects of himself that would be attractive, whereas he will give us his vices. Now many of his vices, of which I am sure he is secretly proud, and many of the uniquenesses that he discovers in himself, I find in myself and believe to be in all persons. I am not referring to those things which might embarrass us, but to his claim, for instance, that it is difficult for him to write. He seems to think that there is something unique about that.

*Cairns:* I have a theory myself as to why the *Confessions* exerted such an influence. The most dangerous book in my library at home, I find, is a book entitled, *The Layman's Handbook of Medicine.* Every time I read that volume through I find that I have all the diseases enumerated in it, and I think that Rousseau occupied in the eighteenth century a similar position.

*Tate:* But don't you think that Rousseau made it possible for mediocrity to think itself distinguished? Anybody can practice this kind of muddled introspection and find in himself things, if he is ignorant, that he could consider unique.

*Cairns:* Rousseau was acclaimed as a great man and everyone who read this book said, just as Mr. Van Doren said: "My heavens, I have all these diseases. I must be a great man too."

*Tate:* Don't you think that we have a great many little Rousseaus in the modern world? The countless autobiographies that come out every year are all in the Rousseau tradition, or most of them, at any rate.

*Van Doren:* They are in the Rousseau tradition if they are strings of stories about how women have fallen in love with the author.

*Tate:* Yes, Rousseau certainly set the pattern for that.

*Van Doren:* Do you believe his stories of his love affairs, incidentally?

*Tate:* I don't know whether I do or not. I'm inclined not to believe them.

*Cairns:* Whether they are true or false, he did innovate intimate literature in France. I think that's a positive quality of the book.

*Van Doren:* I should deny that. I think that Montaigne is much more intimate than Rousseau. Even Pascal is more intimate, although, curiously enough, Pascal is not writing about himself.

*Tate:* He is much more intimate and more impersonal.

*Van Doren:* But he tells us more about himself, paradoxically, than this man does. I do not believe this man.

*Cairns:* Rousseau, however, is intimate in a different sense. Whether you believe the man or not, he does, I think, have a point against Montaigne and Pascal, and that is they tell only the good things about themselves.

*Van Doren:* They didn't seem to think so. They were not calling them good or bad.

*Tate:* I don't believe that Pascal told only the good things. Don't you think that he says a great many things about his own limitations, even his own vices? He had a career as a man of the world.

*Van Doren:* For instance, Pascal at one point is afraid that he is proud. He says: "Perhaps the reason I am writing this paragraph is that I want someone to admire it." If he had been sure of that he would have erased the paragraph. He let it stand because he thought it was true, whoever had written it. But Rousseau is constantly proud.

*Tate:* There is a point about Rousseau's claim to self-knowledge that I'd like to make. He says somewhere in the *Confessions* that all his memories of the past are agreeable, but that all his anticipations of the future are fearful.

*Cairns:* He was a very timorous man.

*Tate:* He identified his memories with his temperament. He thinks of his temperament as something perfect and sacred. I mention this because I'd like to get at the fundamental thing Rousseau believed in. I think of the modern attacks on Rousseau, for example, the great attack by the late Irving Babbitt in a book called *Rousseau and Romanticism,* in which Babbitt said that Rousseau's sentimental belief in the perfection of human nature had done incalculable damage to the modern world, and I am inclined to agree with Babbitt.

*Van Doren:* It's very interesting at this point to remember that although Rousseau says he loves mankind, he seems to hate or to feel maliciously toward every man whom he mentions in this book, every man, at any rate, of note. Some old tutor, about whom the world knows nothing, he may praise.

*Tate:* Some man who was not a literary rival.

*Van Doren:* Diderot, Grimm, Voltaire, Hume and, of course, among musicians (because he fancied himself a musician), Rameau, the great composer of his time, he endeavors clearly, I think, to put down.

*Cairns:* He did not feel that way toward women, although I was going to account for his attitude toward men on the ground that he had a persecution complex, which I think is evident as you read the *Confessions.* His attitude toward Mme. de Warens is one of the most interesting passages in the book. I feel that she herself was the person to whom he really owed his outlook on the world. It has seemed to me, as it has to others, that the golden age which Rousseau wished to bring back to earth was simply a generalization of the life he had lived at Les Charmettes with Mme. de Warens.

*Van Doren:* He owed a great deal to her, although you must remember that he tells us many things about her which she would not like him to have told. I mean, he criticizes her, oftentimes in a way that one who loves someone else would certainly avoid.

*Cairns:* She was also a mystery to him. I do not believe he ever completely understood her, although it has been well stated that she herself in her temperament was Rousseau with the genius left out.

*Van Doren:* She was important to him, of course, because he could love her without having to be afraid of her. This great lover, if he is supposed to be that, was obviously a very incompetent one; he was afraid of most women. I read that in all the stories he tells. This woman he does not have to be afraid of because she is a mother to him.

*Cairns:* Would you accept the view, in the light of what you have just said, that Mme. de Warens is a superior Mme. Bovary?

*Van Doren:* Very interesting. I hadn't thought of that.

*Tate:* What is your opinion, Mr. Cairns?

*Cairns:* I wondered, would you be afraid of Mme. Bovary if you knew her?

*Tate:* No. I don't know—I might have to take that back.

*Cairns:* Rousseau obviously was not afraid of Mme. de Warens.

*Tate:* Why would you be afraid of Mme. Bovary and not of Mme. de Warens?

*Cairns:* Well, I'd rather not answer that, Mr. Tate. Of course, there was another influence on Rousseau's life and that is Diderot. You will recall that . . .

*Tate:* That he quarreled with Diderot.

*Cairns:* He quarreled with Diderot and I think that is quite interesting. Rousseau went to see him at the time the competition was proposed on the subject whether or not the arts and sciences had contributed to the progress of civilization or had hurt it. He went to see Diderot and told him that he was going to compete with an essay on that subject, and that he was going to defend civilization. Diderot said: "Why do that? Everybody is going to defend civilization. Defend savages. Say that their culture is superior to civilization. Then you may stand a chance of winning the prize." That was not an original notion with Rousseau.

*Tate:* No. But that's a very damaging thing to say about Rousseau, isn't it?

*Cairns:* I think it is true, and Rousseau wrote the essay along those lines, won the prize and had to maintain that position the rest of his life, although he didn't really believe it.

*Tate:* Don't you think that he probably came to believe in it? That brings up one of the most interesting psychological facts about Rousseau, the capacity for self-deception that he seemed to have all his life. His literary fame depended upon a belief that he had expressed insincerely and then the fame convinced him that it was a sincere belief.

*Cairns:* You will notice that in his subsequent writings after this essay which gave him his great fame he slowly retreated. His first essay was really in praise of primitive life; his second essay qualified that view; the third essay represented a greater qualification. I think the remainder of his life he was returning to the position he had in mind before he called upon Diderot.

*Tate:* Mr. Cairns, won't you summarize for us Rousseau's fundamental belief?

*Cairns:* Recently I came across a summary by T. E. Hulme.

*Tate:* One of my favorite writers.

*Cairns:* T. S. Eliot admires him very much, and Eliot has endorsed these views. Hulme summarized Rousseau's position in this way: "Man is by nature wonderful, of unlimited power, and if hitherto has not appeared so, it is because of external obstacles and fetters which it should be the main business of social politics to remove." Now Hulme and Eliot disagree violently with that position, and the position they take is that man is by nature bad or limited and can consequently only accomplish anything of value by discipline—ethical, heroic or political. In other words, they believe in original sin.

*Tate:* I wouldn't quite follow that summary. I would agree much more with Irving Babbitt, that man becomes bad—he is not inherently bad—but he becomes bad by refusing to acknowledge limitations. He is more limited than bad. The evil comes . . .

*Cairns:* Why do you think he is either bad or good? Why isn't he neutral?

*Tate:* I think we have a fundamental necessity to think in terms of moral good and evil.

*Van Doren:* I should say that the word "bad" is much more interesting than the word "neutral." Only those men can interest us in our virtue who begin by talking about our weaknesses and our vices.

*Tate:* We have no confidence in them if they don't.

*Van Doren:* We shall learn nothing from a man who begins by telling us we are good, because we know we are not; whereas we can be truly interested in a person who gives us credit for our faults and then tells us that we can still make something of ourselves.

*Cairns:* Is there any way of determining this question whether man is in his original nature either good or bad?

*Tate:* That is one of the fallacies Rousseau entertained: that he could tell what man was in his original nature.

*Cairns:* Isn't that the modern fallacy of Eliot and Hulme: that they can determine he is bad?

*Tate:* Oh, no, they don't determine that.

*Cairns:* It is their conviction that they can.

*Van Doren:* Our old friend Aristotle is on this point very simple and profound. He says man is a rational animal. He means by that that man is mostly an animal but that he has a little reason. The little reason is what makes all the difference. If you translate this into theological terms, man is bad, but he has a little capacity for good—which is what makes all the difference.

*Cairns:* I will go along on the word "limited," but I just can't swallow bad or good. I think he is neutral.

*Tate:* When we say man is wholly bad, we are talking about an essence or a substance. I prefer the word "limitation" too, but the evil is introduced in terms of experience by a refusal to recognize the limitation.

*Van Doren:* I think the reason we find Rousseau writing like an ignorant man, even though he writes extremely well—surely he is a good writer of some kind—is that he doesn't know this thing we have been talking about. That sounds vain, but is he capable of seeing man with any kind of double vision—as actually limited but capable of virtue and strength?

*Cairns:* You quoted Aristotle a minute ago. I'd like to know if you disagree with him in his assertion in the *Poetics* that the author's personality should not intrude, because in the *Confessions* that is one of the principal things we have.

*Van Doren:* Certainly not.

*Tate:* It seems to me that Rousseau gives himself away in the most interesting fashion.

*Cairns:* That is what he intended to do.

*Tate:* Exactly, but in a way which he didn't intend. A common criticism of Rousseau is that he was very infirm in his perception of objective events. "I have but one faithful guide," says Rousseau, "on which I can depend. This is the chain of the sentiments by which the succession of my existence has been marked, and by these events which have either been the cause or the effect of the manner of it. I can easily forget my misfortunes, but I cannot forget my faults, and still less my virtuous sentiments. The remembrance of these is too dear to me ever to suffer them to be defaced from my mind. I may omit facts, transpose events and fall into some errors of dates, but I cannot be deceived in what I have felt nor in that which from sentiment I have done. And to relate this is the chief end of my present work. The real object of my *Confessions* is to communicate an exact knowledge of what I interiorly am and have been in every situation of my life. I have promised the history of my mind and to write it faithfully. I have no need of other memoirs. To enter into my own heart as I have hitherto done will alone be sufficient."

(1806-1873)

# JOHN STUART MILL

# *Autobiography*

*JOHN STUART MILL, the nineteenth-century logician and philosopher whose* LIBERTY *is a classic on the theme of toleration, wrote another classic in his* AUTOBIOGRAPHY, *the most famous portion of which deals with his education. His treatment of the subject is not so much a confession as a complaint; the efforts of his father, also a philosopher, to give his mind the best possible training were so humorless and pedantic that he later concluded himself to have been the worst-educated youth in England, if not the world. The training was good and the discipline was unremitting; the boy read Greek and Latin before most children can read their primers, and well before adolescence he had been made familiar with the chief theories of private and public conduct. But it had been a training of his mind alone; the rest of his nature had not been permitted to develop, and even in the realm of intellect he had been denied acquaintance with art. The result at maturity was a crisis in his soul, a depression of his faculties which only the discovery of Wordsworth's poetry cured. Mill's narrative of this crisis, along with his explanation of its cause, has rightly come to be considered a piece of autobiography which no one can afford to ignore. There is no vanity in its telling, as we often suspect there is in Rousseau's disclosures of personal weakness. Neither is there the fascination, for Mill was, in spite of everything, an utterly sober man. And his book is of value for other reasons than this.*

*Cairns:* It would be difficult to find two men more unlike than Rousseau and John Stuart Mill, whose *Autobiography* we are considering today. In his education and character, Mill is the complete antithesis of Rousseau, who had neither education nor character. But I feel that these two men were alike in that neither had first-rate minds. Rousseau had a gift for effective expression of popular ideas, and Mill acquired at an early age the habit of applying himself industriously. It is his description of his unusual and very early education, when his character and the habit of hard mental discipline were formed, that is one of the most interesting parts of his *Autobiography*. Mr. Tate, do you agree with me in suspecting that had Mill received the ordinary education of small boys of his time we would probably never have heard of him?

*Tate:* I am inclined to agree that we should not have heard of him. His education, I suppose, was one of the most remarkable in all literature. It is true that before he was six years old he could read Greek.

*Van Doren:* But he was reading it, I think, as early as three.

*Tate:* Yes, but by the time he was six he was extremely proficient in it. He read it with great fluency. And I think he was about eight when he began Latin. For some reason his father, James Mill, postponed the Latin. He was very backward in Latin, beginning when he was eight years old. I always see the picture of the little boy, John Stuart Mill, sitting in his father's study looking at a classical text. His father would not permit him to use a classical dictionary, so if John Stuart Mill came to a word he didn't know he would ask his father. Out of that, it seems to me, the terrific dependence that the son felt toward his father, up to the time of his father's death, began.

*Van Doren:* And the father was not there in the study just waiting to be asked questions, either. He was writing his *History of India.*

*Tate:* And he was apparently a very impatient man. All day he had been working in the East India Company. The remarkable thing is that both of the Mills did all of their tremendous intellectual labor in their spare time. Now about his education. He looks back upon it and he seems to find something wrong with it, but I think it is interesting that he says that after all the element of fear cannot be dispensed with in teaching the young.

*Van Doren:* Meaning the element of discipline.

*Tate:* In other words, you can't make education wholly pleasant.

*Cairns:* That is contrary to the tenets of progressive education today.

*Tate:* It seems to me that it is. To go back to the question that you asked me a moment ago: if Mill had been given an ordinary education his powers might have been greatly diffused. Probably the peculiar kind of development he had consisted in taking over his father's discipline completely and then adding a little to it and differing from his father as he developed. He didn't rebel. Without that foundation he couldn't have done anything.

*Cairns:* It is a curious thing that the fault in his education lay in omissions. His father gave him an intensive instruction which Mill outlines in his *Autobiography,* but it is curious what his father omitted. As I read the volume this time, I noticed four omissions. There was a failure to develop Mill's sensibility, his affections, his aesthetic sense, music . . .

*Van Doren:* The things he called feelings.

*Cairns:* Yes, and imagination. There was no physical development. I think that Mill would have been a much finer man, for example, if he had played cricket.

*Tate:* Didn't he take walks? Wasn't that the only form of exercise he ever had?

*Cairns:* That is the only form, but he didn't associate with other boys.

*Van Doren:* There is one very pathetic passage in which he says that his only memory of his early experience with flowers and birds is in connection with trying to remember what to say to his father about what he had read the night before, or the day before.

*Cairns:* There was also a failure to round out his accomplishments. There was no breadth of view. He said afterwards that he obtained a comprehensive outlook from Mrs. Taylor, who became his wife, but I am a little skeptical of that. But the fourth and most important thing of all is that he was not allowed the choice of a point of view. Throughout his life he never had his own point of view.

*Van Doren:* Well, isn't there a fifth one too? He says somewhere that with respect to science, although he had an interest in the experiments with which you perfect your scientific studies, he was never permitted actually to perform such experiments. He merely read about them. It was, after all, a completely bookish education.

*Cairns:* He wanted a laboratory experience and missed it when he dealt with scientific theories later in life. I think that omission is important. His *Logic* would have been a better book if he had known the technique of the laboratory.

*Tate:* Do you think that was wholly a disadvantage? Perhaps a more direct acquaintance with science would have helped him. At the same time, I can't help feeling that he was spared a good deal of specialization.

*Van Doren:* There would have been danger in that.

*Tate:* I don't think his failure to achieve breadth of view has anything to do with lack of scientific studies. I think it was just a freak of his nature, emphasized by his peculiar education.

*Van Doren:* His nature in itself was incomplete.

*Cairns:* I think his opinions on science would have been different if he had had a laboratory training.

*Van Doren:* You remember that one of his efforts throughout his whole life was to apply the rigor of physical science to political philosophy. Perhaps a man could have done it better, or would not have tried to do it at all, if he had known more than Mill did about physical science.

*Tate:* And so his politics became chiefly a logical structure. Later he began to see through that and also the limitations of a scientific education.

*Van Doren:* He was always seeing through things.

*Cairns:* There was one aspect of Mill's education which Mr. Tate did not mention, but which to me was one of the most interesting points in the book. Mill described the influence of Dumont's translation of Bentham on his own intellectual development and he asserted that that single book changed the whole course of his mental life. I couldn't think immediately of any other parallel in the history of thought where a man had been influenced to that extent by one book. I wondered if you knew of any.

*Tate:* Pascal and Montaigne.

*Van Doren:* Blake and Swedenborg. Oftentimes the book which changes a man's life is inferior to the books that he will write.

*Cairns:* You are speaking of the influence of Montaigne on Pascal?

*Van Doren:* And of Swedenborg on Blake.

*Tate:* I think occasionally you'll find authors who attribute their own intellectual revolution to a certain book, but I am inclined to think that they exaggerate it somewhat.

*Van Doren:* Whenever I'm asked this question I am embarrassed because I can't think of any such book; probably in my case it would have to be a list of books.

*Cairns:* I know it would in my case.

*Tate:* Mr. Cairns, what do you think is the chief defect of Mill's education? I am inclined to think in the case of a philosopher it's strange that he should have felt that one book alone turned his mind that way.

*Cairns:* I think, as I tried to indicate a moment ago, that the chief defect was the fact that he never had his own point of view.

That may be attributed to the fact that he did not have the physical virility to combat his father who was obviously an extremely aggressive man. He was influenced as a boy and young man by Bentham, Ricardo and his father, and then in later life by Mrs. Taylor, the woman he subsequently married.

*Tate:* I have often heard it asked by people who haven't studied Mill closely, why it was that a philosophy of association, that is, a philosophy which bases everything on sense perception and observation, should have had so little use for poetry, which of course is the art which gives us many images and particular observations.

*Cairns:* You will recall that poetry had an influence in his life when he went through a severe mental crisis at about the age of twenty.

*Van Doren:* You mean the crisis in which he began to wonder what good it would do him to achieve all of his ends?

*Cairns:* When he asked himself the same question that Rousseau asked himself, the question: Would I be happy if all desirable social reforms were accomplished?

*Tate:* Don't you think that he would have felt that he was living in a vacuum because he would then have had no sensibility; experience would have had no substance?

*Van Doren:* He certainly realized that a happiness consciously driven toward might not be an end in itself. That is the basis for one of the most interesting pages in this book, it seems to me.

*Tate:* Doesn't he make this remark—it's rather Aristotelian in spirit—that he decided that the object of happiness must be pursued indirectly?

*Cairns:* That is the point that Aristotle makes. Happiness must be a by-product, not an end in itself.

*Van Doren:* He is always discovering Aristotle, incidentally. This man, whose education, I should say, was limited as all education in the time was limited, learned how to break through those limitations by the discovery of Aristotle.

*Cairns:* Don't you think that everyone in some degree goes through a similar experience?

*Van Doren:* Surely.

*Tate:* It must seem to us today very remarkable that Wordsworth's poetry gave him a new lease on life.

*Van Doren:* It did the same thing for Matthew Arnold. If you remember Arnold on the poetry of Wordsworth, he talks not so much about its art, about its excellence in the way of poetry, as about what it did for him. It healed him and soothed him. You hear a great deal of that talk during the nineteenth century. Wordsworth was almost a medicine for men who were philosophically sick.

*Tate:* Mr. Van Doren, I think that Mill is really sounder on Wordsworth than Arnold. He has a much shrewder conception of Wordsworth's limitations as a poet, but he acknowledges his tremendous debt to him.

*Van Doren:* Don't you find that Mill for all his limitations, which are clear, is wonderfully able to see those very limitations, and so to be as honest perhaps and as accurate as a man can ever be in writing?

*Tate:* Doesn't he say of Wordsworth that he is the poet for unpoetical natures and that he knew that he himself had an unpoetical nature?

*Cairns:* But he went to Wordsworth, not for Wordsworth's description of nature, but for the emotions derived from nature.

*Tate:* He says that Sir Walter Scott gives you natural scenes much more vividly than Wordsworth. The attitude toward nature was what he got from Wordsworth.

*Van Doren:* He continues even there to talk about his education. Wordsworth was simply one more educator for him, a man who was training his feelings.

*Cairns:* He felt the need of a more rounded life and a more rounded point of view. You will recall that he said he was a well-equipped ship without a sail. Now I take it that feeling was the sail that was missing.

*Van Doren:* There are parallels to this philosopher, at least with respect to his discovery suddenly that he must take account of something that he hadn't taken account of before. A few years ago John Dewey realized that he had made no place in his philosophy for art; so out he came with a volume about art which attempted to place it somehow in a universe which for him had been without it until that moment.

*Cairns:* I think the parallel there is quite striking. Cultivation of feeling became the cardinal point in Mill's ethical creed and he tried to arrive at feeling rationally, just as John Dewey attempted a philosophical justification or rational justification of art.

*Van Doren:* There is a very interesting question here. Do men who have lacks of that sort and who seek, however conscientiously, to remedy them—do they ever find the remedy? For instance, Mr. Tate, would you say that Mill ever knew very much about poetry?

*Tate:* No. His feeling for poetry was only didactic.

*Van Doren:* Very elementary.

*Tate:* He got high moral sentiments from it and he read the ancient poets for the history that they gave him.

*Van Doren:* Don't you suspect that he really preferred Joanna Baillie to Shakespeare?

*Tate:* I'm sure he did.

*Cairns:* I think he indicated that pretty clearly. Would you agree with his own explanation of the crisis, that he felt the need of a more rounded life, or would you agree with the interpretation that his crisis was the result of having a point of view forced on him?

*Tate:* I think the very philosophical position that he held limited him to mere intellectual experience. Sensibility was ruled out on principle. He had a thoroughly rationalistic point of view.

*Van Doren:* And when it came time to remedy that I should say it was almost by definition too late. Don't you think so?

*Tate:* Yes.

*Cairns:* He was ossified.

*Van Doren:* We can't decide so suddenly to have feelings. You don't get feelings that way. And there again I think we must say in his favor that he understood he wasn't getting them wholly or wasn't getting them rightly.

*Tate:* Don't you think that his fundamental misunderstanding of poetry was the assumption that poetry was entirely feeling?

*Van Doren:* If I were going to defend poetry against Mill, which I wouldn't want to do very seriously, I would want to talk not in terms of the feeling in it at all, but in terms of something which he might consider to be strangely intellectual.

*Tate:* But it is something that he couldn't see in poetry at all.

*Cairns:* I think his life, when we read this book, is a very tragic one.

*Van Doren:* Very pathetic. Would you say tragic or pathetic, incidentally?

*Cairns:* Perhaps pathetic is a better word.

*Tate:* Doesn't the pathos come out of the only piece of humor in the book? It is unconscious humor. He says that while he had his depression of spirit he had the despair of Lord Byron!

*Van Doren:* Yet he was an absolutely honest man, I should say.

*Cairns:* Unquestionably.

*Van Doren:* And we appreciate that most, I think, when we find him recognizing and stating the limitations of doctrines which have been forced upon him and which he agrees he ought to hold. No man is more willing to correct himself—as here, for instance. He was indebted to the philosopher Comte. Yet he says: "M. Comte lived to carry out his doctrines to the extremest consequences by planning in his last work the completest system of spiritual and temporal despotism which ever emanated from a human brain, a system by which the yoke of general opinion wielded by an organized body of spiritual teachers and rulers would be made supreme over every action and every thought of every member of the community. It is but just to say that his work is a considerable improvement in many points of feeling over Comte's previous writings on the same subjects, but as an accession to social philosophy, the only value it seems to me to possess consists in putting an end to the notion that no effectual moral authority can be maintained over society without the aid of religious belief. For Comte's work recognizes no religion except that of Humanity. Yet it leaves an irresistible conviction that any moral beliefs concurred in by the community generally may be brought to bear upon the whole conduct and lives of its individual members with an energy and potency truly alarming to think of. The book stands a monumental warning to thinkers on society and politics of what happens when once men lose sight in their speculations of the value of Liberty and of Individuality."

*(1838-1918)*

# HENRY ADAMS

# *The Education of Henry Adams*

*FOR Henry Adams autobiography was a form of history. His* EDUCATION *is as far as a book can be from Rousseau's* CONFESSIONS, *which exposes and exploits a personality. Adams, a historian by profession and a Bostonian by birth, had no interest whatever in the world's opinion of himself. One of the Adams family which has given two Presidents to the United States as well as a number of other notables, his reserve was equal to his pride; so that we must not look in his autobiography for anything local or personal, and in fact we note that of a particularly painful period in his career following his wife's death, he writes not a single word. He himself appears in the* EDUCATION *only as one to whom certain significant aspects of the nineteenth century were clear; it is the time that absorbs him, not the man—whom he always refers to in the third person. The time was one which it was his "education" to understand. Failing to understand it be-*

*cause no man could do so, he decided that his education had never taken place; which was his way of saying what other books of his said, namely, that civilization had become so multiple as to be now quite meaningless. The Middle Ages had known unity; we know only multiplicity. Other times have possessed power; we possess energy. The* EDUCATION, *published privately for other historians, became a widely influential book after its release to the public in 1918. It is still the classic statement of our modern confusion.*

(MR. R. P. BLACKMUR, GUEST)

*Cairns:* The three notable autobiographies, of which *The Education of Henry Adams* is the last, were selected in each instance as representative works of their kind of each of three centuries. Rousseau represents the romanticism of the eighteenth century. John Stuart Mill's *Autobiography* reflects the conscientious, social-reforming obsession of the nineteenth century. In Henry Adams we have the reaction. John Stuart Mill slowly matured to a point of view made explicit by Adams. Mill too late came to realize that man's happiness is not achieved by social reform, that the greatest happiness of the greatest number was not a social problem but a moral problem. Henry Adams found himself in the world created by the Rousseaus and the Mills. Its vulgarity and chaos caused him to stand apart from it, although he did not disdain to write about it. His autobiography is the book in which he inveighs against it, and points out that only through faith can man find in life any meaning, unity or order. Henry Adams always insisted that he was a failure. What do you think, Mr. Van Doren, he meant by that?

*Van Doren:* The statement, obviously, is rich in irony, both conscious and unconscious. Conscious because Adams surely knew that he was in many respects successful and one of the most important men of his time. Unconscious because even he could not know, I think, the influence this particular book was to have. He could not have known, I think, that he had written one of the few books of our time destined to become classics. The failure he is talking about, I suspect, is chiefly his failure, relative of course, as a historian. He would mean by that not that he hadn't written great works of history, but that he had failed or almost failed to find, as he says, that spool on which he might wind the thread of history without breaking it. He was afraid that he had found a break in the continuity of history. Mr. Blackmur, does it seem to you that he is primarily a historian?

*Blackmur:* That is only part of the story, though I think a great part of the failure was merely the failure that goes with making any very great effort of the imagination.

*Tate:* Now, Mr. Blackmur, it seems to me that Adams' failure is excessively dramatized throughout the book. *The Education of Henry Adams* is, as we know, not a straight autobiography. It is highly allegorized and symbolized. He sees himself as Man in the nineteenth century. It's a spiritual history, and that kind of history is bound to fail.

*Cairns:* But, Mr. Tate, Adams' great-grandfather was President, his grandfather was President, and his father was Ambassador to the Court of St. James's. He was trained to feel that he had political obligations, and if he could not realize them he thought he was a failure.

*Tate:* Not only obligations, but he thought he had great opportunities. A great many readers feel that Adams was making claim to a political career on the ground of his ancestry.

*Van Doren:* He did feel that.

*Cairns:* His government never offered him a political position. Whether he resented that I do not know. But he seems to make it clear that unless he succeeded in action he thought that he had failed.

*Tate:* Mr. Cairns, don't you think that there is a parallel between Henry Adams—I admit a remote parallel—and Dante? Dante had a political career in Florence. He was exiled. Adams was never really exiled, except perhaps he was self-exiled at times, but when their political careers failed they turned to something much greater than politics.

*Cairns:* But Adams never had that chance, and isn't his failure the fact that he did not have a political career? Would you agree with that, Mr. Van Doren?

*Van Doren:* It seems to me that history is very important to Adams and that Adams surely did not fall into history with a sense that he was falling downward. I take it, from my reading of this book, that history is to him the one important thing, because the historian in a special sense controls the world.

*Tate:* Then, Mr. Van Doren, what did he mean by "history"? He didn't mean history as his contemporaries wrote it, because he was intensely dissatisfied with that. He was very much dissatisfied with his own history of Jefferson and Madison.

*Van Doren:* He had the desire as a historian to find a significant story in human movement.

*Cairns:* You mean in his own life?

*Van Doren:* No, no. In human movement from as far back as you might want to take it. It was more important to him than it is to most historians to have a theme under which he could order all events.

*Blackmur:* Oh, Mr. Van Doren, in a way, his *Education* is an attempt to dramatize the history of the United States in the nineteenth century in terms of one man, himself. He thought of himself as eminently in a position to get the most out of that history. So you could say that part of his failure was in not getting more, and part of it was in the failure that went with the effort to try to see a unity in the history.

*Van Doren:* But perhaps this unity didn't exist.

*Tate:* Don't you think, Mr. Blackmur, that at times he seems to be assuming, without ever being explicit about it, that perhaps in some other time deeper significance had been found in the writing of history? But is that actually true historically? Was that deeper significance ever found on the mere historical level?

*Cairns:* I want to find out what Mr. Van Doren means. You are suggesting that his failure, as he describes it, was ironical. Do you mean that that is the thread of his narrative, the thread on which he could hang his autobiography in order to give it unity and coherence and form?

*Van Doren:* Yes. Irony supplies the unity of his autobiography.

*Blackmur:* There it is a matter of art. He wanted to make his book a work of art, and he always felt that his composition fell down, partly because he talked too much about his father.

*Cairns:* Do you agree with Adams' statement, Mr. Blackmur, that it was not a personal failure on his part? Although, of course, he is ambiguous on that point, as I read the book as a whole, he attributes his failure to a failure of the period. He said that the moral law was dead and that there was only social anarchy, corruption and self-interest. He attributed the failure to a failure of the nineteenth century and not to some failure of his own.

*Blackmur:* I should assent to a good part of that, yes.

*Van Doren:* As far as art is concerned, the autobiography is, I should say, almost by definition an imperfect art form because it can have no end. This autobiography, like all others, is more successful, let us say, more happy as a book, in its earlier than it is in its later chapters. Adams with this magnificent elaborateness of his runs into multiplicity in his own life and thought, but so does every man who writes an autobiography. No man knows how to end an autobiography except on a note of—well, equilibrium.

*Tate:* What kind of work do you think a man could write in which he can avoid the lame ending that we tend to find in autobiographies?

*Van Doren:* I am interested in the suggestion you seemed to be making a minute ago: that this is more than an autobiography, more than a work of history; that it is a poem perhaps. We are working with art on almost the highest level.

*Tate:* Wasn't he trying really to bring together all the knowledge of his time in terms of his own experience and trying to give it some sort of objective form that people could understand?

*Van Doren:* He was trying to write a book which would say everything that a book of his time could say.

*Blackmur:* You will notice, Mr. Van Doren, that he leaves himself out as much as it is possible for a man to do. Perhaps one should say that it wasn't, in his mind, exactly autobiographical.

*Van Doren:* I am very willing to grant that.

*Blackmur:* He himself never put that phrase on the title page of his book.

*Van Doren:* Nevertheless, in the beginning there are those chapters which we can call nothing but charming, and I mean that in the most dignified sense of the word. Chapters about his boyhood in Quincy and his grandfather particularly, the man whom he calls the President. I think no one ever forgets the story of how the old man, without saying a word, led the boy to school when the boy refused to go.

*Cairns:* Or the portrait of Madame President?

*Van Doren:* By all means. And, of course, Adams' own father.

*Tate:* Mr. Van Doren, don't you think that the success of the portraiture in the early chapters is due to his looking back on his grandparents with some of the innocence of childhood? While they stood for certain ideas, nevertheless he saw them as people. In later life he tended to see people in terms of their ideas and what they represented.

*Cairns:* I was interested in what Mr. Blackmur said: that Adams tried to keep himself out of the book. I think the book as a whole represents his intellectual doubts. It's the autobiography of a mind. But don't you agree, Mr. Blackmur, that there is a personal problem there? In the background isn't Adams always asking himself: "Why was I never offered public office when I was so well equipped for it?"

*Blackmur:* He knew why he wasn't offered public office.

*Cairns:* Why, do you think?

*Blackmur:* Because his style of man was out of fashion. It went out of fashion permanently in Grant's Administration. It had really gone out of fashion in Jackson's, when Jackson beat John Quincy Adams.

*Cairns:* You mean Grant killed the Adams style of man because, as Adams says in the *Education,* when Grant appointed his Cabinet, he realized that he, Adams, was through.

*Blackmur:* If men of that kind were to be made Cabinet members, then there was no room for an Adams.

*Van Doren:* What kind of man do you mean Adams was?

*Blackmur:* It's most easy to put it as he put it himself. He called himself an eighteenth-century man. He was committed to the original experiment of a republican democracy.

*Tate:* Wouldn't that imply the belief in a kind of ruling class, people who did nothing but practice government and took the responsibilities?

*Blackmur:* Yes. Government by men disinterested and able to govern.

*Cairns:* Do you think Adams was pre-eminently equipped for public office? Do you agree with his own estimate of himself?

*Blackmur:* I don't know. He never tried.

*Van Doren:* Of course, the question is difficult to answer because you are talking about two periods, in one of which he might have been and in the other of which he could not have been.

*Cairns:* He was a philosopher, and some philosophers have made good statesmen. Marcus Aurelius, for one. Alexander the Great, perhaps. Are you not suggesting that it is the fault of democracy that the ablest men are not in politics? Are you making that statement as being particularly true since Grant's Administration?

*Blackmur:* I would say that Grant's Administration represented that time when the real power in the country was taken out of directly political hands.

*Van Doren:* And put into what kind of hands?

*Blackmur:* Into the hands of the industrialists, the financiers, the railroad men.

*Cairns:* But you wouldn't say that necessarily in democratic practice the ablest men cannot go into politics?

*Blackmur:* No, I'd not say that.

*Tate:* Gentlemen, I'd like to bring up a question that was implied in what we were just saying. Henry Adams' sense of failure seems to me to be, as Mr. Van Doren was saying a little while ago—it's a kind of irony and perhaps it amounts to no more than that—a profound realization of the contingencies of life. He was born to a career and thrown off; that dislocation of his life turned him into a different kind of man, and made him speculate upon the very basis of life. A very successful man of action tends not to do that.

*Van Doren:* Irony suggests, too, the most famous example of it, Socrates. Socrates was always ironic in saying he was a failure, in saying he couldn't make speeches, couldn't decide things. He couldn't answer questions; he could only ask them. Yet the end of Socrates was a happy end. It was not the gray end that we find this man living.

*Cairns:* But I feel that Mr. Tate is right in following Adams there. Adams said that accident determined everything that he did.

*Van Doren:* I must confess—Mr. Blackmur probably won't like this; it probably isn't true—I have never been able to accept Adams' depression or his pessimism as necessary. I know that it was wonderfully stated, and that, as a result, the literature of America and England in the decade or two after the book was published took the same tone. But I have never been able to feel that that pessimism was necessary either.

*Blackmur:* There's one thing to say there, and that is that none of those who have written about him, from personal knowledge, none of those whom I have met who actually knew him, thought of him as a pessimistic man. His pessimism was perhaps a matter of temper in writing, as many men differ in their letters from their conversation, in their books from their letters.

*Cairns:* It is a curious thing that his great-grandfather, John Adams, in writing a letter to his wife, predicted what he hoped would happen to his descendants, and I should like to read a sentence to you from that letter. John Adams wrote to Abigail: "I must study war and politics that my sons may have liberty to study mathematics and philosophy, geography, natural history and naval architecture, navigation and commerce and agriculture, in order to give their children a right to study painting, poetry, music, architecture, statuary, tapestry and porcelain." That is, of course, exactly what Henry Adams studied. But his dissatisfaction lay in the fact that he did not follow the career that his great-grandfather, who wrote this sentence, followed. He did not want to accept what his great-grandfather had planned for him.

*Tate:* Mr. Cairns, I find in old John Adams' statement a considerable degree of unconscious irony. When the great-grandson studied art and literature, he studied it with a sense of their deficiencies. Mere art and mere literature without something supporting them from beneath—a religion, and that's what Henry Adams was looking for—tended to be empty.

*Van Doren:* John Adams had no conception of what his great-grandson would be looking for—which I agree was religion, was unity.

*Cairns:* He was looking for a faith as a working hypothesis. The faith didn't have to be true, but he needed a faith, he said, in order to give unity to life.

*Van Doren:* As a historian, he would say it did not need to be true.

*Tate:* But for the man, it's different. It must be true.

*Cairns:* He would have to believe it as a man.

*Van Doren:* As all men have to believe something now with the same intensity that people once believed in the Virgin.

*Cairns:* Of course, he said also that he was looking for education and that brings up the question of what he meant by education. I think his position is ambiguous. I wonder if Mr. Blackmur, who is making a special study of Mr. Adams, has any thoughts on that.

*Blackmur:* I have too many.

*Cairns:* Give us one or two.

*Blackmur:* Perhaps the simplest one was found, I think, in the conclusion of the chapter that dealt with teaching in Harvard College, where he says that what he wanted in education was the tools to allow him to meet the life which he found in his own time. That was something that he had not gotten anywhere.

*Cairns:* You mean mathematics, French, German and Spanish?

*Blackmur:* And so on. It would be more than that. In other words, it would be the ability to read and to understand whatever the finest or most valuable work was that was being done in his time.

*Cairns:* He felt that he had an innate capacity; so if he had the tools he could, as I recall the phrase, compete with anybody.

*Blackmur:* I think that's a very good working definition.

*Tate:* Mr. Blackmur, don't you think that toward the end of his life this search for education became, of course, a search for something much more than the word "education" ordinarily implies? He was searching for faith, and when he said that in his time there were two kingdoms of force which had nothing in common but attraction, wasn't he stating the spiritual problem of our age? Two kingdoms of force: one the Christian religion, of which the symbol was the Virgin, the other the new religion of which the symbol was the dynamo that he saw at the Paris Exposition in 1900. The dynamo and the Virgin became symbols of the two poles of his thought.

*Van Doren:* Do you think, Mr. Tate, that he understood the dynamo as well as he understood the Virgin? How seriously do you take the later chapters of this book in which he wonders whether his education was as good as it should have been in science? Of course, he laments that it wasn't good at all, but how much do you think he understands the drift of physics, for instance?

*Tate:* Mr. Van Doren, I doubt whether he understands it very much. Probably just about as much as we do.

*Van Doren:* I don't understand it at all.

*Tate:* I don't either.

*Blackmur:* I think, Mr. Van Doren, there is perhaps a little more than that. He was a close associate of Langley, for example, for many years.

*Cairns:* And he did get a lot out of him.

*Tate:* Wasn't his interest, Mr. Blackmur, philosophical rather than strictly scientific and experimental?

*Blackmur:* Oh, somewhere he admits that. His own experiments were limited to keeping magnets on his desk in order to trace lines of force dramatically.

*Cairns:* And also to show that magnetism could not be explained by contemporary physics?

*Tate:* But to go back to the dynamo that Mr. Van Doren brought up. I don't believe that he took the dynamo as seriously as the Virgin. In fact, I think he had contempt for the dynamo. I think he had tended to develop a contempt for the scientific outlook. Not science as such, but the corruption that the religion of science had brought into modern life, the disorder, the anarchy, multiplicity of aims.

*Blackmur:* I think, Mr. Tate, it was dread rather than contempt.

*Van Doren:* I was going to use that word, too. His fear of the dynamo was not the fear of the Virgin, which is the fear of God.

*Tate:* Don't you remember the beautiful, ironic passage when he first sees the dynamo? He says that one wanted to pray to the dynamo. It is said in irony, and it is a very moving passage.

*Cairns:* That is all symbolical, but I think there is an element of truth in his attempt to find two points of reference: the twelfth and thirteenth centuries as a symbol of unity, and the twentieth century as a symbol of multiplicity. If a historian takes those two points of reference, he can work backward and forward from them. It is more than a metaphor, more than fancy.

*Van Doren:* Although, of course, you can't help wanting to test him a little there. You can't help wondering to what extent he read unity into the thirteenth century and to what extent he read multiplicity into the twentieth century.

*Tate:* That's only relative, isn't it? Certainly Dante had a very difficult time unifying his own experience.

*Van Doren:* It was not too easy for him to unify his experience.

*Tate:* Perhaps it was a little easier then than it is for us, but the problem wasn't solved automatically.

*Cairns:* The only point I was making there is, it seems to me, that it is perhaps the beginning of a genuine comparative method in history, and from that point of view I think his conception of two points of reference was useful.

*Van Doren:* His method is surely very grand and simple. I mean the method of describing two points in history and drawing a straight line through them which is bound to pass through all others.

*Blackmur:* He was very good at making such comparisons, Mr. Van Doren. He had a very useful one in politics, one pole being coal power and the other pole being gun power. The United States and Great Britain, for example, represent coal power, and Germany and Russia—this is as of 1900—would represent gun power, the conflict between the two being foreseeable.

*Van Doren:* What about his prophecies as to international relations? They are very interesting to me.

*Blackmur:* They are more accurate than any others that I have seen.

*Cairns:* Extraordinarily accurate. And in that sense, perhaps, his education, such as he had received from life, was not altogether a failure. He said that the essence of education was to teach the mind how to react with vigor and economy, and I think his mind was quite a vigorous mind and wonderfully economical.

*Van Doren:* His success, it seems to me, was very great. We started by talking about his failure. His success was the kind that Shakespeare had in writing *Hamlet.* Shakespeare may have thought of that as a failure too, because what he was trying to do there probably could not be done by a man. Nevertheless, what we have is something better than any other man has done.

*Tate:* And, Mr. Van Doren, don't you think that the high aim of this book could never be achieved; it could never be fully realized?

*Van Doren:* I take it that that is what Mr. Blackmur meant when he referred to the nature of his effort. The highest compliment we can pay Adams is to describe the nature of his effort.

*Cairns:* He asked what sort of education could have given him power. Do you think that is an unanswerable question? Because, as he also said, society had failed to discover what sort of education suited it best.

*Tate:* Mr. Cairns, don't you think he substantially answers the question? The men who had power in his time were the men who automatically had the kind of education, or lack of it, which permitted them to run society.

*Cairns:* Not necessarily so.

*Tate:* Not to run it successfully—no. He didn't think they ran it successfully.

*Cairns:* They may have run it very badly.

*Tate:* Yes. Might he not have answered the question this way: That to run modern society successfully we'd have to have something different from modern society?

*Van Doren:* Perhaps no man in that society could run it.

*Cairns:* What do you think of the *Education* itself when you compare it with St. Augustine or Rousseau?

*Van Doren:* I was thinking of Augustine a minute ago.

*Cairns:* Would you put it on a level with his *Confessions?*

*Van Doren:* Perhaps not, but Augustine said that education should be such as to make you capable of reading any book or of writing any book.

*Tate:* Gentlemen, I have a passage here which dramatizes nicely Adams' feeling for the thirteenth century and for modern times. "Adams never tired of quoting the supreme phrase of his idol Gibbon, before the Gothic cathedrals: 'I darted a contemptuous look on the stately monuments of superstition.' . . . Gibbon ignored the Virgin because in 1789 religious monuments were out of fashion . . . Without malice, one might find it [*i.e.,* his remark] more instructive than a whole lecture of Ruskin. One sees what one brings, and at that moment Gibbon brought the French Revolution. Ruskin brought reaction against the Revolution. St. Gaudens [the sculptor] had passed beyond all. He liked the stately monuments much more than he liked Gibbon or Ruskin; he loved their dignity; their unity; their scale; their lines; their lights and shadows; their decorative sculpture; but he was even less conscious than they of the force that created it all—the Virgin, the Woman—by whose genius 'the stately monuments of superstition' were built, through which she was expressed. He would have seen more meaning in Isis with the cow's horns, at Edfoo, who expressed the same thought. The art remained but the energy was lost even upon the artist."

# FICTION

(c. 1661-1731)

# DEFOE

# *Moll Flanders*

*D*ANIEL DEFOE *is the most prodigious literary journeyman on record. Besides writing with his own hand the whole of an important newspaper for many years, and besides creating the profession of journalist as it still is known after two hundred years, he was the author of approximately a thousand books and pamphlets, many of them influential in their day and several of them still living classics.* ROBINSON CRUSOE, *one of the most popular books ever written, is the best-known instance of his power to imagine and convey the details of a life, not his own, lived under special conditions. He was seldom recognized in his own time as a writer of fiction, so convincing were the "biographies" he turned out in such great profusion. Any narrative so plain and circumstantial must be true, the feeling was; and only with time have his superb merits, his invention and his verisimilitude, been given the credit due them.* MOLL FLANDERS *has noth-*

*ing of Defoe in it except his genius; it is in Moll and her career that we are absorbed; it is she that we believe without ever asking whether it is possible not to do so. Her disreputable days become a portion of general human experience, while Defoe's art is taken for granted. His art is of the highest, and it will always be studied by those who want their stories to carry conviction. He is also a reminder that prose fiction, of which he is one of the creators, had better remain prose. The poetry of Defoe is unseen, though it is always clearly felt, beneath a deceptively commonplace exterior.*

(MISS KATHERINE ANNE PORTER, GUEST)

*Cairns:* I could not help associating Moll Flanders with Robinson Crusoe when I reread Defoe's novel. He is so realistic that I felt I was reading a true story. Perhaps I ought not to admire Moll Flanders, but I feel that on the whole she is an excellent person, and it occurred to me—although I am not altogether certain—that Moll would have made a fine wife for Robinson Crusoe. I wonder, Miss Porter, if you would agree with that.

*Porter:* Oh, yes, I do, but I think that she made an excellent wife for all her husbands.

*Van Doren:* And would for any man, perhaps?

*Porter:* Oh, I think so. I think she had the qualities that men like.

*Van Doren:* I'm sorry I came two hundred years too late.

*Tate:* Every man is apt to feel that way. Miss Porter, what do you think that Moll had in her character that made her such a good wife, although she was a wife so many times?

*Porter:* Well, she was a woman extremely friendly to men, and she was very resourceful. She was self-supporting. I don't think that's a small matter.

*Cairns:* She was self-supporting in a strange fashion.

*Porter:* Well, yes, in odd ways. But I think if she had been on a desert island, for example, she would have shown the same kind of ready wit and resourcefulness and a cool head in a crisis and a very practical mind.

*Van Doren:* Would she have complained about the difficulties?

*Porter:* She never did.

*Van Doren:* She never seems to be that kind of woman.

*Cairns:* I had only one reservation about Moll Flanders being the wife of Robinson Crusoe. I thought she would make an excellent wife for any man except, perhaps, Robinson Crusoe. Do you think that she would have been content to live on a desert island? Wasn't the mainspring of her action excitement?

*Porter:* Well, yes. But I think she would have found excitement on a desert island too without much trouble. You remember how happily and comfortably she lived quietly when she was young. Then she got a great deal of excitement, even so, out of life.

*Van Doren:* She was no Emma Bovary, was she? Nothing neurotic about her.

*Porter:* Oh, no.

*Tate:* She was not a frustrated woman at all, but if that is true, why, do you think, had she so many husbands? Why didn't she stick to one of them?

*Van Doren:* It was not her fault perhaps.

*Cairns:* It may have been her craving for excitement. I gather it is more exciting to have many husbands than merely one. Defoe seemed to think so. His advertisement of the book stressed the plurality of husbands as an exciting aspect of the novel.

*Tate:* She was constantly being "done in" by her men, wasn't she?

*Porter:* Well, in a way, but it was mostly a question of the marriage portion, you remember. The money always got in the way, and one thing and another. They couldn't last because they had no money, and they separated.

*Van Doren:* Her husbands were always dying, too.

*Porter:* Some of them were dying and some of them were going away to seek their fortunes. Their troubles were largely what we now call economic.

*Tate:* But isn't it true that the only husband who was well-to-do turned out, by one of those malignant chances of fate, to be her half-brother? And she had to separate from him.

*Cairns:* Moll had a characteristic that Robinson Crusoe possessed. She was a solitary person. She was solitary in society because she was an outlaw, and of course Robinson Crusoe was solitary in nature. He was alone—until his man Friday appeared—on an island. And I am still not satisfied that you have answered my question.

*Porter:* Well, I can only remember one thing that she said about herself: that she could never work with a partner. Do you remember? Twice, I think it was, she went with a partner and each time she came to disaster.

*Cairns:* Yes, but she had perhaps a semi-partner at the end—her governess. I forget the name, if any, that she applied to her.

*Van Doren:* She calls her her governess.

*Tate:* By the way, Miss Porter, don't you think the governess is a rather mysterious character? She's a person of great worth. At the same time, she is Moll's confederate in crime. I can't place her. She is the only character, I think, in the entire story who may perhaps be not quite convincing.

*Van Doren:* My notion is otherwise. It seems to me that she was one of the most convincing. I wonder why that is. I should say that here this woman is, by chance, perhaps, and by circumstance, doing certain things, following certain trades of which we might disapprove, and yet carrying into those trades, into those occupations, the character that she was born with, that she always had. She is a very clear-headed and very faithful woman, very faithful to her friends.

*Tate:* That's true, but let me see if I can make the point a little more clearly. Moll, of course, does not lead an ordinary social life. But the governess is obscure because Defoe doesn't spend as much time upon her as he does upon Moll. He doesn't give you enough detail about her. She moves forward and backward, moves up a little into the foreground, then disappears again.

*Van Doren:* That is what I like about the way he handles her. For instance, suddenly you find her very active for no special reason. Do you remember the occasion when she goes to the man whom Moll has robbed? Her main intent is to blackmail him. Suddenly she has the passion to do that. It isn't explained, just as it isn't explained that she wants to help Moll on this occasion or some other occasion. The coming and going of this woman, to me, attests her vitality.

*Tate:* I don't feel that Defoe ought to explain her. I think one of the great virtues of this book is that no action is really motivated. It's like life because you don't see where the action comes from. You can't predict the consequences. Yet it's all beautifully clear.

*Cairns:* I thought you might suggest that that was a defect of the book, that he doesn't really put us inside his characters. We only know them through their actions.

*Porter:* No, I think the great virtue of that book is that his characters explain themselves with their actions and their speeches, and you know as much about them as you could possibly know. You know a great deal more about them than someone you know in life, really, and you understand also their motives; I don't think he has to explain.

*Van Doren:* I quite agree with you, Miss Porter. We find out about the inside of a person, so-called, by his outside. I think it is the outside that tells us. There is nothing else.

*Cairns:* How would you differentiate the characters in this book? It seems to me they are all alike because they are all leading the same kind of life.

*Van Doren:* Well, are her husbands alike? I should say not.

*Tate:* I think they are very different.

*Porter:* They're all as different men as you could possibly imagine.

*Van Doren:* Two of them are, respectively, a banker and a highwayman. I find nothing in common between those two men.

*Cairns:* You may be letting a mere label mislead you.

*Porter:* Their characters are very different.

*Van Doren:* One is a good banker and one is a good highwayman.

*Tate:* They tend to be types.

*Cairns:* That is exactly my point.

*Tate:* That's all right. I have no objection to types.

*Cairns:* I have no objection to types either—in their place.

Aeschylus created types and they are magnificent. Do we want the novelist to give us nothing but types? Don't we want the novelist also to be able to give us individuals?

*Porter:* They tend to be types in everything except the most important thing in a novel, and that is the difference in their human emotions. They all have a different set of feelings about things, which they express very clearly. In their relation, for example, with Moll, each one is quite different and quite separate. They all have a kind of amiability and a kind of benevolence almost, you know, which Moll's personality inspired in them all alike; but they are quite different really, and the characters of the men come out in their speeches and in their actions. They don't seem in the least alike to me, and I thought I knew them very well.

*Van Doren:* Wouldn't you say, Miss Porter, speaking as a novelist, that any character in a novel must be a type first of all?

*Porter:* Oh, naturally.

*Cairns:* I would not deny that a completely unique individual might not appeal to us. We ought to be able to recognize some common characteristics in him.

*Van Doren:* Perhaps he must be seventy-five per cent type.

*Tate:* If he's not a type first we don't understand him; we can't possibly get hold of him; we can't recognize him; he is a monster.

*Cairns:* But the modern novelist would attempt to give individuality to his characters, would he not?

*Tate:* I think, Mr. Cairns, that Virginia Woolf's characters tend not to be types, and for that reason it is very difficult to remember the action of a novel by Mrs. Woolf, although while you are reading the novel it is immensely impressive.

*Van Doren:* Yes, but it's all Mrs. Woolf.

*Tate:* And it's very hard to remember it a year later.

*Van Doren:* The inside of Mrs. Woolf's characters is the inside of Mrs. Woolf.

*Cairns:* That may be a reflection upon Mrs. Woolf as a novelist.

*Van Doren:* It's a reflection upon the theory of novel writing which says that you should get at the inside of your people. A great artist gets the outside. It's the most difficult thing in the world.

*Cairns:* It is difficult also to get the inside. Difficulty does not seem to me to be a sound test.

*Porter:* By getting the outside very clearly and perfectly, there is a sort of radiation. The radiation of personality through the being as presented from the outside.

*Tate:* When we talk about this objective quality of Defoe's, it's not quite the same thing that we get in the ordinary realistic novel of today. It's a very different thing, isn't it?

*Cairns:* The element that is lacking, I think, is introspection, in large part. That is an element that the modern novelist has added which I don't find here to any appreciable extent.

*Van Doren:* But, Mr. Cairns, my objection is that this element of introspection which you speak of has not given us the insides of the characters. It has given us the inside of the author's mind.

*Cairns:* Because second-rate novelists have used this method. But in the hands of a first-rate novelist, it seems to me a valuable element that we should not arbitrarily exclude.

*Tate:* I think I agree, Mr. Cairns.

*Porter:* I think that Joyce is a first-rate novelist and I think that he has come as near to getting completely into the bloodstream of his characters as anyone in the world, and for the most part, I find his characters very monotonous and not half so interesting as an objectively presented character like Moll Flanders. Now I'm not going to interrupt anyone again.

*Cairns:* Miss Porter, we want you to.

*Tate:* Well, Miss Porter, what do you think about this? You've mentioned Joyce. What about Henry James? He seems to combine very subtly these two things, the external observation of the character and the interior monologue. I'm not sure that we remember the interior monologues of James' characters. I remember his novels as a succession of scenes. That's what you take away, and of course the scene is pre-eminently what Defoe gives us.

*Van Doren:* But the interior monologue in James is again, I would say, James himself. The interior monologues in his novels are almost indistinguishable from his prefaces to those novels.

*Tate:* They all have the same style, the same tone—yes.

*Cairns:* To repeat—that may be a reflection on James. However, I enjoy his prefaces as much as his novels.

*Van Doren:* Take a person who is done completely from the outside, as Hamlet for instance, about whom I think we know nothing except the way he looks, the way he talks, what he says, and so forth. Even the soliloquies, I should say, are not indications of what he is inside. And yet we know everything about him.

*Tate:* It seems to me, Miss Porter, that this novel is a "dramatic" novel. That is, it is presented in one scene after another and the author never appears in it at all. That is a great thing to achieve in fiction.

*Porter:* I like the introspective novel very much. I think it has its place and I think we'd be much poorer without it, but I do think that the weakness of it is that when a novelist gets inside of a character, he finds only himself, and the great art really is to be able to look at the world and individuals and present characters that readers will recognize and will know or feel they know. That is a tremendous feat.

*Van Doren:* Once you're inside a person you cannot see him, literally speaking. You see organs or motives or what not that are just like yours. It seems to me very clear that this is the case.

*Cairns:* Would you not like some soliloquies from Moll Flanders?

*Tate:* The whole book is a soliloquy.

*Cairns:* Not in the sense in which we are talking.

*Van Doren:* Mr. Cairns, why do you believe in soliloquies? Why do you think they tell more about a person than his conversation with other persons? I don't see why they should.

*Porter:* Moll is always saying, "I thought this. I said that to myself. I was grieved," and she describes her grief. "I repented," and she describes her repentance in a passage which gives me more the feeling of real grief for sin and a real sense of the soul approaching death than anything else I know in the English language, and she does it all by saying, "I thought this and that. I said that."

*Cairns:* Yes. They are all descriptions about something, but you are never taken inside that something.

*Tate:* Mr. Cairns, doesn't Moll go into a soliloquy occasionally?

*Cairns:* She does occasionally.

*Tate:* She moralizes and she says that she is going to repent, but they are the least interesting passages.

*Cairns:* I can't tell, Mr. Tate, whether you are for me or against me. Where do you stand on this question of introspection?

*Tate:* I think it all depends on who does it and how successful it is. But the safest, and at the same time the most brilliant, thing in fiction is this objective method.

*Van Doren:* Mr. Cairns, I'd like to know more about this inside that you speak of. Character originally means an outline drawn of someone. To be able to draw an outline of someone you have to be outside him, obviously. When we're inside him, there is nothing to see. There is no point of view. But also, what is there inside of a person? If you take a person's skin away from him, what is there?

*Cairns:* I think Miss Porter has given us an example in Joyce's novel. The whole novel is about what's inside Mr. Bloom and Miriam Bloom.

*Van Doren:* I'm interested in your word "about."

*Cairns:* What do you mean?

*Van Doren:* I think you're confessing right there that it isn't the inside. It's about the inside, and so I think the inside of Mr. Bloom is still at a distance from Joyce.

*Cairns:* You must admit that there is certainly a distinction. A distinction can be drawn in this manner: The novelist says, "A does something"; that is one approach. The other approach is: A, a character in a novel, says, "I am going to do so and so for the following reasons," and thinks about it. His thoughts are recorded in the novel. That latter element is what I find lacking in *Moll Flanders*.

*Van Doren:* But why do you believe people when they tell you what their reasons are for what they do? I don't know what my motives are.

*Cairns:* That depends on the art of the novelist.

*Tate:* Yes, I think so, too, Mr. Van Doren. For example, a character in a novel states explicitly his motive. The author shows that it is not his real motive. The false motive becomes dramatically interesting.

*Van Doren:* Of course. But in both cases you're on the outside of that person. You hear him say, "This is my motive," don't you? It's something that happens between you and him.

*Tate:* But don't you think the upshot of the matter is something like this—that the introspection, the soliloquy, is likely to be no good unless it is firmly grounded in a realistic setting? That is to say, unless the character is very distinct from the outside, you don't believe his soliloquy.

*Cairns:* Let us attack that problem from the point of view that you have just suggested, from the point of view of Defoe's realism. Do you think his realism is the result of his shopkeeping experience, or is it a conscious art such as Flaubert employed?

*Porter:* I think Defoe was a first-rate artist.

*Cairns:* I think he was too, but how about his realism? Was it because he was a shopkeeper that in the book he gives you the cost of the stockings, how much the linen was worth, or was his realism a deliberate art?

*Porter:* That may have something to do with his background, his training, because after all he was using a very good method. He was writing about what he knew. Of course, though, that may have something to do with his choice of a character too, because, after all, Moll was intensely interested in the price of things and getting a little money and knowing what things were worth.

*Cairns:* So was Defoe himself.

*Van Doren:* And so was his new audience.

*Cairns:* You would not say that his realism was the realism of Flaubert, would you?

*Porter:* No, I don't think so. It's on quite a different level.

*Van Doren:* I should say that there was very little difference in degree; that is to say, Flaubert looks at a certain class of French people of the nineteenth century with a theory about that class. He doesn't describe that class without the aid of feeling and a theory about the middle class, the bourgeoisie. So, however, does Defoe have a feeling and a theory about the class of person whom Moll represents. I think he was conscious that he was introducing into fiction a new type of person.

*Tate:* But at the same time, don't you think that unlike Flaubert, Defoe is not interested in giving you an analysis of society? You don't see the English social system of the early eighteenth century at all. The realism is close up. It is realism about Moll's immediate surroundings.

*Cairns:* His realism was the realism of the journalist. It is photographic and is designed to picture the society Defoe knew at first hand.

*Porter:* With respect to some of the laws, I always thought that he made rather a good criticism of a certain phase of society when Moll makes her speech to the judges just before the death sentence is passed upon her. He puts into her speech a real criticism of the criminal code; and he does quite often criticize society—rather obliquely, that is true—but he does say that the poverty and the bad upbringing of people is the cause of crime. He does say so, plainly.

*Van Doren:* And weren't you impressed, too, by the fact that he seems to have a certain knowledge—which I should say was social—of the habits of people in a certain quarter of London with reference to marriage?

*Tate:* Yes, but he doesn't draw it up systematically, for example, the way Zola did.

*Van Doren:* Oh, no. I think Flaubert did not do it systematically either.

*Tate:* Zola did, however. He documented his books in great detail.

*Cairns:* Flaubert, of course, was selective for his effect, and Defoe is cumulative in his effect.

*Porter:* But both are very good methods which the artist can use.

*Cairns:* I am not condemning either. I am making a distinction.

*Van Doren:* Can you say any more about the method of Defoe as a novelist, Miss Porter?

*Porter:* I love especially that cumulative method, one episode following another until you find at the very end you have a complete picture, exactly what he wanted you to see and you realize that you've had it in a procession of small pictures that build up to the whole.

*Cairns:* What do you think about the fact that he gives no descriptive detail, no scenery, no houses, no descriptions of people?

*Porter:* He was a city man, for one thing.

*Tate:* Don't you think that there is another reason for that, Miss Porter, and that it proves Defoe's superiority? One vice of the modern novel is the long descriptive passages.

*Van Doren:* Description is always the resource of someone who does not know how to tell a story.

*Tate:* I'm afraid that's true. Fielding has no description.

*Van Doren:* A first-rate novelist never needs description.

*Cairns:* I hope we bring up this point when we discuss Proust.

*Porter:* I don't pretend to know how Defoe does it. It is really beyond me. I've tried to put my finger on it, but when Moll goes on her ship you see that ship.

*Cairns:* But he does not describe it.

*Porter:* No; he doesn't have to.

*Van Doren:* He creates the ship.

*Porter:* He gives you the ship. You see the coach she travels in. You see the house she lives in. She goes into a street and in the strangest way you know the street.

*Cairns:* Flaubert creates the same effect on me, but his method is entirely different.

*Tate:* Paradoxically, don't you think you see the streets and the ship and the coach because he refuses to describe them? He selects one object. Moll puts her hand on one object and holds it. The whole scene comes to life.

*Van Doren:* Or that famous place in the novel where she suddenly sees her Lancashire husband from her window in the inn. She simply walks to the window because she needs air, she says. It is a curious thing. That little statement creates the room, the inn, the street, and the husband.

*Porter:* And when she goes along the country road and meets the honest man, you know, who is going to sell her a horse. There is the country road and there is the man. And not only that, she is trying to deceive him; she is trying to escape; and she has her little thoughts about the way she is deceiving this man and her motives for it, and the whole scene is clear.

*Cairns:* Do you think he is a very great artist?

*Porter:* One of the greatest.

*Van Doren:* I would say that what we have just been saying suggests that he is a great artist. God does not describe the world. He creates it. He doesn't need to describe it.

*Cairns:* No, because He hands it to us and we have to take it. If Defoe does not appeal to us we can put him aside.

*Tate:* Doesn't Defoe give you the scenes almost as if they weren't communicated through words? You tend to forget the language. The object shines through the words.

*Van Doren:* The words are a perfectly transparent medium.

*Cairns:* If he is such a great artist, how do you reconcile his art and his morality? Is he reducing art to a tool of morality?

*Porter:* I think he made quite a few little bows in the direction of the moral fashions of his time.

*Cairns:* You think he is not serious in his morality?

*Porter*: Well, he was a man who wrote political pamphlets for hire, that's true, and he went with the side that seemed to promise him the best advantage, and all that. But I think his morality was strong and sincere; certainly a little commonplace, but real.

*Cairns:* How do you reconcile the happy ending of *Moll Flanders* after such a life of sin and wickedness? How do you reconcile that happy ending with the morality he is preaching in the book?

*Porter:* She repented, don't you see? And it is true that there is a religious idea that repentance is sufficient. Of course, it shouldn't lead to a happy ending as a usual thing, but you remember that in those days—I notice it in studying the Puritans—they really did believe or seemed to believe that God rewarded earthly virtue with earthly good.

*Cairns:* But Moll did not repent until she had a sum of money in the bank and an attractive husband.

*Tate:* Didn't she repent before that?

*Porter:* She repented when she was facing death and thought she was going to be hanged next week. There is almost no religion that will refuse a sinner on his deathbed. Oh, no, she repents at exactly the right moment.

*Cairns:* You mean the right moment at the end of the book when she had all this money, or the moment when she was facing death? She repented, of course, both times.

*Porter:* No, her real scene of repentance, which I think is one of the most exciting things in the book—Defoe promised he would make it interesting, and he did—the great passage in that book is from the time the minister comes to talk with her about her soul and persuade her to repent, until the time he returns to bring her news of her reprieve. Then again she becomes immediately the busy woman of the world—counting her possessions, encouraging her husband, making plans for the future.

*Cairns:* So her repentance wasn't sincere, was it?

*Porter:* Yes, she behaved much better after that. She had a few habits left over that she tried to curb.

*Tate:* She had several habits. Don't you think, Miss Porter, that Defoe may have something else in mind? Is he showing us that a virtuous woman can also on occasion be a thief, that a certain kind of virtue doesn't consist solely in conventional behavior?

*Van Doren:* Yes, and of course it is also fair to remember that his morality was a morality of success. These new people whom he introduces into the world, these middle-class people for a new middle-class audience, are people who have to make their way in the world—a thing that we still have respect for, I should say.

*Porter:* Yes, indeed. It's certainly part of our national faith.

*Cairns:* She was goaded, of course, by poverty, and there is a very fine sentence that I recall from the book. She said, "The terror of approaching poverty lay hard upon my spirits." Perhaps she can be excused on that ground.

*Tate:* Perhaps it's more than a conventional excuse that Moll was deceived in her girlhood by the young country gentleman. From then on it was almost impossible for her to recover and be a respectable woman. She had to live in the underworld from that time on.

*Cairns:* But she did become a respectable woman at the end.

*Tate:* In a way, yes, but I don't think her respectability is really convincing, Mr. Cairns, I must say.

*Cairns:* That is the question I raised, whether or not he is sincere in his morality. I take it we agree that he is not.

*Van Doren:* The use of the word "gentleman" reminds me that when she was a little girl in the workhouse, she said she wanted to be a gentlewoman, and it turned out that she meant she wanted to be a woman who could make her own way.

*Porter:* To make her own living.

*Van Doren:* Speaking of the style of this man, I should like to read a paragraph in which he has created a scene, created all over again the governess whom we were talking about a minute ago, made her talk so that we seem to listen to her talking. The occasion is that on which Moll has been disguised as a man. She runs from those who are chasing her into the governess' house and is not identified there because she has changed her clothes. "When they had thus searched the house from bottom to top and then from top to bottom and could find nothing, they appeased the mob pretty well, but they carried my governess before the justice. Two men swore that they saw the man whom they pursued go into the house. My governess made a great noise that her house should be insulted and that she should be used thus for nothing, that if a man did come in he might go out again presently for aught she knew, but she was ready to make oath that no man had been within her doors all that day, as she knew of (and that was very true indeed). But it might be indeed that if she was above stairs any fellow in a fright might find the door open and run in for shelter when he was pursued but that she knew nothing of it, and if it had been so he certainly went out again, perhaps through the other door, for she had another door into an alley, and so had made his escape."

(1828-1910)

# TOLSTOY

# *War and Peace*

*WAR AND PEACE is generally considered the greatest of all novels. Some of its rivals for this rank would be other books by Tolstoy, since the author of* ANNA KARENINA *is an admitted master of his art. But there is little doubt as to which his masterpiece is; for* WAR AND PEACE *has everything, and has it in baffling abundance. It is as credible as Defoe and yet immeasurably more important; it is as finely organized as a tale of minor proportions would be, and yet it never loses its grasp of a single vast subject. This is Napoleon's invasion of Russia and the retreat from Moscow as witnessed by a host of individuals whom Tolstoy creates with lavish and painstaking ease. These individuals come from all classes and have all degrees of virtue or vice, of strength or weakness, of ugliness or beauty, just as the action embraces almost every imaginable human experience. Sometimes the focus is near and sometimes it is far, as in the famous battle chapters;*

*but it is always clear, or if it is not clear the reason is that Tolstoy wishes to impress upon us the impossibility of seeing such a thing as a battle whole. He can do what he wishes; and we cannot choose but accept his judgments for the same reason that we cannot contrive to disbelieve his narrative, based as it is on the fundamental situations of story. The power of recognition-scenes, for example, is nowhere in literature more simply proved than in his account of the meeting between Natasha and the wounded Andrey.*

*Cairns:* If it is true that *War and Peace* is the world's greatest novel, it might be interesting to ask ourselves why. Mr. Tate, I wonder if you would state what *War and Peace* has that other novels lack.

*Tate:* That is a very difficult thing to talk about. I would say, in general, that *War and Peace* has everything that every other novel has, and in greater abundance. It has a greater abundance of life, every kind of life we know today, or will ever know. The setting of *War and Peace* is the Napoleonic era, but it is no more than a setting. It has every scale of life, every social class, every person living in that time. Yet everything is perfectly plain, distinct, in bold relief. There is no mistaking what Tolstoy is trying to do.

*Van Doren:* You don't think that the reason for the eminence of the book is some single thing in it, some trick which is performed there, some single quality that could be named?

*Tate:* If there are any tricks in *War and Peace,* there are so many that we forget them.

*Van Doren:* I quite agree.

*Tate:* It has everything that every novel has.

*Van Doren:* And more of it.

*Cairns:* It has everything that a novel could have, but I think it has one quality which many novels lack, and that is its epic quality. I am thinking of the term "epic" in two senses: in the Aristotelian sense—though not strictly—of a dignified theme and organic unity and orderly progression; but I am using it more particularly in its common meaning of heroic.

*Tate:* *War and Peace* has epic proportions, but I do not think

Aristotle would have called it strictly an epic. It is too close to history, and there is too much that does not bear upon the plot. But the theme is heroic.

*Van Doren:* Heroic and broad. I was interested in Mr. Tate's reference to the many classes represented here. Do you think it was an advantage for Tolstoy—as perhaps for any novelist—to be able to refer to an ordered society with its many classes in their respective positions?

*Tate:* If there is any secret to Tolstoy's art, it's probably not the secret of Tolstoy. He is not conscious of it. I mean that he could assume the existence of a complete, highly developed society. You remember that although he gives us all classes he doesn't have a theory about any class. He simply presents each class. He doesn't show the class alone; he shows them all as interrelated. For example, the great hunting scene at the Rostov estate. The huntsman has such an established position in society that he talks back to his master, the old Count Rostov.

*Van Doren:* On the hunting field the hunting master is master. But what are the classes here? There is the Tsar, of course—Alexander—at the top.

*Cairns:* And Napoleon whose shadow falls across the novel as it fell across the world.

*Van Doren:* Although Tolstoy does not place him in the class of Alexander.

*Tate:* Tolstoy thought of Napoleon as an example of the "illegitimacy" of the period. He didn't belong to the royal hierarchy of Europe.

*Cairns:* But he treated Alexander, his own Sovereign, as he treated Napoleon. You will recall that his technique, whenever he brought Alexander or Napoleon on the scene, was to introduce either an adjective or some descriptive phrase that would take those men from the pedestal on which they stood. When Alexander was called out to the balcony to address the mob, Tolstoy describes him as munching biscuits. When Napoleon appears on the scene, he refers to his pudgy hands.

*Van Doren:* Of course, he despises Napoleon. He does not in the same way despise Alexander, if he despises him at all; l makes a great deal out of the fact that young men in the ear battles want nothing so much as to die for Alexander.

*Tate:* Exactly. The young Count Rostov, at the Battle Austerlitz, has a wonderful vision of the Emperor. The Emper rides up, and Count Rostov's whole purpose in life at his age we ought to say at his age because he is not mature—is fulfille you see.

*Van Doren:* Let us see if we can name the classes. There is t Tsar. There are the nobility, the counts.

*Cairns:* The court society.

*Van Doren:* There are the princes. What do you understar a Russian prince to be?

*Tate:* A Russian prince is just a gentleman.

*Van Doren:* I was told once that the nearest equivalent English is mister.

*Tate:* He is just a gentleman.

*Van Doren:* A member of an old family. There are the coun and the princes, then.

*Tate:* There seems to be a very large difference between prince and a count. A count is higher. Count Pierre Bezuho whom we shall probably discuss in a few minutes, is very f above Prince Andrey in rank, and one of the interesting featur of this book is the contrast between Prince Andrey Bolkonsl and the Count Pierre Bezuhov.

*Cairns:* Can Mr. Van Doren's question be summed up by sa ing that he describes every class in Russia from the peasant the Tsar?

*Van Doren:* Between the counts and the peasants, do we ha any intermediate classes—merchants, for example?

*Tate:* There is almost no middle class.

*Cairns:* You have the soldier, for one.

*Tate:* He is in a professional class. The old Russian socie very closely resembled the society of the old South in this countr The old South had a very small middle class.

*Van Doren:* The middle class was the subject, if the novel h a subject, of *Madame Bovary.* It is gone here, or has never come into existence.

*Tate:* Do you suppose, Mr. Van Doren, that that class is wholly missing in Russia? We know historically that it wasn't. Don't you think rather that Tolstoy was not interested in it? He was interested in people whose situation in life made them superior to their economic necessities. You had the peasants at the lower end of the scale; they were fixed; they were poor but they had no economic necessities in the sense that a middle class must be economically competitive all the time.

*Van Doren:* The classes he represents here are free for the purposes of fiction.

*Tate:* They can act disinterestedly, as complete persons.

*Van Doren:* I can't help remembering that Tolstoy himself wanted to believe in a classless society; yet as a novelist he takes full advantage of what I take to be a very great opportunity for a novelist, a society which is ranked heavily and strictly.

*Cairns:* I think he regarded himself as something of a historian, and he wanted to give a faithful picture of Russia at the time. We know from his life that he devoted a great deal of time to studying archives and history, particularly his family history.

*Tate:* Isn't it true that two families in this book, the Bolkonsky family and the Rostov family, are in the ancestral line of Tolstoy?

*Cairns:* I think one represented his mother's family and the other represented his father's family.

*Tate:* We have here two distinct types of Russian character.

*Cairns:* Those two types are represented by Prince Andrey and Count Pierre.

*Tate:* You have in Pierre the brooding Russian, and in Andrey the Russian who is trying to be a man of action, but who doesn't quite succeed because he doesn't believe in it.

*Cairns:* You have a third type: the soldier, Nikolay. I think all three of them represented phases of Tolstoy himself.

*Van Doren:* He probably liked to think that he was most like Pierre, who is repeated in *Anna Karenina* as Levin. Tolstoy doubtless thought of himself as a simple, kindly, innocent man. But of course he had this enormous sophistication which comes out in Andrey, who is European; and in Nikolay.

*Tate:* Don't you think that Tolstoy was an innocent and unsophisticated man?

*Van Doren:* I can't say that in view of what he has created here.

*Cairns:* I think that point is valid and is justified. He kills Prince Andrey as a character, but we know that he intended to carry Pierre forward into the succeeding novel, which would have dealt with the Decembrists.

*Tate:* Mr. Cairns, don't you think that a Western European novelist would probably have killed Pierre and preserved Prince Andrey?

*Cairns:* I don't think a Western European novelist could have conceived a Pierre.

*Tate:* Probably not, and for that reason he would have killed him off because he couldn't have handled him dramatically. Prince Andrey is unique dramatically. Regardless of the fact that he has philosophical, even sentimental, moments of introspection, he is at the same time a man of action, and you can always project Andrey into some situation which is action.

*Cairns:* The interesting thing about the novel is that it contains hundreds of characters, and yet they are all individuals to us. A Russian reading the novel may regard them as types and not as individuals, but I think a man of the Western world contemplating Pierre or contemplating Andrey would regard them as individuals.

*Tate:* I'm not sure I do. While I agree they are individuals, first of all they are types. I recall something Mr. Van Doren said a minute ago: that all these characters are framed by their social background.

*Cairns:* We agreed when we discussed *Moll Flanders* that all characters in fiction must in large part be types.

*Van Doren:* Pierre is not a peasant, for instance, and that tells us perhaps ninety percent of what he is.

*Cairns:* Undoubtedly they are types. But I also, perhaps because I am not a Russian, have an impression of individuality.

*Van Doren:* I don't know what an individual is. You cannot contemplate an individual.

*Tate:* Mr. Van Doren, I would say that you can't get an individual until you see him in the circumstances which have molded him as a type.

*Van Doren:* All sorts of things about him would be true of other men. To be sure, there are the particular things that he does, and we relish them. There is no man like Pierre in this book or in the world, if you like. But he is a man, and he is a man about whom you can say things. An individual cannot be discussed. There are no known words which would apply.

*Cairns:* We have been praising this book. Are we taking the position that there are no defects in it?

*Van Doren:* I don't know any, I must confess. I read it always with the greatest absorption.

*Tate:* There may be certain defects of structure, if you think of more limited novels, but in terms of *War and Peace* I can see no defects.

*Cairns:* If it is asserted that *War and Peace* is universal—and I take it we must assert that if we say it is great—then from that position I think it has some defects which a really universal novel would not have.

*Tate:* You mean this particular novel is universal?

*Cairns:* Isn't that implied in our statement that it is the greatest novel? It should have an appeal at all times and everywhere.

*Tate:* It is certainly universal, in the sense that everybody can read it.

*Van Doren:* Yet it starts very decidedly from Russia, from a particular place with a particular atmosphere, as any universal work of art must do.

*Cairns:* I think its ideas are dated, but not necessarily from the point of view of the present day, because I think we are still under the influence of Rousseau. Tolstoy wore Rousseau's picture around his neck. He worshipped him. The book is full of the ideas of the nineteenth century, which may, at some future time, limit its appeal. Furthermore, good critics, prior to the nineteenth century, under the influence of a different climate of opinion, might have been unsympathetic to some of its ideas. The book might have bored them, just as some of us are bored by the religious discussions of the seventeenth century.

*Van Doren:* You speak of its ideas. You don't mean, do you, the ideas that make the novel what it is as a novel? These are, of course, the ideas that Tolstoy had while he was writing it; but the novel as a novel does not seem to me to be composed of ideas.

*Cairns:* No. I mean the ideas expressed in the novel from time to time, the propaganda part of it. Another defect that I find in the book is that parts of it seem to me not to flow from Tolstoy's own personal experience, but were prepared from other books.

*Tate:* What do you mean, prepared from other books, Mr. Cairns?

*Cairns:* Take his discussion of freemasonry. It seems to me that he just read up on it.

*Tate:* Let us examine that. What do you mean, read up on it?

*Cairns:* I think he went to the library and took out a lot of books on freemasonry and absorbed its theory and practice.

*Tate:* Well, why not? The real test of that would be the result in Pierre Bezuhov's character. Is freemasonry convincing in dramatic terms? Is it convincing as Pierre Bezuhov lives out freemasonry?

*Cairns:* I would state it the other way. I think Pierre is convincing in spite of his freemasonry.

*Van Doren:* But it is very important in the biography of Pierre that he at one time or another wants, perhaps needs, this thing and that he gets it. We see him going through ceremonies which are in themselves dramatic. Later on he rejects it all.

*Tate:* The real point is: What is freemasonry to Pierre? Isn't freemasonry to him a kind of universal, rational religion? It's certainly not the old Russian religion of Christianity. It's a belated eighteenth-century rational religion. How can all men get together and love one another?

*Van Doren:* Which is a very important question in his mind. And I think it is made convincingly important. Wouldn't you say so, Mr. Tate?

*Tate:* Yes. But I don't think it has any philosophical importance. It is important in this novel. It's something that takes place in the experience of these people.

*Van Doren:* Here we are talking about Pierre and Andrey, the two heroes of the book—it has at least two, perhaps more—and we are talking about their families, the Bolkonsky family, the Rostov family, and the rest. We haven't said anything about the fact that this novel is supposed by many people to be about Napoleon's invasion of Russia and his retreat.

*Tate:* That brings up a very interesting point. It reminds me of the classical criticism of this novel. Percy Lubbock, the English critic who wrote, I think, the finest book on the novel ever written—*The Craft of Fiction*—says that *War and Peace* is really two novels which are never quite fused together. We have the theme of war, on the one hand, and we have also the private life of these different families, on the other.

*Cairns:* Birth, growth, death and birth again.

*Tate:* Lubbock says that the private life is summed up in youth, the growth of youth into maturity and old age, the succession of the generations.

*Cairns:* The processional march of the generations.

*Tate:* That is a very interesting point from which to view this novel.

*Van Doren:* It is. But we have been talking about *War and Peace* as a novel which concerns the fortunes of many individuals and families.

*Cairns:* Do you think the book has a theme?

*Van Doren:* I think it has a theme, which the whole of the book is required to state.

*Tate:* Can you state it, Mr. Van Doren?

*Van Doren:* Of course not.

*Tate:* None of us can.

*Cairns:* It can be said, as Lubbock emphasizes, that the theme is the ebb and flow of life over a period of about fifteen years. Tolstoy shows us a new generation which grows to maturity and settles into middle age. The book ends on the note of another new generation. That is the dominant theme which Lubbock thinks would have made a better novel if Tolstoy had not superimposed upon it a second theme, of which the hero is Russia. It might also be said that the theme is the age-old struggle between the East and the West.

*Van Doren:* Tolstoy couldn't state the theme, short of writing 1146 pages. That is my way of saying that it is a really successful novel. It is about much more than Tolstoy realized. It is about everything he knew, believed, felt, saw.

*Tate:* But can't we take up Percy Lubbock's idea somewhat as follows: He says that the war and the peace don't go together. I think he is wrong for this reason: that the war intensifies all the emotions that we get in the scenes of domestic life. Those scenes would go on without the war, but the thing that makes them so convincing, so vivid, so dramatic is the fact that they are intensified by this remote influence, which is the war. They are heightened. Every character in Tolstoy's novels, and I think particularly in *War and Peace,* is a normal character with emotions abnormally intensified.

*Van Doren:* You say "this remote war." The war in an important sense is not remote. It is not something lugged in from time to time.

*Tate:* It is not that at all.

*Cairns:* No one could have the idea that it was a novel about Napoleon if that were so. I think what Mr. Tate has said can be stated another way: that the processional march of the generations and the war episodes are so integrated that the reader regards them as a unit.

*Van Doren:* The war for Tolstoy whenever he becomes articulate about it—and when he is articulate he may not be saying anything very important—is a series of marches also. The book is full of marches if you like, of great masses of people and of individuals, of pairs and triplets of people, and of families. In his very theory of the war itself and of war in general, we have something that binds the two halves of the book together. A war for him is something that happens. It isn't caused by an individual. It is something that happens among all the people whom it affects. Well, here is the war going on and here are the people whom it affects.

*Cairns:* An interesting point about the war aspect of the novel is that in the nineteenth century the pacifists regarded it as an indictment of war, and they utilized it as part of their propaganda for nineteenth-century pacifism. When I read the novel today, I don't feel that way. It seems to me that he is absolutely neutral toward war. He is neither for nor against it.

*Tate:* I think the propaganda against war in *War and Peace* suffers the fate of all propaganda. It can be taken both ways. But the war is made so interesting that it could very well be taken as a glorification of war.

*Van Doren:* For Tolstoy—not as a man, not as a thinker, but as a novelist—anything that human beings do has its glory. Humanity is equally glorious in its wars, its peace, its quarrels, its love affairs. I think he can be said to have hated nothing that ever happened.

*Tate:* Do you remember the famous scene preceding the Battle of Austerlitz when Nikolay Rostov is with the detachment which is ordered to defend the bridge? Nikolay is there; it's his first experience of war; he goes through successive phases of courage and fear. That episode seems to be a rather minor thing. But it's a coalescence of the war and the domestic themes. Would you say that that small episode is as important as the grand episodes in which General Kutuzov and Napoleon appear?

*Van Doren:* All the episodes in the book have their importance. Do you ever find that Tolstoy is dragging us through an episode just because he needs it in his novel? Each one of them carries its own conviction as it happens.

*Cairns:* He uses an episode of that sort to give you a picture of a certain aspect of warfare.

*Tate:* Do you think that any of those war episodes could be omitted?

*Van Doren:* We are also, however, Mr. Cairns, learning about Nikolay Rostov as that is happening.

*Cairns:* Everything that Tolstoy does in the novel from the point of view of technique has two objectives. One is to illuminate the character and the other is to illuminate the action as a whole.

*Van Doren:* And of course there are all sorts of incidental things. On this bridge, you may remember, Nikolay hears his first gunfire; it sounds like the rattling of nuts on metal.

*Tate:* Isn't that remarkable? I remember a story of a soldier in the American Civil War who heard musket fire for the first time. He said it was like the falling of a great number of planks, a tremendous number of planks from a great height. They all clattered on the ground.

*Van Doren:* And slapped the earth.

*Cairns:* I wonder if you received from the book as a whole the impression that I received—a sense of sadness. Of course we know that Tolstoy later in life was interested in the basic question: Why live? That is a question that a Western man, it seems to me, would not ask himself. I think the Western man would ask himself the question that Somerset Maugham asked in the novel, *Of Human Bondage*. Has life any meaning?

*Van Doren:* It isn't the same question, is it?

*Cairns:* If the Western man concludes that life has no meaning, he still wants to live. He doesn't question himself and say: "Why should I live at all?" But it seems to me that Tolstoy is asking that question in *War and Peace,* that that is the basic question. Out of the novel as a whole you get a sense of sadness.

*Van Doren:* But not the sense that life is not to be lived. Tolstoy is not sorry that life is being lived.

*Tate:* Don't you think that the sadness in this novel is not very different from the classical melancholy, the *lachrimae rerum,* the tears of things, the melancholy of human life?

*Van Doren:* Or for that matter, the sense of sadness and of terrible error there is in the *Iliad.* The *Iliad* is full of warfare which seems to relish itself, yet from time to time we understand clearly, I think, that for Homer this very warfare is one of the most horrible and magnificent errors ever committed.

*Cairns:* Tolstoy was reading the *Iliad* at the time he was writing *War and Peace;* in fact, Tolstoy compared himself to Homer, and the most distinguishing characteristic of *War and Peace,* as of the *Iliad,* is its epic quality. Not only does it have that link with the *Iliad,* but it also has the link that behind all those mass movements of people there are forces operating. In Homer's epic poems those forces were symbolized by the gods.

*Tate:* I think it is very close to the Christian doctrine that the Christian life is perpetually impossible and perpetually necessary. There is that paradox. Gentlemen, here is a passage from the novel which I think illustrates beautifully Tolstoy's power of depicting the individual episode, the quality of an individual scene. This is the wounding of Prince Andrey which leads to his death. "A whiz and a thud; five paces from him the dry soil was thrown up as the cannonball sank into the earth. A chill ran down his back. He looked at the ranks. Probably a number had been struck. The men had gathered in a crowd in the second battalion. 'M. l'aide-de-camp,' he shouted, 'tell the men not to crowd together.' The adjutant, having obeyed this instruction, was approaching Prince Andrey. From the other side the major in command of the battalion came riding up. 'Look out,' rang out a frightened cry from a soldier, and like a bird, with swift, purring wings alighting on the earth, a grenade dropped with a dull thud a couple of paces from Prince Andrey near the major's horse. The horse, with no question of whether it were right or wrong to show fear, snorted, reared, almost throwing the major, and galloped away. The horse's terror infected the men. 'Lie down,' shouted the adjutant, throwing himself on the ground. Prince Andrey stood in uncertainty. The shell was smoking and rotating like a top between him and the recumbent adjutant, near a bush of wormwood in the rut between the meadow and the field. Can this be death? Prince Andrey wondered, with an utterly new, wistful feeling, looking at the grass, at the wormwood and at the thread of smoke coiling from the rotating top. 'I can't die. I don't want to die. I love life. I love this grass and earth and air.' "

(1871-1922)

# PROUST

# *Swann's Way*

*MARCEL PROUST'S great modern novel in fourteen volumes is the outstanding monument of a literary age which has absorbed itself in the study of psychology.* REMEMBRANCE OF THINGS PAST, *of which* SWANN'S WAY *forms the first part, would be notable for its extraordinary incidental narratives, such as that of Swann and Odette or that of Marcel and Albertine; but its continuing concern is with the psychology of memory, and the author's last devotion is given to the problem of recording the way his mind held in its recesses the whole of a past world. That world, with its Parisian aristocracy into which so many entrances are tentatively made, has, to be sure, a certain solidity which at times can remind us even of so burly a novelist as Balzac; yet most of the time it is a thing of the mind, and Proust's interest is largely confined to the delicate and mysterious mental processes which none of his predecessors in the art of fiction had known so much about. He is so much a connoisseur of these that he is led more or less to specialize in abnormal and even fantastic situations, or in grotesque characters such as the Baron de Charlus. And all this is fascinating even when we recognize it as limited in its importance. In addition, however, Proust has an abundance of natural gift which saves him from the fate of the literary specialist.* REMEMBRANCE OF THINGS PAST *is one of the richest of contemporary treasures, and no reader of it will ever forget its Paris.*

(MR. ANDRÉ MAUROIS, GUEST)

*Cairns:* Marcel Proust uses the story of the disintegration of French aristocratic society as a background on which to record his impressions of psychology, manners, customs, love and, particularly, art and time. Mr. Maurois, would you agree that that is the theme of the novel?

*Maurois:* Perhaps the theme could be expressed in one sentence of Proust himself: "Time, as it flows, is so much time wasted and nothing can ever be truly possessed save under the aspect of eternity which is also the aspect of art."

*Van Doren:* Perhaps it is such a feeling that inspires certain persons like Saint-Simon or Pepys to keep diaries. I have always thought so. For them it must have seemed that time would continue to flow, and everything with it be swept away, unless they imprisoned it in their books.

*Maurois:* Yes. Art, because it gives the past a *form,* saves it from change and disintegration.

*Tate:* Mr. Maurois, don't you think it is interesting that Proust, in power and technique one of the most advanced novelists, should partly return to a very old form of the old novel? His novel is partly a very elaborate personal record.

*Maurois:* Oh, yes, certainly. And you have, included in the book, a short novel which is exactly a classical novel of the old type.

*Cairns:* You mean the section, "Swann in Love"?

*Maurois:* Yes, the second part of *Swann's Way,* so different from all the rest of Proust's work.

*Van Doren:* You wouldn't say, then, that Proust's work is

entirely concerned with society? After all, there are individuals here. And, chief of all, there is Proust himself.

*Maurois:* I feel quite certain that Proust never intended to be the Balzac of his time. His book was not a *Comédie Humaine.* No, he intended to be the Bergson of the novel. He was interested, not in a sociology, but in a new psychology and, to a certain extent, in a new metaphysics.

*Cairns:* He was, of course, greatly influenced in his theory of time by Bergson.

*Maurois:* Bergson was his teacher in philosophy at the Lycée Condorcet in Paris, and had great influence in the intellectual formation of Proust.

*Cairns:* I cannot quite agree with Mr. Van Doren's point about society. You will recall that, as a young man, Proust had two major ambitions—love and society. He wanted to be received in French society; he wanted to have a great love affair. But later on in life he concluded that those two ambitions were not worthwhile, and for them he substituted his interest in time and art. He ceased to pursue love and society for themselves, but stormed them indirectly through the instruments of time and art.

*Maurois:* Exactly. Love and society became for him themes for his art. The true artist always ends in giving up real life in order to see it better, and from outside.

*Tate:* Mr. Maurois, don't you think that Proust looked upon the society of his time differently from, for example, Thackeray in his time? The social framework may be disintegrating, but that isn't Proust's main interest, is it? Isn't it rather the individual consciousness, the secret life of the characters? Don't you think generally that literature tends to be interested in such private experience when the social framework begins to break up? Private experience becomes very important, whereas it wasn't so important perhaps in the age of Racine. Life was much more social.

*Maurois:* Yes, except, of course, that even in the seventeenth century, you also had men like Pascal or La Rochefoucauld who were very much interested in analyzing the feelings of the individual.

*Van Doren:* And Saint-Simon's *Memoires.*

*Tate:* Yes, but I was thinking of the novel as a sort of public form of literature, comparable nowadays to the drama of the seventeenth century. Perhaps the kind of experience we have can not be conveyed in the drama. And isn't it significant that our great writers tend to be novelists?

*Van Doren:* I don't see why we shouldn't take Proust at his word when he tells us that this book came into existence because, at a certain moment of his life, something happened over which he had no control, and which made him remember his past. Do you happen to know, Mr. Maurois, the autobiography of W. H. Hudson, the English writer?

*Maurois:* I've read some of his books.

*Van Doren:* He begins by telling a story something like Proust's. Suddenly—this was in his old age—the whole of his past appeared, as clear as if it were on a map, as if he looked at it from a mountain top.

*Maurois:* Well, Chateaubriand had the same experience. He tells us, in the *Mémoires d'Outre-Tombe,* how, because he had heard a skylark, he suddenly recaptured all his youth, and the atmosphere of Combourg which was to him what Combray was to Proust.

*Van Doren:* One of Proust's points surely is that we do not control our memory evenly. It plays tricks on us. Sometimes it gives us a great deal; sometimes nothing.

*Cairns:* That is one of the points he makes about memory, but I think he is more complex than that. He has a well-formulated theory of time. He regards time as an enemy and he also regards it as a friend. It is an enemy in the sense that it destroys the values that he observes in the external world. It is a friend because, through a strange process that he devised, he was able to use it to recapture the past.

*Tate:* Although Marcel Proust solved this problem in a special way of great originality, isn't he really concerned with the oldest meaning of art—to capture from the wreckage of the past something of permanent significance?

*Cairns:* Oh, I think so. I think it goes back at least to the discussion in Plato's *Symposium* of the thirst for immortality.

*Maurois:* Proust thinks that there are two sorts of memories. The first is at work when you reconstruct a thing just by reason. The second is the intuitive memory which starts working suddenly because you heard a skylark, like Chateaubriand, or drank a cup of tea, like Proust, and because this one sensation resuscitated the whole experience. Proust's theory is that intuitive memory is the only true memory.

*Van Doren:* Yes, through a sort of mystical experience.

*Cairns:* He wanted an involuntary memory—some way of conjuring up experiences otherwise than through reason. His finest experiences came through involuntary memory; but because they were involuntary he could not control them. That was a source of unhappiness to him.

*Van Doren:* He was a great psychologist, just as Saint Augustine was a great psychologist, and his best pages are on memory and time.

*Tate:* Wouldn't it be interesting to compare Proust to Saint Augustine, who, in the fourth century, wrote the greatest imaginative analysis of memory before Proust? Saint Augustine is a Christian moralist, and is concerned with the moral control of this seething life beneath consciousness. Proust wanted to subject it to a different control, which we call artistic control, for lack of a better word. Proust wanted to bring it to the surface; it became the most powerful thing in us. Saint Augustine was interested in suppressing it.

*Cairns:* But I think Saint Augustine was just as much of an artist as Proust. And I think they both made the same point: that you recapture the past through imagination and not through intellect.

*Maurois:* That is quite right.

*Tate:* Mr. Maurois, is it true that in *Swann's Way* it is all memory of this second kind? For example, the section that you mentioned a moment ago, "Swann in Love," was, you said, a small classical novel. Isn't that a deliberate act of imagination, rather than memory?

*Maurois:* Oh, no. Certainly not. As we have already said, that second part is not typically Proustian.

*Tate:* In the beginning of the novel and at the end, we see the boy narrator, and those two parts of the book frame the middle part, which isn't actual memory.

*Van Doren:* As a matter of fact, it happened before he was born.

*Tate:* Now doesn't that bring us around to Proust's technique as a novelist? It seems to me one of the most interesting techniques ever devised.

*Maurois:* But again I think we find this technique only in the first and third part, whereas the second part could be the work of any great novelist. Dickens might have done it.

*Tate:* Or Tolstoy might have done it.

*Maurois:* But, of course, not so humorously.

*Van Doren:* I have been interested, reading again this part of Proust's work, in picking out parallels. Here, among other things, is the story of a man who loves a woman for reasons that he does not understand. He loves a woman whom he does not respect. I am thinking of *Of Human Bondage,* for instance.

*Maurois:* And who is physically not his type.

*Van Doren:* He keeps on saying to himself, "I can't be in love. She isn't beautiful. I don't like to listen to her talk. She is vulgar." He behaves like Philip Carey in *Of Human Bondage,* who nevertheless finds himself more and more in love.

*Cairns:* Isn't it a defect of the novel that it is never explained why he marries this woman?

*Tate:* But he doesn't know, does he?

*Cairns:* Are you speaking of Swann?

*Tate:* Yes.

*Van Doren:* Does anyone ever know why he is in love with another person?

*Cairns:* I am not asking why he is in love with Odette. That problem is the whole fascination of the central portion of *Swann's Way*. Suddenly we are confronted in the novel with the fact that Swann is married to Odette, although he has said: "This woman is vulgar and common and she is just not my style." Those were his words. Then all at once we find he is married to her without any attempt at explanation, except a vague remark, I believe, by another character, which does not disclose anything.

*Maurois:* Proust explains very little—indeed too little. Very often you get the impression that the hero is ten years old, and then suddenly twenty, and then is ten again.

*Cairns:* Do you think those defects are due to his methods of writing, the fact that he wrote the novel all in one draft and then rewrote it and kept adding in the middle and adding at the end and adding at the beginning, so that the whole manuscript finally was quite disrupted?

*Maurois:* It is due to the fact that he doesn't attach much importance to objective time.

*Tate:* No. Wouldn't the method of the novel prevent an explanation of Swann's marriage? The narrator is within the story. Is he entitled to judge the other people any more than they can judge him? Is judgment necessary? Isn't Proust simply rendering a subject?

*Van Doren:* Also there is the theory which he expresses at the end of *Swann's Way,* when he says that no experience was ever more than a thin disk held between the contiguous impressions that compose our life. Do we know experience as we are having it or as we remember it? It has three dimensions.

*Cairns:* Proust said that all he wanted was a single moment of relief from chronological time. By giving his whole attention to that single point, those defects that I have mentioned, if they are defects, are really not important in his theory of the novel. Time is the central theme, and all else is subordinate. There is a further point on which I would like your opinion, Mr. Maurois. Has Proust brought a new sensibility into French literature, a sensibility comparable to that of Montaigne or to that of Rousseau? Proust to me seems closer to Montaigne than to Rousseau from the point of view of sensibility.

*Maurois:* He certainly would be closer to Montaigne than to Rousseau, but I think he is original. He brings us something quite new. I pronounced the name of Bergson. I think we should come back to him. You see, Proust is really the novelist of the beginning of the twentieth century, as Bergson was its philosopher.

*Cairns:* Would you like to state what you understand to be new in Proust's contribution?

*Maurois:* Well, first of all, he sees life much more in detail than anyone before him. To Proust a minute is just as important as two years to any other novelist, and he spends as many pages to describe this one minute as anyone who writes a novel about a complete love story.

*Cairns:* He found the tremendous power of the detail. That is something that other novelists had not observed before him.

*Maurois:* That's one thing. Then another thing is that he had an idea of the relativity of sentiment, much more accurate an idea than anyone before him had. Of course, Stendhal could see that too, but Proust much better.

*Van Doren:* He must have seen human life in a very complicated pattern. Everyone notices as he reads this book the many ironies which arise out of the fact that no one individual is ever completely known by the individuals who associate with him, by the various groups among whom he passes. I take that to be true of life. No one is ever fully known by anyone. Proust reminds us of this more clearly than any other novelist does.

*Cairns:* I could not help but be struck by a parallel in Plutarch when I reread *Swann's Way* this week. You will recall that Plutarch said that he was not interested in what the men he described had done, so much as he was interested in the very minute aspects of their lives, such as an involuntary gesture or a mere glance into the eyes. He thought that revealed much more about the great men of whom he was writing than the mere record of their deeds or the books they had written, and I felt that Proust had somewhat the same technique, that it was the involuntary gesture of a particular man that revealed to Proust the hidden secrets of the man rather than the day-to-day life of the man.

*Tate:* Don't you think that is another way of saying that Proust is very much interested in the problem of personal identity? In what sense do we remain the same over a great many years?

*Van Doren:* Or even within a single year. In what sense are we the same person as we move among our various acquaintances?

*Cairns:* None of his characters, of course, was stationary. The reader is often very much surprised at what happens to Proust's characters. He begins with a particular understanding of a character, and before long he finds that he is confronted with an entirely different character.

*Van Doren:* Who are some of his characters? We haven't named enough persons. There is Swann.

*Maurois:* There is Dr. Cottard, who, at the beginning of the novel, appears as a fool; we discover later that he is one of the greatest doctors of his time.

*Van Doren:* And Swann himself at the house of Mme. Verdurin—who thinks she is running so important a salon—is never taken at his true worth. She has no conception of who or what he is.

*Tate:* And being in a scene that is uncongenial, he commits *gaucheries* that he could not possibly have committed in his own society. He was occasionally surprised at his own behavior. He is not the same man.

*Cairns:* I take it that Proust himself figures pretty largely in the novel. You knew Proust personally, did you not, Mr. Maurois?

*Maurois:* No, I didn't know Proust. My wife knew him very well, but at a time when she was only a girl.

*Van Doren:* He was a strange person at best, wasn't he?

*Maurois:* Oh, yes, a most extraordinary creature.

*Cairns:* Does she have some vivid recollections of him?

*Maurois:* She has many letters. They are very interesting because he took the same trouble to explain small details in writing to a small girl that he would in a novel.

*Van Doren:* Surely nothing was simple to him.

*Maurois:* No, nothing at all. But what *is* simple?

*Cairns:* How much of himself is in the book as a character?

*Maurois:* I think the narrator, the central narrator, is Proust, and he has put a great deal of himself into Swann too.

*Van Doren:* I have often suspected that, and it provides an opportunity to ask a certain question. This is, in my opinion, a great novel, perhaps the great novel of the twentieth century. I think it has a limitation, nevertheless, which can be understood if we remember how much effort is put by the author into the expression and analysis of taste. Thus, Swann is a man who is chiefly notable for his taste, and so is our hero. Our hero is exquisitely sensitive to right or wrong in taste; but less so, I should say, in the realm of action, of morals. If this book has a limitation, it is that its emphasis is upon taste rather than morals.

*Maurois:* I was going to say that the range of Proust is much smaller than the range of Tolstoy or Balzac, but at the same time, in his own sphere, he is just as great a master.

*Van Doren:* In his own sphere he is very great. I was only trying to say that his sphere is not as important as the sphere of Balzac.

*Cairns:* I recall an article you wrote, Mr. Maurois, about the time of Proust's death in *La Nouvelle Revue Française,* in which you compared him to the scientist, to the entymologist, and I wondered what you thought of the so-called laws that Proust generated in his novels. The laws, for example, that we cannot find happiness in another person; that it is impossible to know the external world. Do they strike you as valid generalizations?

*Maurois:* Yes. Of course, they are not exactly scientific laws; experimentation is not easy in the world of sentiment. But Proust had the scientific spirit. That we cannot know the external world is evident.

*Tate:* But was that particularly new? Don't we get it in Henry James? In *The Portrait of a Lady* the whole story is Isabel Archer's gradual insight into Gilbert Osmond, and, at the end of the novel, it is almost like a classical recognition scene. Only then does she have any conception of what he is like.

*Van Doren:* Mr. Tate, I know that you are an admirer of Henry James.

*Tate:* I admire him for much the same reason that I admire Proust. I think they are very much alike.

*Van Doren:* So do I. And I too am an admirer of Henry James. I was thinking of him all the time while I reread *Swann's Way.*

*Cairns:* Do you accept his assertion that we do not profit by experience?

*Maurois:* To a large extent. But I don't think it matters very much. I do not attach particular importance to the laws discovered or illustrated by Proust. To me, his book is a work of art, and it is as such that I admire it.

*Cairns:* He attached importance to them; but I have always felt that the novel would not have suffered if the laws had been omitted.

*Van Doren:* The importance he attached to those laws and to his theories of fiction is something like the importance which Tolstoy attached to his theories. They are quite irrelevant to what the man was saying in each case.

*Maurois:* And what Tolstoy says about history is nearly always wrong.

*Tate:* Proust somehow got his imagination stimulated by Bergson, and it doesn't make any difference whether he understood Bergson.

*Van Doren:* It is personally very important for an artist to have a theory, but the theory isn't important as an ingredient in the art that he produces.

*Tate:* There is a question, Mr. Van Doren, that you brought up a minute ago about Henry James. Don't you think James and Proust are very much alike insofar as they both put the narrator or the "observer" inside the story as the central intelligence? They both carried that technical device very far, farther than any other novelists. I'd like to ask Mr. Maurois, if he is also an admirer of Henry James, what he thinks the relative value of these two writers is in that respect.

*Maurois:* I admire Henry James, but I think Proust is a greater writer.

*Tate:* Why do you think so? He may be.

*Maurois:* First of all, I think he writes better. Proust is not only a great novelist; he is a great poet. James sometimes, but very seldom. Also, I think that though Henry James was very intelligent, Proust's intelligence goes much further.

*Cairns:* Doesn't that go back to the point we made a little while ago: that Proust contributed a new sensibility to the world, something that James did not do?

*Tate:* He felt the world in a new way. I am inclined to think that James represents very much the same thing that Proust does, but that it isn't so highly developed. He is very much aware of the relativity of feeling and his characters are intensely aware of time. But they are constantly engaged in the moral evaluation of their own actions, and Proust's characters seem not to be evaluating their actions. As Mr. Van Doren says, they are largely concerned with sensibility and taste.

*Van Doren:* They haven't moral concern. I should say that Proust's stories, because he tells many stories here, are in themselves more interesting than James's are.

*Tate:* Perhaps they are. I am not sure.

*Maurois:* You can remember Proust's characters much better than James's.

*Tate:* I can't.

*Van Doren:* James, however much I admire him, does tend to flatten out in my memory, whereas the cook here—Françoise—is an old woman whom one couldn't possibly forget.

*Tate:* I admit James doesn't give us what I would call "floating" characters; for instance, Aunt Leonie. Aunt Leonie is just a character loose in the novel. She doesn't affect anything.

She exists in her room with Françoise, her servant, and she is one of the memorable characters in fiction. What does she mean? We don't know what she means. She is just there.

*Cairns:* I think James and Proust probably had the same aesthetic theory that the artist must have a new vision, that he must see reality through the conventional concept. But I think Proust took it much further. Now a problem that worries me in this novel is the story. I don't think the story attracts, in the usual sense in fiction. If the story does not attract, what does?

*Van Doren:* You mean the story of Swann?

*Cairns:* No, the novel as a whole.

*Van Doren:* All I can say is that it is very attractive to me.

*Cairns:* I am speaking of the story interest itself, which seems to me to be largely lacking. The attraction of the novel as a whole is to be found, I think, in what we observed before, the tremendous power generated by a minute treatment of the particular. . . . I see you have a passage you want to read.

*Van Doren:* We were talking perhaps twenty minutes ago about that famous cup of tea which Proust tells us he drank with a madeleine. It is surely one of the most famous passages in the novel, and perhaps a fraction of the passage should be read. He is explaining how the repetition of this experience has suddenly brought a flood of memories to him, and this is one of his ways of talking about the importance of that flood. "When from a long distant past nothing subsists after the people are dead, after the things are broken and scattered, still, alone, more fragile but with more vitality, more unsubstantial, more persistent, more faithful, the smell and taste of things remain poised a long time, like souls, ready to remind us, waiting and hoping for their moment amid the ruins of all the rest, and bear unfaltering in the tiny and almost impalpable drop of their essence the vast structure of recollection."

# DRAMA

(525-455 B.C.)

# AESCHYLUS

# *Prometheus Bound*

THE EARLIEST *master of Greek tragedy whom we know was attracted to vast subjects and to gorgeous spectacles. Aeschylus's treatment of the Agamemnon story, for instance, was grander than that of either Sophocles or Euripides. But he never found a bigger subject than that of* PROMETHEUS BOUND, *nor is one imaginable. The scene is not only a mountain in the Caucasus but the whole of a universe relevant to this mountain and to the Titan who is chained there. The chorus sings and dances like the waves of the far-washing sea, and at no time is the perspective made small. But the theme is theologically great as well. The disobedience for which Zeus is punishing Prometheus is none other than that which he committed when he befriended man by giving him the arts of fire. God, in other words, seems to be playing a jealous role; his cruelty is as unlovable as his prohibition was beyond our comprehension. How is he to be justified except by the conclusion that he is God and therefore beyond the necessity of justification? It is the question of Job and of* PARADISE LOST, *and Aeschylus no less than Milton or the author of the Old Testament drama conceives it his duty to defend the ways of God. How he does so is one of the secrets of his great poem—of its style, its scene, its conception.* PROMETHEUS BOUND *is one of the simplest Greek tragedies, and one of the most magnificent.*

(MR. PAUL GREEN, GUEST)

*Cairns:* Aeschylus said that he dedicated what he wrote to Time. Tonight we are beginning a new year, even a new decade in the sense that the 1930's end tonight. Is there any point in *Prometheus Bound* which has a special significance tonight?

*Tate:* Mr. Cairns, what do you mean by special significance for New Year's Eve?

*Cairns:* As I read the play this week, it seemed to me that one idea that we can draw from it is the necessity of compromise between power, represented by Zeus, and intelligence, represented by Prometheus. H. G. Wells once said that the present age was a race between education and catastrophe. I think he was merely saying what Aeschylus said long ago: that we have to reconcile power and intelligence or face disaster.

*Tate:* I am inclined to disagree with you. You are placing power in the hands of Zeus, I presume, and intelligence is the province of Prometheus. I would say it is just the opposite.

*Cairns:* In this particular play? You are not thinking of his other plays and the fragments of the Promethean trilogy?

*Tate:* Just this particular play. Zeus is wisdom; Prometheus is merely scientific intelligence and stands for the power of mankind. If this play has any significance for the new year, I should say it is probably this: that the modern world or the Promethean world, the world which has everything highly developed which Prometheus gave to man, the world of science without wisdom, is about to destroy itself. I wonder if Prometheus, lying there on the rock, isn't a little bit regretful about it.

*Van Doren:* Is he lying there still, Mr. Tate?

*Tate:* I think so, because the rest of the trilogy that Aeschylus planned or wrote we don't have, and we'll have to assume that he may be lying there.

*Green:* What do you mean, Mr. Tate, when you say the world is destroying itself?

*Tate:* It may be a little difficult to get at this. We are confronted in the *Prometheus Bound* with one of the mysterious paradoxes of human nature, and Aeschylus has given us a myth which covers it. I think we would be very simple-minded if we thought that myth was mere symbolism. It contains an objective, an imaginative projection of a fundamental conflict in human nature; that is, human beings want to get all the benefits of worldly power, and yet when they get them they seem to cause trouble.

*Cairns:* Are we not now, on your analysis, about where we were when Aeschylus analyzed the Promethean myth? Prometheus had given men benefits. He had taught men how to use fire and how to build a house and how to tame waters. Man, on your analysis, abused the gifts Prometheus had given him.

*Tate:* Exactly.

*Cairns:* We come back then to Zeus, representing power. Zeus, if he were still enthroned, would perhaps want to eliminate the human race and create a better one, as he wanted to do in the play, but Prometheus saved mankind from that fate.

*Tate:* But don't you think that in a myth, a feature like the destruction of the human race by Zeus is only an extreme, imaginative statement of a possibility? It seems to me that the power that Zeus represents is very different from the power that Prometheus represents. The power that Zeus represents is, roughly speaking, the kind of power that man should feel that he confronts everywhere in the world, a power that he can't overcome. Isn't it the error of modern man, Promethean man, who thinks he can replace God, that has got us all into trouble?

*Van Doren:* Yes. There is a contemporary poet, incidentally, who takes very much that view: Robinson Jeffers. He represents man in all his poems as being bloated with the vanity of his power and destroying himself; according to Mr. Jeffers, it would be an excellent thing if he continued the process and ceased to exist, so we would have nothing but eagles and rocks.

*Cairns:* I think Jeffers' objective may be realized if things continue at the present rate.

*Tate:* What is this myth that we are confronted with in this play?

*Van Doren:* Mr. Tate and Mr. Cairns and Mr. Green, I am worried because you identified Prometheus with intelligence. I don't find him especially more intelligent than Zeus.

*Cairns:* He knows more than Zeus because he is able to predict the future, and prediction is the essence of intelligent direction. That is his hold on Zeus.

*Tate:* Isn't Prometheus the first scientist? His predictions are scientific.

*Van Doren:* But the thing that he knows is not represented as scientific. He simply knows a secret. Zeus would give anything to have that secret, but it isn't represented, it seems to me, as a special or difficult form of knowledge.

*Cairns:* But the knowledge he communicated to mankind was a new form of knowledge at that particular time.

*Tate:* Wasn't it knowledge as we know it? Hasn't Prometheus given to man, according to this myth, letters and numbers? Isn't all our knowledge encompassed in those two things?

*Van Doren:* Yes, but in the universe of this play, all the arts and all the sciences and all the philosophical disciplines are of little significance, it seems to me. They bulk very small. That little animal called man may be proud of his arts and his letters, but they don't seem to affect the way the world is run. They don't seem to affect the conflict between Prometheus and Zeus, which I should say is a conflict between two Titans.

*Green:* Listening to you gentlemen talk about this subject of conflicts, it seems to me that if we are going to be allegorical or symbolic, then these two conflicts represent man against nature. Zeus is the natural power—that dark, incalculable power of the universe illustrated in nature and the forces of nature, and Prometheus is man's rebellion against those powers and is man's efforts to establish an empire against them. All the way through the dramas of Aeschylus, it seems to me, there is an interest in the rebel—the rebellious man against the inchoate and terrific powers of nature.

*Tate:* Don't you think, Mr. Green, that while he is interested in man's revolt, he is also interested in its results? Do you think that Aeschylus can resolve the conflict? He thinks it is a noble thing for man to rebel, and yet necessarily the rebellion in the long run fails.

*Green:* Man can resolve the conflict by intelligence. The whole trilogy is built on the resolution of this conflict. We only have one extant play, of course, but we must think in terms of the three plays, *Prometheus Unbound* and *Prometheus the Fire Bringer,* for whom the religious ceremony was later created, with the adoration of the human race exemplified in it.

*Tate:* Do you think, Mr. Green, that Shelley's *Prometheus Unbound* may represent what Aeschylus probably did?

*Cairns:* I hope not.

*Tate:* I hope not too.

*Green:* Why do you hope not?

*Tate:* Because I think *Prometheus Unbound* by Shelley is a very sentimental and romantic play.

*Van Doren:* And the reason is that man is so important to Shelley. I insist, as perhaps a minority of one, that man is of almost no importance in this play. I, for instance, do not find that anything is being said or done here to support the thesis that man is rebelling, or that the future of man is involved, or that the career of the world with man in it is involved. I still see it as a conflict between Prometheus and Zeus.

*Cairns:* May I put it another way, because I think Mr. Green has touched on something vital? The play is so elemental—Aeschylus deals with elemental forces—that we all can read what we want into it. It is possible to see in it, for example, the conflict between humanism and humanitarianism.

*Tate:* Go ahead. Tell us what you mean by humanism.

*Cairns:* I am talking about a particular aspect of humanism, represented perhaps by the ruthless aspiration of the Renaissance, in which the greatest sacrifice would be made for an ideal. Opposed to this is the humanitarian movement of the nineteenth century, in the scheme of which ideals would yield to sympathies.

*Tate:* What sort of ideal? Ideal of power or of perfection?

*Cairns:* In this case, it was Zeus's wish for a superior race of men. Zeus is opposed by the humanitarianism of Prometheus, whose wish it was to preserve man as he then existed at the expense of the ideal. Zeus's dissatisfaction with man is analogous to God's anger with man at the time of the Flood.

*Green:* That dissatisfaction is not an arbitrary one. If we want to think in terms of symbolism, allegory, Zeus is identical with the powers of nature against which man has built his creative enterprises. Consider—all of us walk upright, whereas every muscle of our body cries out for all-fours.

*Tate:* Zeus is the all of nature.

*Green:* That is right—nature.

*Van Doren:* May I put in my protest again? I do not find anything inchoate about Zeus. The play begins with his sending a blacksmith with two helpers to nail Prometheus against a mountainside. The blacksmith is more of an artist than Prometheus. He succeeds in binding him there forever. I find that Zeus is an individual who hates another individual. I don't find inchoate forces of nature or anything of the sort.

*Tate:* Don't you think, then, following your suggestion, that we ought to look at the action of the play? The action is something perfectly distinct and literal. All our symbolic interpretation must be based on that. We will have to look at the action before we can tell whether our symbolism is correct.

*Green:* You mean by action what happens in the play?

*Van Doren:* What the audience sees. Mr. Green, is it clear to you what the audience sees here?

*Green:* Yes, in spite of all our fog. For instance, in talking about this play, we haven't visualized the production of the piece as the Greeks saw it. Let us think of a tremendous amphitheater, a wide-stretching stage, and a ritual with plenty of sound and marvelous sight, with costumes, exaggerated gesture and voice—all a kind of religious and fervent creation.

*Tate:* There was an actual religious ritual accompanying this play, introducing it?

*Green:* That is true. So that in addition to what you might call the libretto, the printed words that we read, we should think of everything else that accompanied this libretto, made it live. So the play in those old days certainly was a tremendously inspiring thing apart from any symbolism or allegory we now attribute to it.

*Cairns:* The story is simple: for the duration of the play, Prometheus is seen bound to a rock in the bleak wastes of the Caucasian mountains, with the ocean, which supposedly surrounded the known world, in the background. The drama is, therefore, not one of action, but an emotional drama created by the clash of wills between Prometheus and Zeus. In this struggle of Titanic wills, which will win? Such action as the play affords is contributed by Io, Oceanus, the Chorus and Zeus's messenger, Hermes, who comes to argue with and threaten Prometheus.

*Van Doren:* What did the audience see as the play began?

*Green:* They saw what the script says and more. They saw the festival of Dionysus (Bacchus). And they heard a great deal more than we hear today. They heard the chanting; they saw the dancing; they heard the harp, the flute and, I hope, a tremendous drum, or two or three. Remember the circus and add the church.

*Tate:* I should think, Mr. Green, that while the Greek audience was looking at this myth as a dramatic spectacle, they also had enough sophistication to look at it as symbolism. Certainly there was a certain amount of interpretation going on. Yet they must have felt too that the interpretation was arbitrary, that the main thing was what was actually seen.

*Van Doren:* Namely, a god being chained and nailed to a rock.

*Green:* A man-god. That is the whole point. Don't forget that in this suffering, aspiring world . . .

*Tate:* That is where I would argue with Mr. Van Doren. Prometheus is "top" man. While mankind doesn't figure largely in the play, he is in the background. It seems to me he is just as important as he is in *Paradise Lost.* In *Paradise Lost,* man is a remote creature that they have barely heard about in heaven, and Lucifer goes down to corrupt him. Nevertheless, although mankind is very remote and very small, he motivates the action of this tremendous drama, and I think perhaps he does in the *Prometheus Bound* to the same extent.

*Green:* Oh, yes, the motivation of man is there, because that is the whole purpose of the play—to show man as such, the motivating power.

*Cairns:* Are you suggesting, Mr. Green, that the modern reader of the play must put himself in the frame of mind of the Greek who saw the spectacle in order to appreciate it?

*Green:* The more he can do that, the richer his experience as a reader will be.

*Van Doren:* Then, of course, Prometheus on this rock is visited by a series of persons—including the chorus—who come in and discuss his plight with him. The play is a series of interviews, is it not, with Prometheus? Just as *Samson Agonistes* is a series of interviews with Samson.

*Cairns:* I should like to ask you, Mr. Green, about the character of Io, since we are considering the dramatic aspect of the play.

*Van Doren:* What other aspect of the play is there, Mr. Cairns?

*Cairns:* We began by discussing the symbolic aspects, which I take it may be distinguished for the purposes of philosophy from the dramatic aspects. I am not much on symbolism, and I prefer to read the play as a straight dramatic spectacle, and omit the symbolism.

*Van Doren:* In other words, you prefer to read the play as a play?

*Cairns:* As a play. That is how I should like to discuss it.

*Green:* I think every man ought to consider the play as he sees fit, symbolic or otherwise. You asked me about Io?

*Cairns:* Do you feel that Io in this single part of the trilogy that remains to us is an irrelevant character or not?

*Green:* Maybe she is and maybe she's not, as Jeeter Lester would say. Of course, all the scholars insist you have to take her long spiel about her journeyings over Asia as a kind of travelogue, in which the Greeks were movie-minded and interested, but I like to think of her also as, well, another principle of humanity. Here is the male principle, you might say, this proud, defiant, satanic spirit of Prometheus who is a braggart. And a man has to be a braggart to get where he is getting today according to certain totalitarian findings east of us. But here comes another principle, the warm human one, the pathetic endurer. So I think the two—the male and female—represent guilt and innocence. Guilt with knowledge; knowledge always brings guilt.

*Tate:* Both are suffering. The innocent suffer as well as the guilty.

*Green:* Yes, but Prometheus is a sufferer with a secret of foreknowledge. The secret is the future. Man has that secret, is endowed with it. Io, the poor heifer lady, whom Zeus once loved, and who continues to be persecuted by Hera's gadfly, illustrates, I think, a certain principle in the world.

*Tate:* Why do you think that she has been turned into a heifer? Why does part of her punishment consist in having her transformed into a beast?

*Cairns:* Zeus's wife, Hera, was jealous of Io. She not only turned Io into a heifer, but had her pursued and persecuted by a gadfly; other versions of the myth explain that Zeus turned Io into a cow to hide her from his jealous wife. The Greeks overcame the difficulty of presenting a heifer on the stage by having her appear as a woman with horns.

*Green:* She was a bit like the figures in some of the present-day Silly Symphonies and cartoon pieces, really.

*Tate:* It seems to me there is something more than that.

*Green:* I mean pictorially.

*Tate:* Isn't it this: that when the human being aspires to be a god he becomes a beast?

*Green:* Oh-oh, now you've gone and got profound.

*Tate:* No, it is not my profundity. It is a remark of Pascal's. I think it's very central to the meaning of this play.

*Cairns:* Why can't you accept the customary explanation that Aeschylus is not concerned with love or passion, except in the sense when passion has become an unbearable burden and source of misery to its victims? That is all, it seems, that Io represents. It has also been suggested that Aeschylus did not approve of unequal marriages and wished to emphasize the misery that results from them.

*Green:* What passion? Whose passion are you talking about?

*Cairns:* Zeus's passion for Io.

*Green:* Yes. That is the primitive, instinctive thing I place in that platonic vagueness of primeval matter, the world below being—well, I'd like to coin a word—in the realm that precedes natality.

*Van Doren:* Had Io herself aspired to be divine?

*Tate:* No, it wasn't her fault, but she had been loved by a god, had accepted the love, and her affliction was that she became a beast. It is significant that in the great myth of Leda, Leda and Zeus the Swan, the woes of the house of Atreus all came out of the union of a god and a human being.

*Van Doren:* There is one interesting difference between this story, insofar as it is a story of punishment for disobedience or for reasons unknown inflicted by gods upon inferior creatures, and the same story as it has been told in other literature, for instance, in the Book of Job. There is no indication that the god who is inflicting miseries upon Job is ever going to change. He is eternal, whereas Zeus here is represented as soon to be supplanted by another god. The Greeks had that very interesting sort of evolutionary feeling about their pantheon.

*Green:* That is right. You might say that's the difference between the classical Greek religion and Hebraism.

*Van Doren:* There is always a possibility that the tyrant in Greece's heaven will cease to be. The sufferings of Job, it seems to me, find no relief in any future which can be envisaged. They must be justified against a background which is eternal.

*Green:* The way I read that is this. For instance, the Greek system of knowledge and the Hebrew system of feeling are illustrated in Prometheus, who knew what was to come, and, because of his foreknowledge, he was able to endure. Now Job had mainly his emotions to depend on for his light. He had no final intelligence, no answer to come to him. He raised a lot of questions, but nobody answered him, and he was only submerged under the power of God's exhibitions in nature, terrible wind and I-did-this and I-did-that. So Job says, "I repent. Have mercy on me," and so God did. It seems that in some ways Prometheus' story is a greater story, because of its individual sturdihood.

*Tate:* Don't you think it is a greater story because it is more realistic? It takes account of man's desire to dominate the natural world, and of his determination to do so.

*Van Doren:* I am worried once more, because I don't find any emphasis here upon the notion that man will dominate the world.

*Tate:* Man is Prometheus.

*Van Doren:* Prometheus is a god; he is a Titan co-eval with Cronus, even, the father of Zeus; and he happens to have had this curious desire to do something for man. The conflict is surely between Prometheus and Zeus.

*Cairns:* I think you are overlooking a third possibility. We have referred to the satanic aspects of Prometheus and you have referred to his relationship to Job. He may, however, be viewed from the standpoint of the three figures: Satan, Christ or Job. To which one is Prometheus most closely related?

*Tate:* Mr. Cairns, I have an idea that I don't think will find much favor here, but I shall express it anyhow. It seems to me that, in our Western history, Christ, Satan and Prometheus tend to be identified. The Christ of liberal theology, the Christ that we know today, is a humanitarian figure. He is secular, no longer divine. He is the superman; he is even, according to Bruce Barton, the super-salesman devoted to "service." At best he is the noble man, the good man. He is the bringer of benefits to human society, just as Lucifer and Prometheus were bringers of those benefits.

*Cairns:* The parallel, of course, is that Prometheus suffered as Job suffered, perhaps unwarrantedly. His satanic aspects, I think, have been brought out in the fact that he rebelled against Zeus, and his relationship to Christ is found in the fact that he suffers for mankind.

*Tate:* I think that is very true. Even in the literal story there is a parallel. But I think Mr. Van Doren's point hasn't been discussed enough. In what respect is Prometheus connected with man? I see him, if you will allow a little more allegory, as a symbol of a certain kind of knowledge in man which man does not come by naturally, so to speak. That is, man has achieved rational scientific knowledge, a certain dominion over the world, but he hasn't achieved wisdom. I repeat that Prometheus represents knowledge without wisdom.

*Cairns:* Prometheus is, of course, a god. The only human being in this play is poor Io, who appears on the stage as a cow. But Prometheus represents man in his willingness to suffer for him. He is associated with Lucifer in his act of rebellion against divine law.

*Tate:* What would you say about Milton's Lucifer? He is the light-bringer; that is what his name signifies. He is Prometheus.

*Van Doren:* He is for knowledge. He argues against prohibitions against knowledge.

*Tate:* The knowledge, I think, is pointed up very much in the scientific direction by Milton. Lucifer's lieutenant, Mulciber, digs for gold and for the useful minerals even in heaven.

*Van Doren:* We should make it clear among other things that even a Greek who had no gift for symbols and had no talent for interpretation might have enormously enjoyed this play.

*Cairns:* As a dramatic spectacle.

*Van Doren:* That is what I think a play is.

*Tate:* I agree that we enjoy it that way primarily.

*Van Doren:* He would have enjoyed it as much as he enjoyed the *Agamemnon,* where you have a magnificent king arriving home from Troy, hesitating to enter his house, but walking finally over the red carpet, through the marble door behind which he will be murdered by his wife. So here you have this great fellow chained to the mountainside, visited successively by the persons who come in—chiefly, of course, Io, but also the Chorus. Here, against this great black rock to which a god is chained, dance these maidens who are the daughters of the ocean.

*Tate:* What about those daughters of the ocean, Mr. Van Doren? I think they are wonderful.

*Van Doren:* To me it is enough to say that they are pieces of foam flying up from the sea against a black rock.

*Green:* No, I don't like that.

*Cairns:* I think the virtue of Aeschylus on that point is that he has taken these ideas and given them form. He has made the ocean speak. He has made the mountains and the foam speak, and has actually brought them forth on the stage. I know no other dramatist who has done it as successfully as Aeschylus. I think perhaps Marlowe might have, if he had lived longer.

*Van Doren:* But by the time he died he still was not able to handle it.

*Cairns:* But Marlowe has been described as "a beardless Aeschylus." He too dealt with elemental forces—superb and terrible. The scale on which he worked was vast.

*Tate:* He didn't believe in his symbols. Marlowe's symbols tended to be very thin. They were not the full-bodied figures that you get in Aeschylus. Aeschylus' symbols are very complex. I think that Mr. Van Doren's point is one that we must not forget; that is, no matter how much you symbolize these characters, they remain characters, and anything you say about them is much thinner than they actually are. I am going to read something in just a minute to illustrate this very point.

*Green:* Before we get to that, can't we sum up all this talk that we've had here and come to a conclusion? We've got to have conclusions, you know. I should like to have a little say-so that out of Aeschylus' *Prometheus* I get a sort of statement for the future conduct of man.

*Cairns:* I think the play is so elemental, as I said before, that none of us could ever agree on what it means.

*Green:* If anything—and all things.

*Tate:* Here is Prometheus' conception of the future conduct of man. "Listen to the sad story of mankind who like children lived till I gave them understanding and a portion of reason. Yet not in disparagement of men I speak, but meaning to set forth the greatness of my charity, for seeing they saw not and hearing they understood not, but like as shapes in a dream they wrought all the days of their life in confusion. No houses of brick raised in the warmth of the sun they had, nor fabrics of wood. But like the little ants they dwelt underground in the sunless depths of caverns. No certain sign of approaching winter they knew, no harbinger of flowering spring or fruitful summer. Ever they labored at random till I taught them to discern the seasons by the rising and the obscure setting of the stars. Numbers I invented for them, the chiefest of all discoveries. I taught them the grouping of letters to be a memorial and record of the past, the mistress of the arts and mother of the muses."

(1564-1616)

## SHAKESPEARE

# Antony and Cleopatra

*AMONG Shakespeare's major tragedies, and that is to say among the major tragedies of the world,* ANTONY AND CLEOPATRA *is the least popular. This is because it does not lend itself to the actor's art. There are many scenes and many persons, and the thread of action is not strong or straight. But those who know Shakespeare well are particularly devoted to a work which shows him always at the peak of his power as a poet. In addition, Shakespeare creates in this play, besides a multiplicity of ingredients, a new concept of the hero and the heroine. For Antony and Cleopatra are represented in the maturity of their last loves, and as there is nothing simple about their feelings so there is nothing elementary about the story which their speeches tell. They are beyond romantic illusion; they have been everywhere and seen everything; and each knows that the other is not to be trusted. Yet each loves the other with that sort of love which founds itself upon fact rather than fancy, and which can express itself with quarreling quite as perfectly as with lyric adoration. Antony knows that Cleopatra is vain, treacherous and unstable; yet he is willing to lose Rome for her, and he cannot be sorry, when her deception has caused his death, that he had lived only for her. Cleopatra is never sure of Antony; yet in the presence of his dead body she announces that he was king of the world. Both lovers are infinitely changeable and perennially fascinating; and they have the honor to inhabit Shakespeare's most sophisticated play.*

(MR. JOSEPH WOOD KRUTCH, GUEST)

*Cairns:* Because *Antony and Cleopatra* covers so wide an area, it would be helpful if Mr. Van Doren stated the story for us at the beginning of the discussion.

*Van Doren:* The play begins with Antony in Egypt, where he has fallen completely in love with Cleopatra, to the extent of forgetting his obligations to Rome. He is reminded of them by Octavius Caesar, the man who is going to be Augustus, the first Emperor. At first Antony refuses to take the reminder seriously, but eventually we find him in Rome making his peace with Caesar, and for political purposes marrying the sister of Caesar, Octavia. Then he is in Egypt again, the connection broken between him and both Octavius and Octavia; and soon he is having a war with Octavius, clearly a war that will decide who is to rule Rome and the world. He loses both important battles in this war, partly through the failure of Cleopatra's army and navy to support him; and the play ends with the death first of him and then of Cleopatra.

*Cairns:* Mr. Van Doren, would you agree that there are two themes in the play: the love theme, which I take it is the minor one, and the political theme, which I consider the major one?

*Van Doren:* There are those two themes. I daresay there are others too. Certainly those two are important, love and public life.

*Krutch:* I would agree that the two themes are there, but I disagree as to the emphasis upon them. The best way to begin a discussion of *Antony and Cleopatra* is to consider it as a love story. To say that may not seem to get you far, but it would, I think, lead into the center of the play, especially if you then asked yourself what kind of a love story it is.

*Cairns:* But doesn't the love story only become dominant after the political struggle is over?

*Krutch:* The political struggle is over, as I remember, somewhere about the middle of the third act, so that the two climactic acts are really concerned almost exclusively with the love story.

*Cairns:* The third act and the fifth act?

*Krutch:* Yes.

*Tate:* Mr. Cairns, do you think that you can separate these two themes? We abstract them in discussion, but I'm not sure that they are not really one subject. The chief characters, Antony and Cleopatra, are public figures, and their private lives can't be separated from their political significance.

*Cairns:* Are you suggesting that Antony's love for Cleopatra is really a political device, that he's not really in love with her?

*Tate:* By no means.

*Cairns:* How do you intermingle the love story and the political story?

*Tate:* I think Shakespeare intermingles them; I don't. It seems to me they were actually intermingled, and it is our job to try to find out if they can or cannot be separated. I don't think they can. In other words, the burden of proof is on you for that point.

*Van Doren:* Surely you don't think Shakespeare, in the course of writing this play, was consciously handling themes? He must have thought he was telling a story.

*Tate:* It seems to me that the political theme, if it exists separately at all, merely frames the action, and that is characteristic of all of Shakespeare's tragedies. Somehow, this violent action emerges out of normal life, and as it rises to its climax, people are destroyed, and then at the end order is re-established. You might call that a political idea if you wish.

*Krutch:* I should like to suggest that that question of the two themes and their relationship might be straightened out by returning to my original suggestion that we consider the play as a love story and then ask what kind of a love story it is. If you do that, the first thing you'd say would be that one of the essential characteristics of this love story is that the love is between two people who are very much aware of the fact that they are acting on the largest possible public stage. It is not a private love affair, like the one between Romeo and Juliet. It is a love affair between two people who know that the world is watching them; that the rise and fall of empires may depend upon them. They refer to that again and again. Antony at the very beginning says, "Let the wide arch of rangèd empire fall." They are always aware of the fact that they are acting on the stage of the world.

*Cairns:* It seems to me that you are denying that this is an infatuation.

*Krutch:* I don't know exactly what you mean by that.

*Cairns:* I mean, to come up to Dryden, that the world is well lost for love.

*Krutch:* We have not come up to Dryden. I don't think Shakespeare had come up to Dryden. You are introducing a different subject.

*Cairns:* No, I am defining infatuation. It seems to me that Shakespeare intended to portray these lovers as infatuated lovers.

*Van Doren:* Yes, but they are lovers who are supremely intelligent, wholly experienced and politically competent. They are infatuated, but they are not drunk with their infatuation as younger persons might be or as persons who are more simply sensuous could be. These people, for all the frankness of their love, curiously fail, it seems to me, to give the impression of sensuality which many people attribute to them.

*Tate:* Mr. Van Doren, don't you think that their sensuality is not wholly personal? It is a part of the pagan pomp and display of their age and of their station in life.

*Van Doren:* Yes. You would agree with me, Mr. Tate, I daresay, that they are infatuated.

*Tate:* Oh, very much so.

*Van Doren:* But it isn't the sort of infatuation which blanks the intelligence or blanks consciousness.

*Cairns:* We ought not to forget, also, that they were two proud persons. Do you agree, Mr. Tate, that they have their eye on the main chance, as I understand Mr. Van Doren's point to be?

*Tate:* To some extent, yes. But that isn't the exclusive motive. They have their eye on the main chance insofar as they are both rulers. They are interested in their political situations, but it is not the main chance in any crude sense. I cannot see that they look at their love affair from that point of view.

*Van Doren:* They are in love with each other almost in spite of their desire not to be. Antony from time to time makes that quite clear.

*Tate:* Don't you think that pride governs their tragic end? Caesar is going to take them in triumph through the streets of Rome, and they will not submit.

*Cairns:* That is why I used the word "pride."

*Tate:* What is this pride? Is it simply that she would be humiliated at such treatment? She would also be humiliated because in yielding she would be betraying Antony.

*Krutch:* I am interested in the question as to what extent their love is merely a sensual love. I agree that it is not, and yet I wonder if any of you have noticed the fact that though this is undoubtedly a great love, it is not in any ordinary sense a romantic love. There is no idealization. There is no mystical suggestion about the character of this love. It is not only founded on sensuality, but the sensual aspects of the love furnish all the images and all the thoughts. It is a curious example of the love which can be presented as a great love, in no sense trivial, and yet not in any way conventionally idealized.

*Cairns:* You have put your finger on a limitation which hampered Shakespeare. You must remember that Cleopatra on the Elizabethan stage had to be represented by a boy and, for that reason, Shakespeare excludes all direct manifestations of passion or sensuality. Otherwise the boy would have been made ridiculous.

*Krutch:* Juliet had to be acted by a boy also. There is a great difference between Juliet and Cleopatra.

*Cairns:* It was romantic love in Juliet's case. It is difficult for me to think of Antony and Cleopatra as star-crossed lovers in the Romeo and Juliet class.

*Van Doren:* I don't know whether I care to accept this distinction between romantic and sensual love. Juliet seems to me much more sensual than Cleopatra. Her imagination is heavily sensual.

*Krutch:* Yet Juliet envelops her sensuality in a poetry which is conventional, in the sense that the poetry of Cleopatra is not.

*Van Doren:* But the poetry of Cleopatra, like the poetry of Antony, is in itself, in terms of its language, its imagery, not sensual. What are the things they are talking about? They are talking about their quarrels, about the way they walk on the streets of Alexandria, pretending to be other than what they are.

*Krutch:* I mean simply that they don't talk about this love as being something primarily of the soul. It is quite frankly something of the body, as they discuss it.

*Cairns:* In that sense it certainly is sensual.

*Van Doren:* I would not say of the body. I would say of the mind too.

*Tate:* I would agree with you.

*Van Doren:* Of their whole lives. It is not intellectual, or at any rate intellectualized.

*Krutch:* But the symbols which it finds for itself are continually fleshy symbols rather than spiritual ones.

*Tate:* Don't they think of themselves, Cleopatra as the queen and Antony as one of the triumvirs? Don't they think of their love also in images of material power? Physical but not sensual.

*Van Doren:* I don't find the symbols to be fleshy. The things I remember are curiously refined. I say "curiously" because of the reputation of these persons as lovers. They are refined in all sorts of directions. To be sure, they are frank, and the reference is to love which is physical.

*Tate:* Are they refined in the ordinary sense in which we use the word today? Isn't it rather that their refinement consists in the language in which Shakespeare lets them express their violent natures? Isn't the refinement Shakespeare's?

*Van Doren:* I meant that their ideas about their love were

refined away, or moved away, from primitive forms of expression.

*Cairns:* Do you agree that Antony was sincerely in love with Cleopatra, or was it merely a sensual passion with him? Was it love in the sense that Romeo and Juliet were in love, but in a more mature way?

*Krutch:* You are asking us to make a distinction which is very difficult to make offhand. I don't think they had the kind of illusions about themselves that Romeo and Juliet had. Plainly, they are knowing people.

*Cairns:* There was a mutual distrust at the beginning which seems, in Shakespeare's hands, to develop finally into comradeship and perhaps love. I am not sure of the depth of the love.

*Krutch:* Just before Antony's suicide, he denounces Cleopatra.

*Van Doren:* There is always mistrust.

*Krutch:* It is a love in spite of itself.

*Van Doren:* These people have absolutely no illusions about each other or about themselves.

*Krutch:* They don't believe that they are twin souls in the sense that Romeo and Juliet believe that they are twin souls.

*Van Doren:* My point about their sensuality is that they are even past the illusion that sensuality can be an end in itself. That is why their language does not need to be sensual in its imagery. I am not trying to defend them against the charge of being sensual persons.

*Cairns:* It seems to me that you may be doing Antony an injustice, or at least reading him differently than I read him. His point of view appears to be that of a successful warrior who has one-third of the world or one-half of the world under his control. What he wants from the world, having this great power, is pleasure, and particularly sensual pleasure.

*Van Doren:* But the pleasure that Antony took in Rome, in the days of Julius Caesar, was a pleasure in drama, in games, in revelry, in play of all sorts.

*Cairns:* Perhaps we can get at the point through another approach. The most serious criticism in modern times that has been made of the play was formulated by George Bernard Shaw. He accused Shakespeare of romantic sensuality. He pointed out that Circe in ancient times turned heroes into hogs, but that Shakespeare in this play had turned hogs into heroes. Shaw condemned the play as immoral. Against that view, however, is Goethe's opinion that the play was really highly moral, that it taught that achievement and indulgence are incompatible.

*Tate:* Mr. Cairns, I think that both Shaw and Goethe are wrong.

*Van Doren:* They both sound like nonsense to me.

*Tate:* The play is neither moral nor immoral.

*Cairns:* Do you think it is completely neutral?

*Tate:* That is a different question. Let's say it is neither moral nor immoral, or it is both. It seems to me that you cannot abstract one *motif* from it and say that it is the whole thing. For example, there is no poetic justice in the play, no punishments and rewards.

*Cairns:* Can't you ask the question: Are these a pair of old fools, or are they lovers on a very high plane?

*Krutch:* They are neither.

*Cairns:* What are they?

*Tate:* They are just what they are. They are Antony and Cleopatra.

*Van Doren:* They have some gray hairs. Each one of them has lived a long time and had many love affairs. Each has been through everything. Each knows all the tricks of love and all the deceptions and illusions of love.

*Cairns:* They are completely disillusioned.

*Van Doren:* Completely disillusioned and in love with each other. It is very seldom that you find a love which can survive disillusion. This one has survived it, and that is the amazing thing about it.

*Cairns:* Are you agreeing with Mr. Tate on the point that the play is ethically neutral?

*Van Doren:* Shakespeare is never neutral in human affairs. Shakespeare takes mankind very seriously because he loves it.

Shall we say simply in the present case that he was not conventional?

*Krutch:* Shakespeare does not, I think, anywhere clearly pose this question of love versus honor or pose clearly the question: Was the world well lost for love? At least he does not intend to suggest an answer. He leaves the question completely in solution. Plutarch didn't leave it in solution. Dryden didn't leave it in solution. But Shakespeare did.

*Van Doren:* And Shaw doesn't either.

*Krutch:* And Shaw doesn't either, of course. Shaw is on Plutarch's side, not on Dryden's side.

*Cairns:* Do you find anything ennobling in the characters?

*Krutch:* I find something ennobling in them, not in any conventional sense, but simply in the sense that they are great, and greatness is always ennobling.

*Van Doren:* One sign of their greatness is the way they talk, isn't it?

*Krutch:* Of course, they talk a language better than any language anyone ever talked.

*Cairns:* I think you can find something ennobling in the minor characters. I think Enobarbus' remorse after he deserted Antony is inspiring, and I think the servants who died with Cleopatra are, perhaps, ennobling.

*Tate:* It seems to me that the loyalty of the attendants is merely conventional. That is something that you find in all Elizabethan plays.

*Krutch:* And they are minor characters. The great characters, Antony and Cleopatra, have risen above the necessity for such demonstrations of nobility. They are noble in themselves.

*Van Doren:* They are noble even when they are contemptible, curiously enough.

*Tate:* Their contemptibility is on a very grand scale.

*Van Doren:* A contemptible thing that Cleopatra does only enhances her finally in our judgment, just as it does in Antony's. He forgives everything that she does, and the world forgives them both. Their nobility consists in being able to love so much.

*Krutch:* Their nobility also consists in their ability to find words. Cleopatra, for example, speaks of music, "moody food of us who trade in love." Now, trading in love and being aware of the tricks of the trade is ordinarily an ignoble thing, but when Cleopatra states it in that language, it suddenly seems to lose its ignobility.

*Cairns:* Since we obviously think the play is a great one, I should like to ask Mr. Krutch, who is a professional drama critic, why it has not been a success on the stage.

*Krutch:* Simply because it is too difficult. As Shakespeare developed, he came to ask more and more of his actors and actresses. He came also to ask more and more of his audience. The parts are almost too difficult to act; the language is almost too compact and too fine to be caught on the wing. It just demands almost too much of both performer and audience.

*Van Doren:* Mr. Krutch and I attended a performance of it by some students at Columbia University, and we were more impressed than we expected to be. I mean, the play was surprisingly viable. Wouldn't you say so?

*Krutch:* Very much more than I would have thought or that I had thought when I saw unsuccessful productions.

*Van Doren:* And one very interesting thing about the occasion was this: that when Cleopatra first came on, certain members of the audience seemed to say to themselves: "Ha! Ha! This is that famous lover of Egypt. This is that infamous queen"; and they felt the temptation to snicker a little. But all at once, with one or two speeches, she quieted them. She rose above any such conception of herself and expressed herself as a great and tragic woman. Do you remember that moment?

*Krutch:* Absolutely.

*Cairns:* Were the full forty-two scenes played?

*Krutch:* Oh, no.

*Cairns:* I was interested in his technique in constructing the play. One of the most remarkable things is the contrast Shakespeare brings out between Rome and the East and between the passionate Antony and the passionless Caesar.

*Krutch:* That is a very important point which should be brought up. The contrast, as you say, between the daylight, practical world of the Romans and the mysterious and, perhaps, evil world of the East seems to be a theme almost as important as the contrast between love and honor. I am not sure but what Shakespeare had a certain contempt for the Romans because of their almost schoolboyish limitations.

*Van Doren:* They were speechmakers.

*Cairns:* But against that is the power I feel all through the play of Rome. You find it in the very opening scene, and it seems to be an oppressive power. In every action you feel this tremendous influence.

*Van Doren:* Yes, but the power of Egypt is much greater. The power of Egypt envelops the power of Rome. At the end, Antony, the greatest Roman of them all, because he is surely a much greater man than Octavius, is willing to die in Egypt.

*Cairns:* He is a much greater man as Shakespeare paints him. I am not sure that historically he was a greater man.

*Van Doren:* Oh, I don't care about that. In this play, surely, Antony is the great man. Octavius is a boy.

*Cairns:* But Octavius is the cold, calculating administrator who in the end overcomes his master, Antony. He was the pupil of Antony in his youth, but the final victory is his. Rome is triumphant.

*Van Doren:* From a political and military point of view, Octavius wins, but in the atmosphere of the play, Antony wins.

*Krutch:* Perhaps Octavius wins simply because he lacked the imagination and the sensibility to which Antony fell victim.

*Van Doren:* Octavius would not have been capable of losing a world.

*Tate:* Don't you think that these elaborate contrasts that Shakespeare develops throughout the play bring up another question: the problem of motivation of the action? Is Shakespeare really interested in the motivation? And the motivation raises another question about the morality of the play. When you have a character acting in terms of morality, the character is motivated usually by a single purpose, something very definite and simple; and if he does not succeed, he is destroyed. But here your characters are not really motivated. What is Antony's chief motive? We don't know. I think there is a series of developing contrasts toward the end until one force overwhelms the other. Egypt absorbs Rome.

*Cairns:* No doubt that is a characteristic of this play. The change in fortunes is shown through action and not through theorizing.

*Tate:* That brings me to another question then, Mr. Cairns. Is this a tragedy in the sense that *King Lear* is a tragedy?

*Cairns:* In the Aristotelian sense?

*Tate:* I don't know whether *King Lear* is a tragedy in that sense or not. It may be. But is it a tragedy as is *King Lear* or *Hamlet* or *Macbeth?*

*Krutch:* I would say not, if by that you mean a tragedy which can be abstractly presented in the form of its themes or its conflict. I think that *Antony and Cleopatra* is much more musical, impressionistic. It is not primarily logical. It is a poem.

*Tate:* Mr. Krutch, do you think that the conclusion of the play proceeds from any definite flaw in Antony's character? In *Macbeth,* we see the whole action developing out of a certain weakness in Macbeth himself.

*Krutch:* No, I don't think you see that same thing.

*Tate:* There is something a little more complicated than that.

*Van Doren:* That is why I was a little embarrassed in the beginning when Mr. Cairns asked me to summarize the story. Any summary of the story omits so much. There are not merely the episodes, the incidents, but all this atmosphere, this sponge-like character of Antony.

*Tate:* That is why I objected to having the love *motif* separated from the political.

*Van Doren:* I say Antony is a sponge. I mean that as a compliment. You squeeze him, yet you don't get his essence. He is all through the veins of that sponge.

*Cairns:* Let me ask an Aristotelian question. Do you pity Antony and Cleopatra?

*Van Doren:* I admire them and envy them.

*Cairns:* You don't pity them?

*Van Doren:* Well, I am very sorry at the end that either or both must die. Much goes out of the world, as each one of them is aware.

*Tate:* But are you sorry that Lear and Cordelia die?

*Van Doren:* My feeling is clearly very different there. As a matter of fact, you almost have to be glad.

*Cairns:* How do you feel, Mr. Krutch?

*Krutch:* I do not regret it at all. It is necessary. Antony is the last man in the world to whom this is likely to happen. He is a Roman, he is an old man, he is sophisticated, he is ambitious and everything else. But he is the ultimate victim of love because he is the man who seems least likely to be the victim of love. Therefore, the play is the ultimate triumph of love.

*Cairns:* And if you're quite cynical about it, you may even think that he is financing his Eastern campaign through Cleopatra's money.

*Van Doren:* Cleopatra probably did not think so, or at any rate, did not care. Frequently one of these lovers surprises an unworthy motive in the other, yet he is angry only for the moment. Eventually all is forgotten. Antony, asking for a kiss from Cleopatra, after one of their quarrels, and getting it—just one kiss—says: "Even this repays me." Cleopatra, shortly before her death, could not have been thinking badly of Antony if she could pay him this magnificent compliment. It is after his death.

*"His legs bestrid the ocean, his reared arm*
*Crested the world. His voice was propertied*
*To all the tuned spheres, and that to friends;*
*But when he meant to quail and shake the orb,*
*He was as rattling thunder. For his bounty,*
*There was no winter in it; an autumn 'twas,*

*That grew the more by reaping. His delights*
*Were dolphin-like, they showed his back above*
*The element they lived in. In his livery*
*Walked crowns and crownets; realms and islands were*
*As plates dropped from his pocket."*

# CRITICISM

(384-322 B.C.)

# ARISTOTLE

# Poetics

*THE* POETICS *of Aristotle is the earliest work of literary criticism we have, and it is still the best. The reason may be that its author was interested in more than literary criticism. He was a philosopher in this as in all his books, and his human view remained the widest possible. Turning his attention to poetry, he asks what it is and what it does; nor is he prejudiced as Plato was by the conviction that it is at best an "imitation." Aristotle's respect for poetry bases itself upon the perception that it is a form of knowledge. He means by poetry the art of representing the actions of men, chiefly in story, and, among the forms of story, chiefly in tragedy. His definition of tragedy, arrived at after an examination of many works produced for the theater of his day, continues to be valid in other times and conditions. For his powers of analysis, which no man has surpassed, took him straight to the essentials. He announces these in the quiet voice of one who assumes them to be commonplace, and the very ease of his thought will deceive the casual reader into supposing that because Aristotle was first in the field he was bound to hit upon profundities. But the fact is that criticism has never improved upon his discussions of the tragic hero, of pity and terror, of beginning and middle and end, of revolution and discovery, of poetry and history, of unity, of metaphor. That is to say, criticism still busies itself with Aristotle's "simple" sentences, interpreting them and testing them by the knowledge of themselves which is available to all men. Aristotle is still the wisest of critics, because he was the wisest of men.*

*Cairns:* Aristotle's *Poetics* is a different type of book from any we have discussed before. It is short, only fifty pages, but pregnant with ideas that have dominated Western critical thought. I take it that the basic question Aristotle is attempting to answer is: What makes literature meaningful to us? In answering this question, he develops three principles which pervade the book. He says that the function of poetry is imitation, that the object of imitation is to portray the universal, and finally, that the test of poetry is whether or not it gives us pleasure. Those principles appear to me to constitute the essence of his book. At the same time, I think they are highly ambiguous and need a great deal of clarification.

*Van Doren:* You mean by ambiguous, I daresay, rich in possible meanings. Or do you mean confused?

*Cairns:* I think they are rich in possibilities, not confused.

*Van Doren:* It might be appropriate to raise the question at this point: How is it that Aristotle can assume that we shall take pleasure in the form of literature which he is almost exclusively interested in here, namely, tragedy? How can tragedy give us pleasure?

*Tate:* I think we ought to ask Mr. Cairns to read us Aristotle's brief definition of tragedy, so we can see just what Aristotle is talking about.

*Cairns:* Aristotle says that "tragedy is an imitation of an action that is serious, complete and of a certain magnitude; in language embellished with each kind of artistic ornament, the several kinds being found in separate parts of the play; in the form of action, not of narrative; through pity and fear effecting the proper *katharsis,* or purgation of these and similar emotions."

*Van Doren:* I am interested in the fact that he does not use the word pain anywhere. The opposite term to pleasure is pain, and I note that Aristotle does not say a tragedy causes us pain.

*Tate:* But he does refer to a kind of work that might give us pain; that is, the portrayal of a character who is merely pathetic. He says that tragedy must excite both pity and fear, that the peculiar way in which tragedy arouses and directs those emotions gives us a purgation of them; but this is not painful. Now the word purgation has tantalized critics for two thousand years.

*Van Doren:* Is it your assumption that as a result of this purgation, we feel, on the whole, pleasure?

*Tate:* Yes, but among the nineteenth-century critics, it was not so much pleasure as moral elevation. They thought that the purgation of pity and fear gave us a certain moral elevation, which I am inclined to doubt very much.

*Van Doren:* You doubt that we are improved.

*Tate:* I don't think we are improved. I think our perceptions of life are extended. We are aware of a greater range of experience. But it seems to me that purgation is a rather practical word. It is a medical term. We must not forget that Aristotle was a physician.

*Cairns:* That is my objection to the phrase. I myself do not think that the theater is a hospital. I do not believe, as one of Aristotle's commentators has observed, that we go to the theater to get rid of emotions, but I think we go to the theater to have them more abundantly. Milton's interpretation of our point has always interested me. He said that tragedy tempered or reduced pity and fear to just measures with a kind of delight stirred up by reading or seeing those passions well imitated. In other words, he said, tragedy is a kind of homeopathic treatment, curing emotions by means of an emotion like in kind, but not identical.

*Tate:* Do we not get out of a tragedy, of a Sophoclean tragedy particularly, not only the emotions of pity and fear, but their completion in a full cycle? The form of the tragedy is perfectly balanced. Our emotions have, corresponding to the action, a beginning, a middle and an end; the action is complete, and so is our experience. That gives us a certain intellectual clarity, and permits us to entertain those emotions with equanimity.

*Van Doren:* To enclose them. To find them finished. Life perhaps does not provide a beginning, a middle and an end for our emotions, but tragedy may.

*Tate:* Yes. Nobody's experience is ever complete in the sense that a tragedy is complete.

*Cairns:* I am not sure, however, that that is the pleasure that Aristotle is talking about. Some commentators have taken the view that the notion of catharsis or purging is merely an attempt to answer Plato. It is an argument of Plato's carried one step further. Plato condemns the theater because it arouses those emotions. Aristotle in an aside answers him in the sense that if you were arguing with a prohibitionist, you might say, "Well, wine is a medicine," or, if you argue with a Puritan, you might say that dancing is exercise. But I do not think that that is the essence of dancing or the enjoyment of wine or of tragedy.

*Tate:* Shouldn't we be misinterpreting Aristotle if we said that the whole meaning of tragedy is in the purgation? That is just part of it.

*Cairns:* I think that the aspect of Aristotle's theory we are discussing is merely an aside.

*Tate:* Yes. All works of art have their practical consequences, since we are human beings and we read them, and we are in the world of action and they affect our actions. But it seems to me to be wrong to say that the practical consequences are the whole meaning of tragedy.

*Cairns:* I should like to make our discussion of Aristotle's notion of tragedy a little more concrete by an example. I read Aristotle's definition of tragedy a few moments ago. There is a novel that actually has the word "tragedy" in its title, Theodore Dreiser's *An American Tragedy.* Do you think that is a tragedy within Aristotle's meaning?

*Van Doren:* No, because Aristotle has written a sentence or so which would disqualify it, as a complete tragedy at any rate.

It is a sentence which occurs among several in which he describes the tragic hero. The hero first of all must be a great man; and it seems obvious that the hero of *An American Tragedy* does not begin by being a great man. His fall, the catastrophe he suffers, may be pathetic. There may be something in his story which arouses us to want to change the laws for the average citizen, but it cannot, I think, arouse in us pity or terror. Clyde Griffith was a slight person.

*Cairns:* Would you say, then, that Aristotle was being arbitrary in his definition of tragedy?

*Van Doren:* Arbitrary in what sense?

*Cairns:* That he has devised what is known as a verbal definition.

*Van Doren:* By no means.

*Tate:* Shouldn't we bear in mind, Mr. Cairns, that Aristotle is not saying what anything ought to be? This book is the result of observation, of something that actually was—and is. It is based on Greek plays as he saw them. He is not laying down laws. It seems to me that is one trouble with the interpretations of the *Poetics.* Later the neo-classical movement in the Renaissance attempted to erect the *Poetics* into a system of legislation regarding the drama. It became a book of rules.

*Cairns:* It has been observed that it may be a defect in the *Poetics* that Aristotle had in his bookcase just the Greek classics. Suppose he had had in his bookcase Balzac, Thackeray, Tolstoy and other novelists. Perhaps his definition might have been different.

*Tate:* I think he could have easily provided for all those novels in terms of his discussion of character. Mr. Van Doren has already touched on that in connection with Clyde Griffith.

*Cairns:* Perhaps, in that case then, he might have changed his definition of character.

*Van Doren:* Aristotle is probably answering Plato also when he discusses imitation.

*Cairns:* Yes, Plato had certainly disparaged the term.

*Van Doren:* Plato seems to have meant, when he called poetry an imitation of life, that it is no more than a copy of it without anything being done to life in the process. Aristotle seems to be doing something philosophical with the word. It is comparatively easy to see how imitation can be philosophical. If you want to imitate anything—that is, to represent it, to restate it, to re-form it—you have to understand it; you have to perceive its essence. And that is an effort of philosophy.

*Tate:* What is Plato's point of view when he discusses this question in the *Republic?* Would he not say that if we understood the object of imitation, then we would refuse to imitate it? Our understanding of a material object would instruct us in its imperfection, which should not be imitated. Only the idea should be imitated. But Aristotle had a different conception of the object which was being imitated: It was a good thing to imitate it.

*Van Doren:* I should say that Aristotle on the whole had more interest in what we are in the habit of calling life than Plato did. He was more willing to accept life as it occurs.

*Cairns:* Still, Aristotle says that it is the privilege, even the duty, of the poet "to tell lies skillfully"; he must learn the true art of fiction.

*Van Doren:* We have said that this is a book about poetry. How does it happen that it applies, if it does apply, to what we are in the habit these days of calling fiction, which is written in what we call prose?

*Tate:* Aristotle meant by poetry not necessarily something in verse. He makes that quite clear.

*Cairns:* He meant by "poet" anyone whose work was an "imitation" as he defined that word. It made no difference whether the medium was verse or prose.

*Van Doren:* Verse is a non-essential element.

*Tate:* Poetry, he says, as a rule, is song, meter and rhythm, but that is not the main thing. Poetry is related to the word *poesis*, something made or created, or, let us say, imagined.

*Van Doren:* I should say that for him the art of poetry is substantially the art of telling stories.

*Tate:* Manipulation of plots and the relations of the characters in terms of plot.

*Van Doren:* And modern fiction would always benefit by a scrutiny of the sort that Aristotle provides.

*Cairns:* It would benefit immeasurably; but not, of course, in the sense that there should be a strict observance of any so-called rules to be found in the treatise.

*Tate:* Aristotle says that tragedy has certain qualities, that it has diction, has thought and so on. In fact, there are only two things that tragedy, as Aristotle saw it, had that are not possible in modern fiction, and they are the spectacle and the song. The novel does not have spectacles because it is not on the stage, and it is not sung. Modern fiction is losing the plot, and in both Balzac and Flaubert, we see its decline. This has a definite connection with the kinds of characters we get in modern fiction. They are passive and are not the kind of characters who can develop in action.

*Van Doren:* We get in many modern novels the whole life of a man, beginning perhaps in his childhood and going on through his marriage and through his professional or business career.

*Tate:* Aristotle provides for that too, does he not? He says that unity of character does not mean unity of plot. That is, if you have a man named John Smith running through a novel, it does not mean that the novel has unity in terms of the plot. Smith remains a unit, but the plot is disorderly.

*Van Doren:* The biography of a man is not necessarily a plot.

*Cairns:* He goes even further. He says that dramatic action is not developed with a view to the representation of character; character comes in as subsidiary to the action. The incidents and the plot are the end of a tragedy and without action there cannot be a tragedy; there may be tragedy without character.

*Tate:* We get that principle in Homer. Aristotle says that Homer omits certain characters that were traditionally attributed to the *Odyssey*. They would not fit into the plot.

*Van Doren:* A famous novel of our time which is biographical in form, namely, *Of Human Bondage,* by Somerset Maugham, follows the hero from the time he is a little boy until he is married and has settled down in his profession of doctor. It might be Aristotle's point that Maugham's novel might be more interesting if the events in which we find Philip Carey, the hero, had a greater unity. At the end, you may remember, Philip Carey looks back over his life so far and says: "I can find no meaning in it except insofar as the pattern of any life has meaning if we are absorbed as we follow the intricacies of that pattern." Maugham has there very conveniently referred us back to Aristotle. A tragic hero, according to Aristotle's definition, would be capable of looking back over his life—Shakespeare's tragic heroes always did—and saying, "It was this or that."

*Tate:* There is James Joyce's *Portrait of the Artist as a Young Man.* We know that it is largely, though not strictly, autobiographical. And it is significant that at the end of *The Portrait of the Artist,* the hero, Stephen Dedalus, says that he is going on to other things. He is going to have a new life elsewhere.

*Cairns:* In other words, it is not a complete action. But there is something, I think, that the modern novel has that probably Aristotle could not foresee and that possibly makes up for the loss of plot. In the finest modern novel you get a body of sensuous detail. You get observation of a scene; you get atmosphere built up, which tends to carry interest to the reader. Aristotle explicitly says that he subordinates diction, or language, to action.

*Van Doren:* And decoration. He makes that subordinate, too.

*Cairns:* The nineteenth-century novelist did not try to picture life as better than it is. This is what Aristotle wanted in tragedy.

*Van Doren:* Does Aristotle use the word "better"? The translators are responsible for that. Some of the translators have cheated. I should say he means more significant, more unified, more understandable.

*Cairns:* He seems to say that the characters of Homer are "better" than those of ordinary reality in the sense, to use his phrase, in which "the ideal type must surpass the actual." It is in that meaning that Aristotle's Greek is usually translated by the English word "better."

*Tate:* Did you mean, Mr. Cairns, that in giving us "life as it is," a nineteenth-century novelist was trying to photograph society, to give us the cross-section? For example, Balzac.

*Cairns:* Let us take an example we used before—Dreiser. Dreiser pictured Clyde Griffith as Dreiser thought he really was. Now Mr. Van Doren objects to that as not being tragedy because Clyde Griffith is not a man of heroic proportions, but it may be that to the modern mind, Aristotle's definition of tragedy is not adequate if it forces us to deny that *An American Tragedy* is a tragedy.

*Van Doren:* I should say it was entirely adequate. He is taking care of a great deal of modern fiction when he lets us know it is history. If he could read it now, he would call it history, not poetry.

*Cairns:* That may be. Aristotle was a wise man, and he might surprise us if he came back and rewrote the *Poetics.*

*Tate:* With very few exceptions, he would say that the characters are passive, and not of heroic proportions. There has been a lot of discussion about what Aristotle meant. It seems to me that, by heroic proportions, we mean a man who is possessed of a conception of his human dignity which is fairly rigid and continual. He himself, his human nature, the human side of his character, is not adequate to his conception of what he ought to be. He breaks down; for example, Oedipus. Oedipus has a powerful religious sense of obligation. At the same time, he has certain human frailties. He was arrogant; he was capable of quick anger; he was headlong; and he was destroyed. But at the same time, he was a very great man.

*Van Doren:* Or there is Hamlet, who had a conception of what it is to be a gentleman, a conception such as no man, even he, could live up to.

*Tate:* Or Macbeth, for example. Macbeth's downfall is due to an excessive development of very fine qualities. All those qualities which made a great feudal lord.

*Van Doren:* Including, incidentally, a great sensitiveness to his own deeds, because he trembles with fear at what he is about to do.

*Cairns:* I am worried also by Aristotle's conception of pleasure. Do you think that he means it is our pleasure that is the test of poetry?

*Tate:* It seems to me that in the *Poetics* pleasure is one of those words that Aristotle probably threw off, like purgation, which he assumed that everybody would understand. He could not foresee the complications that the word would have for us.

*Cairns:* No, I cannot go that far. I think that he laid down a fundamental principle, namely, that the end of art is to give us pleasure.

*Tate:* I should have to question that, although most criticism since Aristotle has assumed it. The trouble is that in the nineteenth century you get special psychological theories and even metaphysical theories of pleasure. Coleridge, for example, interpreted pleasure in terms of sensation, and I think that is misleading.

*Van Doren:* The trouble is that the word pleasure has assumed a light value, which is too bad. It has become impossible to use it. But I should say that any work of art, quite obviously, must give us pleasure.

*Cairns:* We might say that it gives us intellectual pleasure.

*Tate:* But that would not necessarily take us very far in interpreting this passage.

*Cairns:* If you accept the principle that the end of poetry is to give us pleasure, it raises the whole relativistic question in modern criticism. Does it, for example, make the valuation of poetry subjective?

*Van Doren:* No, though we do have to consider what pleasure means to the individual. I hope he does not mean by it something distinguished from profit, for instance. Pleasure includes profit. Pleasure involves the entire occupation of myself or yourself with whatever we are attending, the life of a man or the music of a lyric.

*Cairns:* Aristotle meant the pleasure that the average cultivated man in the community felt. That reminds me that the world has taken pleasure in Aristotle's little treatise for several thousand years, and I suppose that there are few books in its field more profitable today for the modern reader.

*Tate:* I think he ought to read the book to understand and to discriminate the different kinds of plots that are possible. After all, there are only certain kinds of people. There are good people; there are bad people; there are people who fall from prosperity to adversity and *vice versa*—they come up and down in the world. Aristotle compares persons and situations and says that none of them in itself is a tragic character or a tragic situation. He says that we expect we can get pleasure from many kinds of literature, but we must not expect from tragedy pleasure that is not proper to it.

*Cairns:* Do you agree with that, Mr. Van Doren?

*Van Doren:* Yes, and a further reason for reading the book today is that it is the wisest discussion of poetry we so far have had. Take it as a piece of literary criticism. We read reviews; we read articles; we are very much interested in criticism. Well, this book remains fundamental in literary criticism. It says things which have become, if you like, commonplace, but which only a very distinguished man can either say or understand.

*Cairns:* That is a mistake the modern reader may make. He may think it a commonplace to read in Aristotle that a play must have a beginning, a middle and an end.

*Van Doren:* That is just the point. Most plays are not wholly satisfactory to us because they lack one or two of those three things. We may not easily know why they are unsatisfactory to us, but a reading of Aristotle would often make it clear. As in the case of O'Neill's plays, for instance.

*Tate:* They are incomplete.

*Cairns:* Do you mean in the sense that at the end the meaning of the whole is not quite clear to us and is not linked to the beginning with inevitable certainty?

*Van Doren:* There is still more to say.

*Tate:* In *Hamlet,* it seems to me, nothing more is required.

*Van Doren:* There is nothing more. That statement should always be possible at the end of a tragedy. *King Lear,* on the other hand, is not a perfect tragedy because it is all end.

*Cairns:* I should like to read, since we have been discussing Aristotle in connection with modern novels, his paragraph in the *Poetics* that bears most closely on that point. He says, "It is evident from what has been said that it is not the function of the poet to relate what has happened but what may happen, what is possible according to the law of probability or necessity. The poet and the historian differ not by writing in verse or in prose. The work of Herodotus might be put into verse and it would still be a species of history, with meter no less than without it. The true difference is that one relates what has happened; the other, what may happen. Poetry, therefore, is a more philosophical and a higher thing than history, for poetry tends to express the universal; history, the particular. By the universal I mean how a person of a certain type will on occasion speak or act according to the law of probability or necessity, and it is this universality at which poetry aims in the names she attaches to the personages. The particular is, for example, what Alcibiades did or suffered."

(1729-1781)

# LESSING

## *Laocöon*

*G*OTTHOLD EPHRAIM LESSING *was important in the re-creation of German literature in the eighteenth century after hundreds of years during which it had been stagnant. No service he performed was more valuable, to Germany and to the world, than the critical one, for he was possessed of wisdom and an unusual power of analysis. This power is best seen in the famous* LAOCÖON, *where Lessing convicts all Europe in his time of a confusion among the arts. Every art has its limits within which it must live; it can live only there, and indeed it can live most fully when boundaries are not only accepted but welcomed. Poetry, for instance, can never do the work of painting, though schools of descriptive poetry existed in the belief that it could. The result was not painting, and neither was it poetry; or if it was poetry it was defective because the attempt it made was in the nature of the art impossible. There is no virtue in attempt-*

*ing the impossible. So with poetry and sculpture; they have different geniuses, and to forget that fact is to honor neither. Other pairs of arts were being confused and still are in spite of the warning which Lessing so clearly issued. His analysis is the most useful tool which a modern critic has at his hand when he wishes to separate history from fiction, music from poetry, or rhetoric from both. The modern critic may not share Lessing's conceptions of time and space as categories of art, but he is bound to benefit by a study of his predecessor's rigorous and fearless method. Great critics are few, and Lessing is one of them.**

* *Mr. Cairns was unable to be present for this discussion.*

(DEAN CHRISTIAN GAUSS, GUEST)

*Tate:* The *Laocöon* of Lessing was first published in 1766. Lessing had been very much concerned about the differences among the arts, particularly the difference between poetry and painting. The discussion begins, or rather centers around, an analysis of the famous "Laocöon group," a piece of ancient sculpture which had fascinated critics through the centuries. You recall that the "Laocöon group" is made up of the Trojan priest, Laocöon, and his two sons, who are being destroyed by a serpent; they are being destroyed because Laocöon had warned the Trojans of the treachery of the wooden horse. Mr. Gauss, may I ask for your general estimate of the book?

*Gauss:* I should say that in the history of criticism of the last two hundred years, this is probably the most important single critical work written by a man of that time.

*Tate:* Would you tell us just why you think so? What do you think is the capital merit of the book?

*Gauss:* There are several. If I were going to pick out the single point that strikes me as most important, I would say it is the fact that here for the first time, clearly, Lessing made a distinction between the limits of painting and the limits of poetry; that is, he tried to show what the painter can do well and what the poet can do well. And he reached certain conclusions on that score which caused a revolution, one might almost call it, in the field of poetry.

*Van Doren:* Don't you think that the reason this man could bring about a revolution in criticism as well as in writing was that, as a critic, he deserved both of the adjectives you have used:

"single" and "clear"? It has always seemed to me that a critic, if he was able to say one thing clearly, either in a single book or in all the books that he wrote, might very well achieve immortality. I mean, one thing that we can remember and use.

*Gauss:* I think that is true. That really makes it a critical masterpiece. If a man has said one thing clearly that really abides with us and that we remember with satisfaction and feel its significance more and more, we have to concede that that man wrote a masterpiece of criticism.

*Van Doren:* And that one thing in the case of Lessing has to do with the limits of an art?

*Gauss:* Yes.

*Tate:* Mr. Gauss, will you explain to us what the phrase, "the limits of an art," means? It is a very interesting question, and not very well understood today by a great many poets and artists.

*Van Doren:* If I may interrupt before Mr. Gauss answers the question, I should say that most people today or at any time, whether they are critics or artists, and certainly if they are laymen contemplating criticism and art, take it for granted that art has no limits, or, at any rate, that a given art has no limits. They may be deceived into thinking so by the fact that a given artist seems to them to be able to do anything; and, of course, that is the illusion he should create.

*Gauss:* I think that is true; but that was the error of a great many people in the eighteenth century. It was because they failed to realize that there are these limits that poetry particularly had gone off on a false line and you had any number of volumes of poetry which were purely descriptive or attempts to describe things in terms of words that could only be described, as Lessing tried to point out, in terms of painting.

*Van Doren:* You mean that poetry was trying to be painting?

*Gauss:* Poetry was trying to be painting and, as a matter of fact, they had been following what they thought was ancient authority because one of the ancients (Lessing calls him "the Greek Voltaire," because he did not like Voltaire very well)—Simonides—had said that painting is a silent poem and that a poem is a talking picture, and so they felt that the fields of poetry and painting were co-ordinate; whereas, Lessing tried to show that the means which the painter uses make it possible for him to deal only with one single moment, one given thing, and he deals in terms of space and form. He can only place things that exist, that co-exist, whereas the poet cannot do this, because, if he is describing a beautiful woman, for instance (and Lessing takes up a number of such descriptions of beautiful women in great poems), the poet has first to describe, as for instance Ariosto does, a woman's hair and then her brow and then her nose.

*Tate:* Excuse me, Mr. Gauss. Doesn't Lessing also go into Homer's failure to describe the famous Helen of Troy?

*Van Doren:* Or rather his refusal—he did not want to.

*Gauss:* He says that refusal shows that Homer was a very great artist, because he realized that no poet could draw in words a description of Helen of Troy which anyone could visualize and recognize. No one of us, no poet, Lessing said, could describe any beautiful woman in such detail that you would recognize that woman on the street, that you could pick her out of two hundred people.

*Tate:* And yet, doesn't Lessing say that an obligation of the poet is also to give us a picture? But that it is a different kind of picture from that of the painter?

*Gauss:* Yes, because Lessing says that the poet deals with successive stages or events, things in process, and he has to use time because his phrases fall consecutively and not together, whereas you look at a painting and you see the hair and the brow and the eyes and the nose and the lips of the beautiful woman all at once, but the poet can only describe one after the other and you lose the sense of the instantaneous impression.

*Van Doren:* That is why the subject matter of poetry has to be things which succeed one another in time.

*Tate:* Lessing believed that the characteristic thing in poetry, which is in time and proceeds from moment to moment, is a series of actions. Do you not think that he was incomplete in his failure to discuss lyric poetry?

*Gauss:* I think the type of poetry that Lessing was really concerned with and really had in mind was epic poetry or, to a lesser degree, dramatic poetry, that the distinction that he makes would not be true of reflective poetry, of the Greek choruses, for instance.

*Tate:* What about Wordsworth? There are many magnificent descriptive passages in Wordsworth, and yet we all seem to agree that Wordsworth is a great poet.

*Van Doren:* I should say that when Wordsworth is a magnificent poet and is describing, his descriptions have action; I mean, his descriptions are of persons or of things that in some sense have movement. Now when Wordsworth was younger—was a typical eighteenth-century poet—he published a book called *Descriptive Sketches,* which is the sort of thing that Lessing was protesting against. I think Lessing would not have protested against the later Wordsworth.

*Tate:* Now, how would you describe the movement of action in Wordsworth's *Prelude?* It is an autobiographical poem of his inner life, the development of his inner consciousness.

*Van Doren:* Yes, but if you consider any of the passages which you remember without difficulty, you will find them to be such passages as that in which he describes himself skating as a boy. That passage is one of the fullest of motion that I know. Likewise, his account of the boat that he stole, and of its movement through the water like a swan. After all, he is not giving you a picture of anything. He is giving you the sense of motion.

*Tate:* I think that is true. Perhaps we could develop this point a little more and understand it better if we turn to drama. It seems to me that in *Antony and Cleopatra,* the main effect is pictorial. I believe we can more or less agree that the action, strictly speaking, is unmotivated. There was no real psychological motivation for the behavior of any of the characters.

*Van Doren:* I am sure that Lessing is a great critic because we can use him so easily. That is to say, he explains why it is that

*Antony and Cleopatra,* though a great poem, is not a great play. It is one of Shakespeare's greatest poems, but the one which is least dramatically forceful.

*Tate:* Mr. Gauss, do you agree with that?

*Gauss:* I think that is correct. I should say that is the least forceful dramatically of the Shakespearean plays.

*Tate:* And yet we seem to agree that it is a great poem. Lessing is talking about poems, isn't he?

*Van Doren:* But when I use the word "poem" there, I am not using it in its fullest sense. I would agree that the fullest sense of the word "poem" calls in the end for something which tells a story successfully. If you like, I am willing to admit then that *Antony and Cleopatra* is not *the* greatest poem of Shakespeare. *Hamlet* is a greater poem because it also tells a story.

*Tate:* Don't you think, however, that *Antony and Cleopatra* has another element in it which Lessing, as a neo-classicist, might neglect? He remarks somewhere that the language of poetry as a medium is not so difficult for the poet as the medium of paint and canvas is for the painter. Probably because we use language as our natural inheritance. The chief thing that the poet must learn, says Lessing, is how to represent action. Don't you think that he ignored something in the language of poetry that may tend to qualify his general theories if we give it due importance?

*Van Doren:* His general theory, I think, when it remains general theory, is always good. For instance, I don't happen to think that language, although surely an important part of poetry, is the necessary part. This is best shown by the fact that the better a poem is, the easier it is to translate, the more of it comes through in a different language. I would even go so far as to say that Lessing's analysis is valuable in a discussion of lyric poetry.

*Tate:* I am surprised to hear you say that. I should like to get your reasons.

*Van Doren:* Doesn't it throw a great deal of light on the triviality of Imagist poetry? Imagism was an attempt to make a stationary poetry, which is a thing that poetry cannot be. About twenty years ago, as you know, in England and America there was a school of lyric poetry called Imagist, and its theory was, among other things, that the short poem can be best when it approaches motionlessness. There was the effort to paint little pictures that were quite frozen, quite fragmentary, in the hope that they would be valuable for themselves. When you think of a great lyric poem, you think of a poem which is moving. A great lyric poem is also somehow dramatic, even narrative.

*Tate:* One of the most profound critical observations of our time is the remark made by T. S. Eliot that perhaps for two hundred years lyric poetry has ceased to be dramatic and has thus lost a certain power. That is one reason, at any rate, why it has lost interest for the public at large. Do you think there is any truth in that, Mr. Gauss?

*Gauss:* That might very likely be true. It is certainly true that that type of lyric poetry has lost a good deal of its appeal, and I am wondering why, whether it may not be because some of the poets themselves realized their inability to do in verse what they set out to do. There is a story of the son of Titian that Alfred de Musset, one of the famous romantic poets, tells: Titian started to paint a portrait of his mistress, but as he continued the painting, he finally decided that no matter how good the painting might be, it could not quite equal a kiss of the original, and that life was somehow far ahead in its intensity of anything that the painter or the poet could do. He therefore turned the picture to the wall and from that time never painted any more. Of course, the poet is supposed to be following after life, never quite being able to reach its intensity, its *lyric* intensity, and that was just because there was nothing dramatic in it; he was simply trying to reproduce in words the intensity of emotion or sensation which is, of course, much more direct in real life than it can ever be on the printed page.

*Van Doren:* But on the other hand, wouldn't you have a certain distrust of an artist, whatever his medium, who felt despair because his art was not what life is? That is another confusion, if you like. Art is not supposed to be life, art is not trying to be life. Art has its own intensities.

*Tate:* Doesn't Lessing say that poetry, since it cannot present objects in space as painting does, must lean upon the reader's previous knowledge of the things that the poet is representing? And for that reason, Lessing supports what you gentlemen have just been saying, that there are certain things that he cannot render in poetry. He cannot render the picture; he can only assume it. There is another point concerning lyric poetry I should like to bring up. If you consider the fact, which Lessing emphasizes constantly, that poetry is a succession of articulated sounds, don't you think that the value of the sound may have something to do with the value of lyric poetry? Lessing, it seems to me, tends to neglect that feature of poetry.

*Van Doren:* That would be why lyric poetry translates less well than narrative or dramatic poetry.

*Tate:* I think of a line which seems to be descriptive—Shakespeare's "The multitudinous seas incarnadine." If we think of the natural object, the sea, to which that line refers, we see that it is not a literal representation of the sea at all. There is a new interest, beyond representation, introduced by means of the use of language. Don't you think, then, that Lessing's theory of imitation, which he borrowed from the ancients, somewhat limited him?

*Gauss:* It limited him very much. I think that is probably the most serious single weakness in Lessing's point of view, that he did realize that what the poet had to do was to appeal to the imagination rather than to direct visual images. That is why he praises Homer very properly for not having attempted to describe Helen of Troy. He simply showed the effect that Helen's passing in front of the old men had upon them; then, when they conclude that it is no wonder that the Greeks left home and made war for ten years for such a beautiful woman, the reader has the sense that this was a beautiful woman passing, much more than if Homer had tried to describe her hair and brow and eyes.

*Van Doren:* You would not say that the line about the "multitudinous seas" was a better line than "To be or not to be, that is the question," would you, Mr. Tate?

*Tate:* Not better. The two lines have entirely different purposes and different situations.

*Van Doren:* The line, "To be or not to be, that is the question," which is very easily translated, might actually be a line more fitting in a play and more powerful in a play than "The multitudinous seas incarnadine," which is excessive to the purpose of the play it decorates.

*Tate:* It is a difficult question to decide. I once read a modern Greek translation of *Hamlet,* and I remember the way a phrase in that very soliloquy was translated. When Hamlet says, "Ay, there's the rub," the Greek translator wrote, "There's the Gordian Knot." That was easily translated, but is "Ay, there's the rub," a distinguished passage in itself? A distinguished line?

*Van Doren:* No. Although the important question, it seems to me, is what Hamlet is saying in the passage; "rub" and "Gordian knot" might both be good. The idea behind either phrase might be more important than the phrase.

*Tate:* Are we saying perhaps that the greatest poets can be easily translated? Do you think that is true? We are always complaining about the badness of translations.

*Van Doren:* Well, who are the great poets? Homer, Dante and Shakespeare, aren't they? They are all relatively easy to translate.

*Tate:* Yes, I suppose so. What do you think, Mr. Gauss?

*Gauss:* I think in general I would agree with Mr. Van Doren. The great epic poets certainly seem to be the easiest to translate. The one that translates perhaps least well of all the ancient poets is Pindar.

*Van Doren:* A lyric poet.

*Gauss:* A lyric poet. Of course, if you really have action and successive stages of action, action in process, the poet can render it very well. Somehow or other, it seems to translate and go into other languages much more successfully than the attempt to translate, let us say, an ode of Pindar's or a lyric poem of Petrarch.

Petrarch is another man who has never been very well translated.

*Tate:* Couldn't we formulate a general rule, that the less action we get in a poem, the more difficult it is to translate?

*Gauss:* Yes.

*Tate:* Because the poem which does not have much action depends for its effect largely upon subtleties in the language.

*Van Doren:* Which may be very fascinating to a person who knows that language.

*Tate:* The line that I quoted a minute ago, "The multitudinous seas incarnadine," would be probably an example. Shakespeare has both kinds of language. The general action can be translated, but the niceties of language are more difficult.

*Van Doren:* We should make it clear that when we assign limits to an art, we are not implying that that art has any limitations in its power to please us, or to impress us. For instance—there is a certain paradox here—the more a given artist understands the limits of his art, the more powerful he becomes. Shakespeare or Rembrandt does not leave us with a sense of limitation at all. So in motion pictures—for this book might become the foundation of a system of criticism for the motion picture, because you have in the very name motion picture the two kinds of art that Lessing is talking about: motion, or poetry; and picture, or painting. A good motion picture when it comes along is probably good because the man making it seems to understand perfectly what a motion picture can do. He is not trying to do more or less than that—certainly he is not trying to do less—and so he completely occupies us.

*Gauss:* I think that is very true, and I believe you were saying in a conversation shortly before this discussion that if the presentation of motion pictures were made with a fuller realization of what can properly be done in movie technique, we should have very much better movies.

*Van Doren:* And movies that seemed less limited, too.

*Gauss:* I think the most important limitation, the type of limitation that the poet puts upon himself, really makes for concentration of effect. Old Goethe had a famous line in which he said,

"When working under limitations, the master really proves himself." He knows what those limitations are and he knows he is working within the sphere in which a certain concentrated effect can be produced.

*Tate:* I was just thinking of a famous modern poet, Hart Crane, who died eight years ago. He wrote a poem called *The Bridge,* an epic poem in a lyric style. The lyric style simply would not sustain what he was trying to say, although it is a very interesting poem.

*Van Doren:* When a work of art is relatively feeble—I don't mean that *The Bridge* was feeble, but it was unsuccessful in a sense—we can often say that the reason is it is attempting to be something other than what it can be.

*Tate:* Do you think it is possible to state Lessing's point of view in a few words? Isn't it a mark of a great critic that his principles can be reduced to something very definite and very clear?

*Van Doren:* Certainly.

*Tate:* There is his distinction between space and time as the respective mediums of painting and poetry. Would you say, Mr. Gauss, that that perhaps is central to his argument?

*Gauss:* I think that is the central point of the whole.

*Van Doren:* At the beginning of Chapter 16 of the *Laocöon,* he makes a full statement—full although brief—of the significance of his distinction between space and time. He says: "Subjects which or the various parts of which exist side by side may be called bodies. Consequently, bodies with their visible properties form the proper subjects of painting. Subjects which or the various parts of which succeed each other may in general be called actions. Consequently, actions form the proper subjects of poetry. Yet all bodies exist not in space alone but also in time. They continue and may appear differently at every moment and stand in different relations. Every one of these momentary appearances and combinations is the effect of one preceding and can be the cause of one following, and accordingly be likewise the central point of an action. Consequently, painting can also imitate actions but only by way of suggestion through bodies. On the other hand, actions cannot subsist for themselves but must attach to certain things or persons. Now insofar as these things are bodies or are regarded as bodies, poetry too depicts bodies but only by way of suggestion through actions."

(1772-1834)

# COLERIDGE

# *Biographia Literaria*

*THE author of* THE ANCIENT MARINER *is famous for a few successful poems and for a great quantity of literary criticism which survives for the most part in an unfinished state—notes for lectures, unrevised periodical essays and reports by others of his conversation. He was a wonderful talker, and preferred the monologue to any tighter medium of expression. His genius for criticism shines out in many a fragment, notably in his lectures on Shakespeare; but it appears most systematically in his* BIOGRAPHIA LITERARIA, *where he finds the autobiographical form uniquely suited to his nature. Even then he is miscellaneous and uneven. Yet there is a permanent importance in his narrative of the literary revolution which he led at the end of the eighteenth century with the help of William Wordsworth. This was the first of a series of revolutions which the following two centuries were to undergo, with the result that we are now familiar with the psychology of literary manifestoes. The field of poetry over which Coleridge and Wordsworth fought may seem at first glance to be a limited one; it is the field of language or diction. But under Coleridge's generalship it widened into the field of poetry itself, and as usual in literary revolutions a number of truths were rediscovered. Coleridge is one of the three or four great English critics, not because of his theories, which a lesser man could have, but because in his mind there was dimension and power, and because in his love of poetry at its best the whole of his remarkable nature shone forth.*

(MR. EDMUND WILSON, GUEST)

*Cairns:* It was agreed in the discussion of Lessing that he had a contemporary value, that he had not only a historical value, but that he stood for something important in criticism and writing today. Can the same point be made of Coleridge? Has he a present value for the contemporary critic and writer? What do you think, Mr. Wilson?

*Wilson:* I think he has. Coleridge is a unique figure in English criticism. I suppose that there is no other case of an English writer, a first-rate English creative writer, who had read so enormously as Coleridge had and who wrote criticism.

*Tate:* Mr. Wilson, what do you think his merit as a critic is? I am not sure that it is possible to state it in a few words. Could you isolate any special characteristic which is of importance today?

*Van Doren:* May I extend the question? Discussions of Coleridge center about his principles and judgments, and I suppose by judgments is meant judgments of particular authors or works. Would you think his principles or his judgments were the more valuable?

*Wilson:* His judgments were probably more important than his principles, if you can separate them. His theories themselves, if you mean by that his principles, I have never been so much interested in, especially their metaphysical aspects.

*Tate:* Do you think his distinction between the fancy and the imagination is a valuable distinction?

*Wilson:* I think that there is something in it as he implies it.

*Cairns:* Not very much, would you say?

*Tate:* I would disagree with you, Mr. Cairns.

*Van Doren:* Could you state the distinction, Mr. Tate?

*Tate:* I will try to state it very briefly; in fact, much more briefly than Coleridge states it.

*Van Doren:* Coleridge never states anything briefly.

*Cairns:* He never developed it to the point of making a real distinction between the two notions.

*Tate:* I think he never quite got around to it. The *Biographia Literaria* is not long enough for his purpose, but it is long enough probably for ours. The distinction between fancy and imagination, while it would not permit anybody to judge a poem, to distinguish a bad poem from a good poem, gives us a certain way of thinking about poetry. For example, he thinks of fancy as a passive faculty. He calls it a mode of memory which is divorced from space and time. That is, it is nothing but reverie. Images float through the mind which are not checked by any real experience.

*Van Doren:* He calls that mechanical memory.

*Tate:* Yes, mechanical memory. On the other hand, the imagination which he calls the esemplastic power—he made up a fancy word for it . . .

*Cairns:* He did not make it up. He took it from Schelling.

*Tate:* He claims it.

*Cairns:* He claimed it, I know, but Schelling coined it.

*Tate:* Apart from that, anyhow, the esemplastic power is the vital and unifying power. It is the faculty that brings all the disconnected elements together and unifies them into a whole.

*Cairns:* Is that conception important today in criticism? Has it been important either in criticism or in poetry?

*Tate:* It is important today for this reason: The advance of science in the last hundred years, particularly since Coleridge's time, has tended to discredit the imaginative powers.

*Van Doren:* It was the whole stock in trade, incidentally, of Poe as a critic of poetry. Poe used the distinction to separate the sheep from the goats among contemporary versifiers.

*Tate:* I don't think he used it very well, do you?

*Van Doren:* No. But it seemed to him perfectly satisfactory.

*Cairns:* He had no more success than Coleridge with the idea.

*Wilson:* Don't you think he probably got it from Coleridge?

*Van Doren:* I believe he did.

*Wilson:* He never admits that he did, but from the dates, he could have done so.

*Van Doren:* I am sure he did.

*Cairns:* Poe prided himself, like Coleridge and Arnold, on his cosmopolitan outlook. I have no doubt he picked up the idea from Coleridge. He was very sensitive to foreign influences.

*Tate:* You mean Poe's famous letter to "Mr. B." I think he got it all from Coleridge.

*Cairns:* The most ambitious attempt in modern times to develop that notion is in I. A. Richards' book, *Coleridge on the Imagination,* and I must say that the book seemed to me to complicate the problem unnecessarily.

*Tate:* It tries to translate Coleridge into the language of experimental psychology, and it does not quite come off.

*Van Doren:* I imagine that if you asked Shakespeare which was the more important gift for a poet, he would say fancy. He might be wrong, and certainly he would be wrong from Coleridge's point of view, but the faculty in Shakespeare's own mind which he relished using was his fancy—or his invention, as the seventeenth century said.

*Cairns:* The distinction is not very important, unless it is tied in to a systematic development of a general theory of aesthetics. Coleridge did not do that and, so far as I know, no one subsequent to Coleridge has done it. The idea is just left in the air.

*Wilson:* Yes. But I think it is important, because it is a part of his ability to distinguish between the first rate and the second rate in literature.

*Van Doren:* But did that depend upon this distinction?

*Wilson:* No, I don't think it did, but the distinction was part of his attempt to explain why great poetry was great and why Cowley, for example, was not so good as Milton.

*Cairns:* I should like to suggest an answer to the question that

I put to you at the beginning of the discussion. I think, myself, that Coleridge is not important for his metaphysical or his psychological ideas, but for his method. As a critic, his contemporary value lies in his method, that is, what he did when he criticized a poem. And the great thing he did, it seems to me, was to keep his eye right on that poem and throw out the window all his metaphysical notions and all his psychological conceptions. He came right down to the question: Why is the particular poem good or bad?

*Wilson:* That is perfectly true.

*Tate:* Isn't it a question, Mr. Cairns, whether a critic's theoretical ideas can in the long run be separated from his practical observations? I am not sure.

*Van Doren:* It is dangerous to do that.

*Tate:* I think they tend to move together. You may value his practical observations more, but I think it is very dangerous to say that you can throw the theory out altogether.

*Van Doren:* The same is true of the poet. Take his friend Wordsworth. Mr. T. S. Eliot has pointed out that it is unsafe for criticism to despise the ideas of Wordsworth. The ideas of Wordsworth in one sense did not make his poetry, and yet the poetry would not have existed without them. They were necessary for Wordsworth. He had to be that serious in order to write poetry at all.

*Cairns:* But I am not throwing out all Coleridge's ideas. He introduced some valuable ones. For example, his catholic method of looking at literature. If he were alive today, I feel that he could appreciate both T. S. Eliot and Saintsbury. He would not have to reject one or the other because he liked one or the other.

*Van Doren:* Of course, his distinction between the fancy and imagination, while very interesting and probably useful, is capable and has been capable of debauching criticism, if not poetry. I should say that the flatness and meagerness of a great deal of poetry since his time stems from the worst part of Wordsworth, which was written out of the theory about the imagination that said it was a way of speaking the truth. Poets since his time have thought that all they needed to do was say something "true." That does not necessarily make a poem.

*Tate:* Don't you think that Wordsworth misinterpreted Coleridge's meaning?

*Wilson:* Coleridge certainly did not mean that.

*Tate:* He did not mean didactic truth at all.

*Cairns:* He meant what he termed philosophical truth. Under the influence of the contemporary German philosophers he tried hard to work out a complete philosophical system of his own. The *Biographia Literaria* was his most ambitious attempt in that direction.

*Tate:* He thought of poetic truth as equal in validity with philosophical truth, and Wordsworth was interested in philosophical truth. He got it confused with the imagination.

*Van Doren:* Coleridge's conception is actually very complicated and difficult, and it is almost impossible to transmit it. You can absorb it into your understanding, but you cannot quote it, you cannot wrap it up in a package and take it away. You cannot even apply it.

*Tate:* Don't you think that perhaps the confusion lies in his failure to distinguish very clearly between his idea of poetic "pleasure"—that is, poetry must give us pleasure—and metaphysical truth? He also says that poetry gives us truth. Now is pleasure truth? Obviously it is not all the time, and I don't think he ever quite gets out of that contradiction. He gets muddled up in it.

*Cairns:* In a philosophical system, pleasure might be the test of truth. But Coleridge never made that point clear, if, indeed, he ever entertained the notion.

*Van Doren:* Coleridge is fascinated by opposites. He loves to list the opposites which must co-exist in a great mind.

*Tate:* It interests me to speculate on why Coleridge was so incomplete. Mr. Wilson, what do you think about that? He rambles, he starts a discussion, does not finish it.

*Wilson:* Of course, his character was in a sad state of decay by the time he wrote the *Biographia Literaria,* and his demoralization is reflected in the worst way in this book. It is not too strong to say that it is the product of a diseased mind, and in order to read it at all you have to get over a good deal of irritation and even disgust with Coleridge.

*Cairns:* I think the question can be answered also specifically in the case of the fancy and the imagination, an idea which he took again from Schelling, and when Schelling ran out of ideas on that particular subject, Coleridge ran out too and just stopped discussing it. He says in his book that he gave up any further analysis on the advice of a friend, but I think he would have stopped anyway.

*Van Doren:* What about this diseased mind, Mr. Wilson? Are you referring to his disease of doubt and hesitation?

*Cairns:* Or are you thinking of opium?

*Wilson:* His whole situation was certainly very neurotic. He was full of opium. He was subject to horrible fits of gloom and inability to make up his mind to do anything.

*Cairns:* Do you think that that influenced his prose writing very much?

*Wilson:* Yes, I think it influenced it deeply. The book is so incoherent.

*Cairns:* It has been said of him, of course, that he never wrote a book, including this one.

*Wilson:* I think that is perfectly true.

*Cairns:* That he was an author absolutely incapable of writing a book.

*Wilson:* He said that from the moment anything presented itself to him in the line of a duty, he found himself unable to do it.

*Van Doren:* He was almost incapable of finishing anything, of doing anything rightly and completely, and, of course, he was tormented by this himself. He recognized the fault. Even in conversation he could never somehow end his thought. He was always getting in deeper and deeper.

*Cairns:* He had one interesting characteristic, however, which has often been observed. He was stimulated by Wordsworth, and

I think he did better than Wordsworth. He was stimulated by Schlegel and he did better than Schlegel, and he was stimulated by Schelling and did better than Schelling.

*Van Doren:* But he was also a man who stimulated other men. He surely was a great stimulant for Wordsworth. The theory is advanced by Mr. Garrod of Oxford that Wordsworth's great period as a poet, which lasted only ten years, coincides exactly with the ten years in which Wordsworth and Coleridge were close friends. Once their friendship broke down, Wordsworth began to be the impossible poet he was in his old age.

*Wilson:* That is probably true.

*Tate:* Is it possible that Coleridge's failure to finish anything is one thing that has made him interesting to writers of our time? I think of Paul Valéry, the French poet, who is always complaining of the great difficulties of writing. He is worried about the possibility of finishing anything, and he even dramatizes it publicly. He is always writing about it.

*Wilson:* T. S. Eliot, when he was here, ended a lecture by saying, "Farewell! The sad ghost of Coleridge beckons me from the shades."

*Van Doren:* Of course, it is not a merit not to be able to finish anything, is it? Are we suggesting that there might be something glorious about the incapacity?

*Cairns:* He had a positive quality that excited the young men of his time, and apparently it reached on into later years, because Walter Pater, in his piece on Coleridge, said that he himself felt that the greatest thing in Coleridge was the excitement of the literary sense he was able to communicate.

*Wilson:* Plainly that is what is in his prose writing that really makes it great and valuable.

*Cairns:* Do you find that, yourself?

*Wilson:* Yes.

*Van Doren:* I find this book exciting, don't you, Mr. Wilson?

*Wilson:* Very.

*Van Doren:* The excitement mounts as you read.

*Cairns:* You find the whole book exciting?

*Van Doren:* Yes. I mean as a book. Some parts are more exciting than others, but the whole is incandescent.

*Cairns:* I should like to give a sample of Coleridge's criticism, a sample of what I mean by his method and which will also illustrate what I think Pater had in mind in the phrase "excitement of the literary sense." He has a few lines on a famous poem, Wordsworth's *Daffodils.* He discusses just four lines:

*"They flash upon that inward eye*
*Which is the bliss of solitude,*
*And then my heart with pleasure fills*
*And dances with the daffodils."*

Coleridge says of those four lines: "It is a well-known fact that bright colors in motion both make and leave the strongest impressions on the eye. Nothing is more likely to than that a vivid image or visual spectrum thus originated may become the link of association in recalling the feelings and images that had accompanied the original impression. But if we describe this in such lines as the first two, 'They flash upon that inward eye Which is the bliss of solitude,' in what words shall we describe the joy of retrospection when the images and virtuous actions of a whole well-spent life pass before that conscience which is indeed the inward eye, which is indeed the bliss of solitude? Assuredly we seem to sink most abruptly, not to say burlesquely, and almost as in a medley, from this couplet to, 'And then my heart with pleasure fills And dances with the daffodils.' " I think that is a fair specimen of his criticism. I quote it not because I agree with everything that he says. I agree with his criticism of the first couplet. It just doesn't make much sense to me. I have some doubts about his criticism of the second couplet.

*Van Doren:* But you like it because it is exact.

*Cairns:* I like it because it is exact. He has discarded all his theories of poetic diction, all his theories of fancy and the imagination, and he has only one thing before him, that is, these couplets. He is a man of extraordinary taste in the history of criticism, and he is giving his reaction to it. For that reason I find it interesting.

*Van Doren:* If you take this book as a whole, you find it delivering to the reader an admirable, not to say magnificent, criticism of Wordsworth generally.

*Tate:* The defect he finds in the *Daffodils* is Wordsworth's general defect. Coleridge has a very keen eye for it. At the same time, I don't quite agree with Mr. Cairns when he says that the analysis is just an application of Coleridge's good taste. It seems to me that Coleridge's psychological bias is very much in evidence. He is looking at the poem not in the terms of the organization of the images, the metaphors; he is looking at it in terms of some psychological effect on the reader, and it seems to me that the general result of this bias through Coleridge's influence up to our time is to focus our attention upon our own personal experience and the personal experience of the poet. Hence we get off into biography and autobiography, and the poetry tends to be left behind.

*Van Doren:* Poetry, in other words, has been pretty largely personal and psychological during the past century, and I quite agree with you that Coleridge and Wordsworth, both as critics and as poets, have had a great deal to do with establishing the trend. All contemporary literature runs to psychology. Fiction does too.

*Tate:* What do you think about that, Mr. Wilson?

*Wilson:* There is another aspect of Coleridge in this book but which you find more explicitly expressed in his lectures on Shakespeare and his miscellaneous writings on literature. He had very brilliant insight into the relation of works of literature to their social and historical backgrounds.

*Cairns:* I can think of a characteristic example of that: his lecture on *Romeo and Juliet,* which was in large part a defense of school flogging.

*Wilson:* I don't know whether I ever read that.

*Van Doren:* Where was this?

*Cairns:* It was when he was called upon to deliver his lecture on *Romeo and Juliet.* I am not referring to the printed lecture which he polished. I mean the one he actually delivered.

*Tate:* Did he mean that Romeo should have been whipped?

*Cairns:* No. Coleridge was much interested in the flogging system in the schools, and he was all for it. He would take the occasion when he delivered his *Romeo and Juliet* lecture to defend the system elaborately.

*Van Doren:* Perhaps he thought Juliet should have been spanked.

*Wilson:* He also has a very interesting discussion of the difference between Greek literature and Chaucer. He shows that in the unity and structure of the Greek sentence and the Greek play, nothing is allowed prominence at the expense of anything else. With this he contrasts Chaucer's *Prologue,* which is a series of simple statements standing more or less by themselves and reflecting the more democratic kind of life back of it. The more individualistic kind of life, rather, I want to say.

*Van Doren:* One sign of his stature is, as Mr. Wilson suggested earlier this evening, that he admires the greatest poets the most. He has no doubt about Shakespeare's eminence. He has no doubt about Milton's or Chaucer's. Or Dante's. The impact of Greek poetry upon him is very great. You can always trust his judgment.

*Cairns:* You can trust his taste. One of the interesting things in the history of criticism is the rareness of that quality.

*Tate:* It seems to me that for his time he was remarkably good on the seventeenth century. In that period the critics tended to neglect the metaphysical poets, but Coleridge realized that Donne was a very fine poet and that Cowley was not. His judgment of that period is largely our judgment today.

*Wilson.* The great thing about him was that he covered such an immense amount of ground and was able always to see what was good and to grade it more or less, to see its relation to other things.

*Cairns:* How do you feel about his controversy with Wordsworth? Do you feel that he was right, or was Wordsworth right?

*Van Doren:* In his controversy over the language of poetry?

*Cairns:* Yes. Did Wordsworth follow his own theories and,

if he did, did he write great poetry when he followed them or not?

*Wilson:* No. Coleridge was nearer right about that.

*Tate:* I think he was too. He takes it up at the fundamental point. Wordsworth says that the language of ignorant people, who also happen to be rural, is the purest language of all. Through it, he thought, you got simple emotions expressed without artificiality. Coleridge is devastating on that point. He argues that the language of rural people is either a degeneration of educated language or, if pure, too restricted in range for great literature.

*Van Doren:* Coleridge there had the broader view. You can always trust him to have a broad view.

*Cairns:* Do you feel that the problem he is discussing is a real problem? Do you think there is a problem of poetic diction? It was a great question in eighteenth- and nineteenth-century criticism, but I have always doubted if the controversy on the point was concerned with anything vital.

*Van Doren:* I would put the problem of language, as he treats it and as Wordsworth treats it, along with the problem of psychology. Let us call it all the question of how poetry gets written. It is of secondary importance in criticism. The criticism of the nineteenth and twentieth centuries has been vitiated by an obsession with it. What do I mean when I say that literature is obsessed with psychology? I mean that our only question is how we think, not what we think, the inference being that it is almost impossible to think at all. Yet, by a miracle, it sometimes happens; so we should investigate how it is done.

*Wilson:* That appears particularly in the modern criticism of poetry rather than in the criticism of other branches of literature.

*Van Doren:* Decidedly.

*Tate:* I agree with what you say about that, but at the same time, I think that this minute criticism of poetic language today has a historical explanation. There is an attempt at present to find out whether poetic language differs from scientific discourse, and while I don't think that the problem can ever be solved, it seems historically necessary right now. People have got to discuss it. Because of the great prestige of science, poetry and the arts are on the defensive.

*Van Doren:* And of course the necessity for Coleridge to discuss a theory of language was historical. The pressure on him was a pressure from the eighteenth century, which had a bad theory of psychology. He substituted a theory not much better, but he was almost forced into doing so.

*Cairns:* Isn't the true argument against Wordsworth's theory of a language from real life—isn't the sound argument: What do the great poets do?

*Tate:* Yes, that is very true. The great poets have written in many different kinds of languages.

*Van Doren:* They used all the language that existed.

*Wilson:* Wordsworth has a good case against the poetic diction of his time. That was a special situation.

*Tate:* Doesn't every literary revolution tend to exaggerate the defects of the preceding generation?

*Van Doren:* And Coleridge's wisdom—for after all, in spite of his being rather absurd and long-winded and incoherent, he is somehow a wise man—comes out when he makes a remark just like yours, that a weak mind when it is reacting against error always runs into the opposite error. It never finds the truth which encloses or defines the mean between them.

*Tate:* You are not saying there, are you, Mr. Van Doren, that Wordsworth had a weak mind?

*Van Doren:* Coleridge was not referring to Wordsworth. Neither was I saying, although I might do so, that Coleridge was wise because he agreed with you.

*Tate:* I suspect irony in that compliment.

*Wilson:* Wordsworth's taste was terrible about his own poetry. He might have had that bad theory and written much better poetry. His poetry would not necessarily have to be so bad.

*Van Doren:* He seems to have had very little sense about his own.

*Cairns:* And Coleridge, of course, reacted to the other extreme against the theories of his day. He reacted against relativism in favor of an absolute position. He was seeking for an absolute position but never found it.

*Tate:* No, he never really established it. I have in mind his famous description of what the poet is and of what the poet does.

*Cairns:* He never did establish it, because I think it is impossible to establish it.

*Tate:* But don't you think that the value of absolute critical theory is its effect on practice? Even absolute theories may have a pragmatic value.

*Cairns:* I certainly would not contest the point that he had a tremendous influence.

*Tate:* Do you think the influence was for the good of poetry? That is the question. Here is his famous passage on poetry: "The poet, described in ideal perfection, brings the whole soul of man into activity, with the subordination of its faculties to each other according to their relative worth and dignity. He diffuses a tone and spirit of unity, that blends, and (as it were) *fuses,* each into each, by that synthetic and magical power, to which I would exclusively appropriate the name of Imagination. This power, first put in action by the will and understanding, and retained under their irremissive, though gentle and unnoticed, control, *laxis effertur habenis,* reveals itself in the balance or reconcilement of opposite or discordant qualities; of sameness, with difference; of the general with the concrete; the idea with the image; the individual with the representative; the sense of novelty and freshness with old and familiar objects; a more than usual state of emotion with more than usual order; judgment ever awake and steady self-possession with enthusiasm and feeling profound or vehement; and while it blends and harmonizes the natural and the artificial, still subordinates art to nature, the manner to the matter; and our admiration of the poet to our sympathy with the poetry."

*(1822-1888)*

# ARNOLD

# *Essays in Criticism*

## FIRST AND SECOND SERIES

*No critic of the nineteenth century has continued to wield a wider influence than that of Matthew Arnold. He contrasts with Coleridge as order contrasts with disorder; with him all was clarity, and there is no "poetry" in his criticism. His work as a poet was done before he took up the instrument of analysis, which he used thenceforward in the purest spirit of prose. His style, with its reiteration and its irony, restored a classic note to English criticism which it had recently lacked; and an air of cool superiority, while it infuriated opponents, helped in the long run to make his ideas prevail. Whether in essays of scope, such as* The Function of Criticism at the Present Time *and* The Study of Poetry, *or in the lesser exercises which defined the essences of single authors, Arnold was lucid and unforgettable. His respect for ideas, and for the foundation which they supply to all literary work, gave each of his* Essays in Criticism *an intellectual force which is rare at any time, but which was especially rare in Victorian England. He was a notable coiner of phrases—"high seriousness," for example, and "touchstones of poetry"—but his distinction is finally greater than that. He combined brains with sensibility, and he wrote as one who will not and cannot be contradicted.*

*Cairns:* Matthew Arnold, like Coleridge, had a great influence on the young men of his time. He influenced them in two directions. He revalued the past for them, particularly the romantic past, and he formulated a set of critical principles which appealed strongly to them. It would be interesting to know, Mr. Tate, which side of Matthew Arnold you find more valuable as you re-read him.

*Tate:* Arnold is a very complex critic; his critical statements have a deceptive simplicity. His great value today is not in his specific literary criticism so much as in his social criticism. He had a very fine perception of the relation between a writer and his society. His poetic criticism tends to be rather arbitrary, and it is very hard to follow.

*Van Doren:* Mr. Tate, your answer, I take it, more concerns Arnold's address to the contemporary situation than his evaluation of older writers.

*Tate:* He sensed a crisis in literature, and it is a crisis that we still feel. There was a new kind of social organization that was very conspicuous in his time because it was new; that is, the industrial organization. You remember, Mr. Cairns, he made the wonderful epigram (he was very good at epigrams): "Industrialism has materialized the upper class, vulgarized the middle class, and brutalized the lower class." A remark like that indicates something of the problem that he was dealing with. He felt that the great creative energies of the past were being blighted, and the result for him was indecision, a dilemma that he expressed in his magnificent poem, *The Scholar Gipsy;* it plagued him all his life.

*Cairns:* I wonder if Arnold's epigram was based upon one by Flaubert, who said that the revolution of 1789 destroyed royalty and the nobility; that of 1848 the bourgeoisie; and that of 1851 the people. Arnold led a strange kind of life for a poet and critic; and it may be that the dissatisfactions of that life are at the root of the dilemma he felt. He was the son of Thomas Arnold, the famous master of Rugby and a man of strong opinions. Matthew Arnold was an inspector of schools throughout his life and traveled a great deal on the English railroads.

*Tate:* Didn't he do a great deal of his writing on trains?

*Cairns:* So I understand.

*Van Doren:* Is that a strange life for a poet and a critic? I consider trains to be very interesting places.

*Cairns:* I should think he would want his materials around him, to be alone in a room and to have the opportunity to reflect upon what he proposed to write. Leonardo da Vinci said that if you are not alone in a room you are only half yourself.

*Van Doren:* The perfect place to write is often not the best place. Robert Frost has written some of his best lines in hotel rooms between trains.

*Cairns:* Thackeray always wrote at loose ends too—in clubs and hotels; but for a man doing scholarly writing, such conditions are unsatisfactory.

*Tate:* Don't you think that the sustained effort required for criticism can be better realized in a study?

*Van Doren:* No, I don't happen to believe that. I am more and more astonished by evidence that writing, good writing, comes about by accident. When we are best prepared to do it, when we have all the leisure in the world in which to do it, we may not have anything to say. Whereas when we are pressed to speak, we may have much. Matthew Arnold was also a lecturer, you may remember, and toured this country.

*Cairns:* Yes, he came to America, and I recall that he said America had produced only two distinguished men—George Washington and Alexander Hamilton—both of them Englishmen.

*Van Doren:* He was once present at a dinner party in Hartford, Connecticut, and was astonished because his friend William Dean Howells was spending so much time talking to a man with a shock of white hair in a corner. He asked his hostess who that fellow was and learned that it was Mark Twain. He said in his very snobbish voice, "Oh, does he go in for that sort of thing?" She replied, "Yes, he does, and let me introduce you to Mr. Clemens." He was introduced to him with the result —I think it was to his credit—that he spent not only most of that night with Mark Twain but also most of the next day. He saw the quality in Mark Twain much more clearly than any other Americans did, although he started out by being a snob about it.

*Cairns:* When you said that he was a snob, you did not mean that he was a social snob; you meant he had a high standard of excellence.

*Van Doren:* I probably should not have used the word. It is merely this: that he believed in excellence as any of us surely does, but he had a way of talking about excellence which was sometimes intolerable to his listeners. There was condescension in his voice. He seemed to say: Those of you I am addressing don't have the same feeling for excellence that I do.

*Tate:* Didn't he feel that it was his special mission to enlighten his generation in England?

*Van Doren:* Oh, he was a great man for enlightening!

*Tate:* Doesn't that lead us into some of Arnold's more serious ideas? What is the function of criticism for Arnold?

*Cairns:* He formulated three principles. He insisted upon the necessity of design, proportion and wholeness in a poem; he insisted on what he called the "grand style"; and he said that literature, or poetry (he used the terms interchangeably) was a criticism of life. One of the interesting things about Arnold is the vocabulary he used. Throughout his life he kept repeating the phrases that he coined, phrases even from his very first critical piece—the fine preface that he wrote to the 1853 edition of his poems.

*Tate:* Mr. Cairns, don't you think that one of the main functions of criticism for Arnold—he repeats it in one of his set phrases—is to release into society a current of true and fresh ideas?

*Cairns:* He always insisted that criticism must discover the ideas upon which creative literature must rest.

*Tate:* And that no writer can function without a background like that.

*Van Doren:* He probably uses the phrase twenty times in his famous essay, *The Function of Criticism at the Present Time.* G. K. Chesterton had an amusing way of describing the effect of Arnold's repetitions. He said he talked like the patient teacher in an idiot school. It seemed to him quite incredible that we should understand anything upon his saying it once. He has to say it twenty times.

*Tate:* I believe that that is very effective at times.

*Cairns:* When he repeats a phrase, doesn't he repeat it in a slightly different situation to throw a little more light on it? In many respects Arnold is a beautiful dialectician. He manipulates his arguments so that there is constant new light being thrown upon them.

*Van Doren:* Perhaps you misunderstood me. Chesterton was admiring Arnold.

*Cairns:* He was a great admirer of Arnold.

*Van Doren:* He was admiring his rhetorical art. For all my own admiration, I cannot help sometimes being amused by him. There is something about this really great critic which is also preposterous.

*Cairns:* I think that it takes a special effort today to understand Arnold, because his vocabulary, such as "culture," "criticism of life," the phrases "sweetness and light," "to know the best that has been thought and known in the world," "the business of poetry is to ennoble us in our living," sound today when we read them as if they had been written by the late Dr. Frank Crane or Elbert Hubbard.

*Tate:* Isn't that, Mr. Cairns, because the phrases of great writers are eventually debased? Some of Arnold's ideas got vaguely into Elbert Hubbard. We think of them in terms of the people who debase them.

*Cairns:* That well may be. Nevertheless, it requires an effort to understand them, but one which I think is worthwhile. Those phrases may embody something of value.

*Van Doren:* Of course, his influence on a higher level has been pervasive and constant. For instance, his essay *The Function of Criticism at the Present Time* goes so far in praise of the importance of criticism as to say that perhaps it would be a better thing now, that is to say, then, for all writers to pause in their attempts at creative work and become critics. We need criticism at the moment, he says, so that we can be creators later on. He is quite pessimistic too. He does not expect to see a great period of creative activity again in England while he lives.

*Tate:* It seems to me that the influence of that point of view in Arnold has been very bad, particularly in academic circles. Matthew Arnold fixed all the poets in a final hierarchy for professors of English everywhere. They take Arnold as the ultimate authority, and they don't have to judge the poets for themselves.

*Cairns:* But don't you think that Arnold's point, which Mr. Van Doren has just summarized, has an element of truth?

*Tate:* No, I don't think so, Mr. Cairns, or at least I can doubt it to this extent: an age cannot deliberately set about criticism and decide to resume creative activity ten years hence.

*Van Doren:* Arnold is a wonderful writer and often deceives us into agreeing with him. He puts our minds to sleep. For instance, he tells us that the reason Shakespeare was so great a creative artist was that in his time there flowed a current of new and fresh and true ideas. He does not offer us any evidence that this was the case. We remain free to suppose that the reason that Shakespeare was good may have been that he was good. He also says of Goethe that Goethe could have been better than he was if a current of true and fresh ideas had been moving in

Germany. I am not sure that the connection between ideas and creation is what he says it is, or is as simple as he says it is.

*Cairns:* Let me give you an example. I assume the phrase "current of fresh ideas," or "the application of ideas to life," is what he means by his other phrase, "poetry is a criticism of life," that that is the real meaning of that famous remark.

*Tate:* It is difficult to understand, though.

*Cairns:* I know it is difficult, but we shall come back to that. Let me speak of an unrelated field. Maitland, perhaps the greatest of legal historians, referred to the toughness of a taught tradition. I am sure that the legal system as we know it could not exist today without the constant criticism of a trained professional class. If you abolish that trained class, the legal system as we know it would disappear. It may be true that just as our legal system is sustained by professional criticism, so literature is sustained by similar criticism.

*Tate:* To go back to the point about Shakespeare: there was no doubt a current of true and fresh ideas, but the significant point about ideas in Shakespeare's time was that the critics had not supplied them. There were not any critics in Arnold's sense. The sixteenth-century critics tended to be quite pedantic; they were not aware of their background as something to be "used" by poets.

*Cairns:* Yes, I do not care who supplies the current of fresh ideas so long as they are supplied and there is a standard of excellence for the writer.

*Van Doren:* There was no standard of excellence for Shakespeare. Shakespeare created his standard, if you like.

*Cairns:* He certainly did. He was also in competition with other playwrights and he saw how bad they were. They gave him a standard of what to avoid.

*Van Doren:* It seems to me that Arnold's conception of the function of criticism is misleading. His claims are too great for it.

*Cairns:* I think that comes out in his suggestion that at a given time literature can pause and be critical, so that later on it can be creative. I am sure that creation does not follow criticism in that sense.

*Tate:* There is a sense, however, in which criticism helps to clarify certain specific problems for any imaginative writer; for example, it can clarify his position with reference to his predecessors.

*Van Doren:* Oh, surely.

*Tate:* But Arnold's general criticism, the criticism of literature in relation to society, which was his strong point, is not very fruitful for the writer, but is often illuminating for the general public.

*Van Doren:* He was right, certainly, in saying that the most perfect literary situation would be one in which true and fresh ideas were immediately and simply available to all persons with or without the benefit of criticism; but he seemed to say that lacking such felicity, any particular generation could by mere intellectual effort and critical will produce the equivalent of these ideas. I don't think it can be done.

*Tate:* I don't think so either. But don't you think that Arnold tends to contradict himself? I imagine if he were alive today he would confess it. He says that he never expected to see a great period of creative literature in England. At the same time, he begins his famous essay, *The Study of Poetry,* by saying that the future of poetry is immense, that we are going to rely more and more on poetry because religion is failing us. We shall have to get from poetry what we formerly got from religion. He claims a great deal for criticism at one moment and a great deal for poetry at the next. And he is never quite clear about it.

*Cairns:* I think the terrible thought occurred to him that somebody might try to put Herbert Spencer's *Principles of Sociology* into verse. He was worried about the conflict between poetry and science, and he tried to resolve it so that poetry had a future as well as science.

*Van Doren:* Mr. Tate, I think you have touched upon a very important side of Arnold when you observed that he expected poetry somehow to do the work of religion, that poetry was going to take the place of religion, whose potency had been lost. In reading the critical essays of Arnold, I was especially impressed by his tone. He always takes us back, I think, to a notion of a particular responsibility which poetry now has. That is why I think he expects too much from poetry.

*Cairns:* He was influenced by the Greeks in that respect. He wanted noble actions and noble thoughts, which he, I have no doubt, thought of, when expressed in poetry, as a substitute for religion.

*Tate:* In the essay that serves as a preface to the 1853 edition to his poems, he says poetry must have a noble action; that action in the Aristotelian sense is the basis of poetry. And he says it does not make any difference in what period of history the poet gets the action. He is confessing really that nineteenth-century civilization does not afford any great actions, and he advises the young poets to go back and study the Greeks and use their subjects if possible.

*Cairns:* He said so specifically, and he took as examples some well-known poets of the nineteenth century and compared them, to their great disadvantage, to the Greeks.

*Tate:* Think of his point about Keats' *Isabella.* He says that it contains more brilliant lines than all the extant tragedies of Sophocles, but that a tragedy of Sophocles is a considerably greater poem. The modern poet, in other words, can write lines but lacks a real subject. Doesn't the lack of a poetic subject today have some connection with Arnold's excessive demands on criticism? Doesn't he expect criticism to perform for the writer the function that religion once performed in giving him a powerful motivation? Criticism will tell the poet where to get his subjects.

*Cairns:* That is the point I made a few minutes ago: that he thought of poetry and criticism as a substitute for religion. It was a notion he developed from his study of the Greeks. Another idea he found in the Greeks was sanity. That was a point he made in the 1853 preface. By sanity, I take it, he meant disinterestedness. He thought criticism should be completely disinterested. I don't know whether that is possible.

*Van Doren:* He was always asking Victorian England to do by an exercise of the will what Greece had done easily and without an exercise of the will. If the Greeks were noble, they were not noble because someone was telling them to be noble all the time. Their notion of themselves seems actually to have been that they were a very disorderly, passionate lot of men.

*Cairns:* Arnold, of course, limited himself in his study of the Greeks, so far as one can tell from reading his essays, to two or three—Homer, Sophocles and, perhaps, Theocritus.

*Tate:* But in his poem *Empedocles on Aetna,* which he significantly suppressed because the subject was "passive suffering," not action, he was dealing with a late Greek, a man, he says, who had some of the same problems that a nineteenth-century European would have, that is, a man who was afflicted by doubt, hesitation and divided aims. But he suppressed the poem because in his view it had no action. It is interesting that the late W. B. Yeats revived that view of poetry. He said that passive suffering was not a subject for poetry. Don't you think that interest in passive suffering, or this feeling for man as a creature who is at the mercy of the external world, explains Arnold's interesting remark about the weakness of modern poets? It applies to modern poets today: we are interested in the detached line, even the phrase. Arnold sums up by saying that we require nothing else of the modern poet if he satisfies "our rhetorical sense and our curiosity."

*Cairns:* He thought the Greeks had a sense of wholeness and the nineteenth century had a sense of detail. I think he performed a useful service in taking us back from the beauty of detail to the beauty of the whole. You will recall that he tells the famous anecdote about the Greek comic playwright Menander, to illustrate the Greek artist's interest in his art as a unit. Menander was asked how his new comedy was progressing. He replied that he had finished it although he had not started to write it.

*Van Doren:* Arnold performed many valuable services, although in his famous prescription for discovering whether a poem is good or not, in his essay called *The Study of Poetry,* he goes in to an astonishing extent for detail. He seems to say that you can decide whether a poem is great or not if it has one great line in it.

*Tate:* That is a very curious contradiction, isn't it? Arnold believes in the value of structure in poetry, and he even uses Goethe's word, "architectonic." Yet he represents Dante with one line.

*Cairns:* But it is interesting that his selections show on the whole a very fine taste.

*Van Doren:* I hate to be picking at Matthew Arnold, whom I do admire, but I should say that his taste was incomplete. All these examples, all these touchstones, are, for one thing, serious. Arnold seems to be blind and deaf to the quality of wit in poetry, which is a quality that I personally consider necessary to greatness. He wants poems to be, on the whole, melancholy, sad, sonorous—"religious," in other words. Poetry to him must have almost a liturgical value.

*Cairns:* We come, I think, directly from that point into his conception of the grand style, which he defined in terms that you have used.

*Van Doren:* He wants an organ playing.

*Cairns:* He said that the grand style, or the "great style," which is perhaps a better term . . .

*Van Doren:* I think "great style" is a better term.

*Cairns:* I prefer it, myself. He said that the great style arises in poetry when a noble nature, poetically gifted, treats with simplicity or severity a serious subject.

*Tate:* At the same time, he did not feel that Shakespeare had the great style.

*Cairns:* No, he had Homer in front of him when he devised his definition, and he thought he had Dante. Whether he really appreciated Dante or not I do not know.

*Tate:* I think he was dead wrong about Dante because Dante has every kind of style.

*Van Doren:* Well, so does Homer for that matter. One of the glories of Homer is that he knows how to be simple, rapid and natural. The little words in Homer are some of the most important words.

*Cairns:* The little words are important, and his definition does not admit the little. However, I think you can take his definition of the grand style and generalize it so as to include Homer and Dante and Milton. He also undoubtedly had Milton in front of him.

*Tate:* Don't you think that when he attributes the great style to Dante he means the lofty intention of the whole poem? Its subject is the most sublime in Christendom. But the quality of the style, line by line, and as the scenes change, is not Arnold's great style at all.

*Van Doren:* If the subject of Dante is great, and surely it is, one sign of its greatness is that it is various. It is as various as the world. All sorts of things come into it and are treated by Dante.

*Tate:* I have always had a strong suspicion that Arnold preferred Milton to Shakespeare, and I believe we could find evidence to prove it.

*Van Doren:* In his essay on Milton, he really seems to say that. He is present at the unveiling of a memorial to Milton's second wife. He says substantially that Milton is the only English poet who has a great style, who has continually a great style.

*Tate:* He gives his case away when he says that the genius of Shakespeare cannot be imitated, or if we do try to imitate Shakespeare we do it at the risk of disaster. But you can imitate Milton because you can imitate the great style.

*Cairns:* I think he is partly right when he says that. His real point was that the young writer should not set out to imitate Shakespeare. He should not have Shakespeare before him as a model.

*Tate:* Well, is Milton any better? Are we to prefer a poet because he gives us something to imitate?

*Cairns:* I feel that Shakespeare is so far above Milton that it is just impossible for anybody to attempt to imitate him successfully.

*Van Doren:* The curious thing about imitating Shakespeare is that there is nothing to imitate. That is to say, Shakespeare has no style. Or rather, he has a thousand styles.

*Cairns:* Shakespeare has the grand style at its best, for he has every conceivable style.

*Van Doren:* Yes, an enormous flexibility.

*Cairns:* He has every style in perfection.

*Tate:* Shakespeare can say anything he wants to say, which Milton could not do and which Matthew Arnold could not do.

*Van Doren:* Homer could say anything he wanted to say.

*Tate:* So could Dante.

*Cairns:* Do you think Homer has lines equivalent to "I am dying, Egypt, dying" or "The rest is silence"?

*Tate:* Well, not precisely equivalent to those lines because he did not present situations like the death scenes of Antony and Hamlet.

*Cairns:* I think they are examples of the grand style in spite of their apparent simplicity.

*Tate:* Wouldn't Arnold call them the pathetic style? They move us but are they elevating?

*Cairns:* He probably would have. Nevertheless, a sound theory of the grand style would, I think, cover them.

*Van Doren:* Arnold is one of the most intelligent men who ever lived, and one of the best rhetoricians, and he reminded us of greatness. The criticism of his time like the criticism of any time tends to grow trivial, to forget greatness. The only trouble is that he always spoke about it with a capital G.

*Tate:* And he has his hierarchy of poets; he is bent upon arranging them all in their right places.

*Cairns:* That is a defect. He very much underestimates Chaucer, for example.

*Van Doren:* Because Chaucer is funny, and Arnold was worried; Arnold was not secure enough in his critical principles to know how to take care of irresponsible gaiety and good humor.

*Cairns:* That is right. He said that Chaucer lacked the high seriousness.

*Tate:* Isn't it curious that Arnold as a religious man neglected the great religious poets of the seventeenth century? He says nothing about them.

*Van Doren:* For instance?

*Tate:* He says nothing of Donne. He could not have liked Donne.

*Van Doren:* Donne was not so well known in his time.

*Tate:* No, but there were also Herbert, Vaughn, Crashaw, Marvel. I think he tends to neglect them because they are witty and ironic. Can you imagine Arnold liking "A Hymn to God the Father," in which Donne puns on his own name?

*Van Doren:* You have brought us within reach of a defect in Arnold there. A religious poet for him is Wordsworth, whose religion, of course, is a substitute for the real thing. It is one of the social religions which infested the nineteenth century.

*Cairns:* Would you today rank Wordsworth as he ranks him? That is, as one of the three great poets—Milton, Shakespeare and Wordsworth.

*Van Doren:* I might. I rank Wordsworth very highly. But I rank him for reasons that Arnold never recognizes. Arnold, for instance, does not seem to have had the ear to recognize the beauty of the beginning of *Resolution and Independence.*

*Cairns:* Yes, his musical ear was defective.

*Van Doren:* Something was curiously lacking there, in spite of the fact that his verse often has fine music in it.

*Cairns:* Would you put Chaucer above Wordsworth?

*Tate:* I would.

*Van Doren:* Oh, I probably should too. But I don't know, I never can rank poets.

*Cairns:* A great poet should be treated as unique.

*Van Doren:* We have said a good many times this evening

that Arnold valued poetry as a substitute for religion. His whole generation was seeking substitutes for religion—in society more than in anything else. This is his classical statement of the position: "The future of poetry is immense because in poetry where it is worthy of its high destinies our race as time goes on will find an ever sure and surer stay. There is not a creed which is not shaken, not an accredited dogma which is not shown to be questionable, not a received tradition which does not threaten to dissolve. Our religion has materialized itself in the fact, in the supposed fact. It has attached its emotion to the fact and now the fact is failing it, but for poetry the idea is everything; the rest is a world of illusion, of divine illusion. Poetry attaches its emotion to the idea; the idea is the fact. The strongest part of our religion today is its unconscious poetry."

# POETRY AND PHILOSOPHY

(c. 98-55 B.C.)

# LUCRETIUS

## On the Nature of Things

*LUCRETIUS wrote a long poem* ON THE NATURE OF THINGS *in order to free men of their fears. What men most fear is the unknown will of those who rule the universe, the apparently capricious actions of the gods. His message in brief is that there are no gods; or if they exist, they give no thought to man on his little earth. The universe is not ruled; chance operates everywhere, and the only law is that of alternative growth and decay. But this is an impersonal law, and the advice of Lucretius was that we learn to accept it. An Epicurean by training, he longed to relieve mankind of the suffering which is caused by the disappointment of impossible desires. The death of desire, particularly for a future life, will bring the only peace available to our minds. Lucretius thunders against superstition and argues against religion; and to support his contention writes a treatise on physics. There is such a thing as matter, and it is uniform everywhere; it is composed of atoms which are alike but which chance assembles in a variety of forms. These forms will in turn be broken up and succeeded by others. And there is nothing for a man to do but recognize the process, even though it covers his case too. The best armor against death is freedom from its fears. The wise man is he who wants nothing that he cannot have. So Lucretius insists in the noblest expression which materialism has ever been given. His poem is standard for its theme; and incidentally it is an imperishable disproof of the theory that poetry cannot afford to be didactic.*

*Cairns:* As you gentlemen are aware, very little is known about Lucretius. I would like to read the one sentence which has survived from antiquity that describes his life. It is from St. Jerome and it is as follows: "Titus Lucretius, the poet, was born (that is, in 95 B.C.). Later he was driven mad by a love-philtre, after he had written several books in the intervals of insanity; Cicero subsequently corrected these books. Lucretius died by his own hand in the forty-fourth year of his life." That is the only thing recorded of Lucretius, who, of course, was an Epicurean and who seemed in his career to have followed the injunction of Epicurus: "Hide thyself and pass through life unknown." I have no regret that we don't know more about Lucretius. I am content to take everything that we know about him from his poem.

*Van Doren:* I agree with you. We know nothing about Homer whatever. We have not even an apocryphal sentence concerning him.

*Cairns:* We are not even certain that he ever lived.

*Van Doren:* We may assume that this biographical sentence which you have read is prejudiced, because a Father of the church would have less use for Lucretius than for any ancient writer.

*Cairns:* I believe every statement that St. Jerome makes has been disputed by Lucretian scholars.

*Van Doren:* In our next discussion we shall find Dante, for instance, putting Lucretius in his hell.

*Tate:* Mr. Van Doren, do you wholly regret this apocryphal version of Lucretius' life? There is a very fine poem by Tennyson about Lucretius which is based upon this legend.

*Van Doren:* I do not regret the existence of the legend. All legends are very interesting. I simply agreed with Mr. Cairns that it is not regrettable that no full-length biography is available.

*Tate:* I certainly agree with you. It seems to me that biography almost never explains good poetry.

*Cairns:* You would not take the position that the fact that Shakespeare left his second best bed to Ann Hathaway helps you in your interpretation of Hamlet?

*Van Doren:* Not at all.

*Cairns:* From the poem, however, the commentators have concluded certain things about Lucretius. I think we can determine that his main objective was truth. In this pursuit he was helped by a good mind. I think he was poetically sensitive; he was aware of the beauty of nature. I think also that we might say his outlook was unusual. I base that on his attack upon love and also upon the pessimism with which he awaits the coming destruction of the world.

*Van Doren:* Pessimism, do you say? Why shouldn't we call it optimism? He is ready to accept the end of the world.

*Tate:* He is ready to accept it because the end of the world will be merely a re-combination of the atoms in other shapes, and although we shall not be there to see those re-combinations, it will not make any difference because at present we are merely combinations of atoms.

*Van Doren:* His whole poem argues against the judgment that any given thing which is going to happen to us is either good or bad.

*Cairns:* Perhaps I should have said, "the melancholy pleasure that he took in the coming disappearance of the world."

*Tate:* Do you think that the melancholy pleasure that he felt in the coming, universal catastrophe, was wholly an expression of his temperament or do you think it was an extension of the Epicurean philosophy? His Epicurean philosophy is unusually interesting. An understanding of Lucretius would clear up many popular misconceptions about it.

*Van Doren:* The word "epicurean" is inverted in popular use. The epicurean is popularly supposed to be a person who is gluttonous for pleasure, whereas we find here a man who, to be sure, considers that pleasure is the only positive good we can have, but who is interested in pleasure in an extremely chaste way.

*Tate:* A very refined, ascetic sort of pleasure. It is pleasure, isn't it, Mr. Van Doren, only in the sense . . .

*Van Doren:* It is an absence of pain.

*Tate:* Yes, it is an absence of pain, not positive pleasure. All our knowledge, according to Epicurus, consists of sense perception. That is the whole extent of our knowledge.

*Van Doren:* The epicurean lives, according to his lights, the most reasonable life possible, the life that makes the fewest demands upon fortune.

*Cairns:* Mr. Tate has put his finger on the essential point in Lucretius' philosophy: the whole philosophy stems from one main principle. The whole philosophy that Lucretius expresses flows from the notion that sensation—and not reason—is the basis of knowledge.

*Tate:* The kind of knowledge that we arrive at through sensation is knowledge according to nature, and Epicurus held that men should live according to nature. They could not do that until they knew what nature was, and to know that is Lucretius' purpose here, isn't it?

*Van Doren:* That is where Epicurus himself comes in, because it was his philosophy of nature, or his science if you like, which Lucretius began with.

*Cairns:* And Epicurus, of course, had derived it in the main from Democritus.

*Tate:* I cannot think that Epicurus' scientific interest was very serious.

*Cairns:* Epicurus' interest was not primarily scientific. But Democritus, from whom he borrowed his ideas, was a serious scientist; Lucretius' main interest seems to have been to combat superstition and fear of death.

*Tate:* What I meant by my statement, Mr. Cairns, was rather this: Was Lucretius' interest primarily scientific, or was he trying to get at the "nature of things" chiefly in order to tell men how to live? Was it the nature of the world or was it a moral philosophy that he was chiefly interested in?

*Cairns:* It was both. He wanted to know: What is the stuff of the universe? What is the universe made of? He found one theory—the atomic theory—which depended upon sensation and which answered all the contradictions that were apparent in the other physical theories of his time. But from the sensational doctrine, upon which the atomic theory was based, and from the atomic theory itself, he also deduced his doctrine of pleasure which purported to teach men how to live.

*Van Doren:* But I gathered from Mr. Tate's question that your answer might mean this: that the science of Epicurus and Lucretius was necessary to their faith; that is to say, they needed to believe that the world was what they said it was.

*Cairns:* That is more true of Epicurus than of Lucretius. And not at all true of Democritus.

*Tate:* I was really driving at this point: Isn't there a dogmatic element in this scientific materialism?

*Van Doren:* Yes, just as there is in materialism today.

*Tate:* Didn't Lucretius fail in scientific interest to the extent that he was not concerned with the actual cause of a given event? In the notion of causality he followed his master, didn't he, in assuming that it was sufficient to find a number of possible causes?

*Cairns:* Lucretius abandoned the idea of first causes.

*Tate:* You spoke of his theory of sense perception. There are some very fascinating deductions that he draws about the size and distance of the sun.

*Cairns:* That follows strictly from his premise. The logic of his poem should not be minimized. He starts with the premise that we only know things through sensation. Now, what is it we know? We know, for example, that the sun and the moon are just as large as they seem.

*Tate:* And isn't there another very interesting proof, from Lucretius' point of view, of the distance of the sun? We know that the sun is only a short distance away by the amount of heat we receive from it. If we stand at a certain distance from a fire and receive a certain amount of heat, and if we find that that is the same amount of heat we receive from the sun, it follows that the sun is only as far away as that fire is.

*Cairns:* I do not see how he is open to attack if you admit his premise and give him the instruments that were available at that time.

*Tate:* It is perfectly logical.

*Cairns:* My last statement needs a little qualification because the Greek physicist did not take advantage of all the instruments available at the time. The Greek physicist studied only the part of the universe which a gentleman should study. He did not go into the arts of the mechanic. The working of iron and bronze was quite advanced, and the Greek physicist could have learned something if he had looked at what was actually done with bronze and iron; but it was beneath the standing of a gentleman to do that.

*Van Doren:* But Lucretius has no laboratory, and I myself do not see what follows from a doctrine that our knowledge consists of sensations, except that we have knowledge of sensations. What else can I have knowledge of, according to any materialist?

*Cairns:* The matter should be looked at historically. Before Epicurus, Parmenides had rejected the senses. He said the senses misled us, and he gave examples of optical illusions which Lucretius discusses. Democritus followed and rejected reason (which had been accepted by Parmenides) because reason depended upon the senses. He was followed in turn by Epicurus who went back to sensation as the true basis.

*Van Doren:* But could you answer my question? What do we know besides sensations if our knowledge comes from sensations? What knowledge do we have of anything of which the sensations are sensations? What knowledge do we have of the sun, or of objects?

*Cairns:* Are you arguing for a sensational materialism?

*Van Doren:* No. I am wondering what knowledge there is for Lucretius besides his sensations.

*Cairns:* There is mathematical knowledge.

*Van Doren:* Is that a matter of sensation?

*Cairns:* Apparently not. Bertrand Russell has defined mathematics as the subject in which we never know what we are talking about or whether what we are saying is true. This seems to me to divorce mathematics entirely from sensation.

*Van Doren:* Lucretius is unable to convince me, however much I love his poem, that he has knowledge or that I must believe what he says.

*Cairns:* That, of course, is the difficulty with materialism ever since it was first formulated. It cannot explain either consciousness or life. But then neither can any other philosophy.

*Van Doren:* No, because here is Lucretius going to great lengths to establish that everything is material, including the mind. Well, once he has established, if he has established it, that the mind is matter, then he cannot even address a sentence of exhortation to us with the expectation that we shall understand him or change our minds.

*Tate:* If you accept complete determinism, how do we know what we ought to do? How can Lucretius tell us? He has shown us that we have a complete material determinism which ends in death. Then having reached that point, he tells us that we should not regret death. How can he say *should,* how can he use a moral "ought" there?

*Van Doren:* How can you say *should* or *must?*

*Cairns:* That is correct. The problem that Lucretius poses is: Is man exempt from the chain of causation that he has described in the physical world? Is man, of all the objects in the universe, the only one that is exempt?

*Van Doren:* He does not seem to say that, does he?

*Cairns:* I think that is what Lucretius is trying to say. I don't agree with you when you say that he is a determinist so far as man is concerned. I think that Lucretius believes in free will for man.

*Tate:* Let's hear your point on that, Mr. Cairns. I don't follow you.

*Van Doren:* And while you are at it, Mr. Cairns, you might take care of Spinoza too, because both of those men, like Bertrand Russell in our own century—Russell was copying Lucretius in his famous essay called "The Free Man's Worship"—write books asking us to believe a certain way after they have demonstrated that it is impossible for one to believe in any other way than that way in which one has been determined.

*Tate:* In taking Spinoza, you have a different kind of determinism. It is not based on sense perception. It is an intellectual determinism: all the world is so rigorously determined intellectually that will and purpose are really irrational in it.

*Van Doren:* But the order of all things and the order of all thoughts are determined for Spinoza. Therefore, he has no more right than Lucretius or Bertrand Russell to ask us to think this or that.

*Tate:* The great question that it seems to me the determinist fails to answer is this: If our knowledge is completely determined and our experience is determined, with what do we know that determinism? How are we free to know it?

*Cairns:* I don't want to argue the theory of determinism. All I want to do is to show you why I think Lucretius believed in free will.

*Van Doren:* Mr. Cairns, you say you are going to show us from a passage in Lucretius that he believed in free will. What I want to know, and what I think Mr. Tate wants to know, is whether he has a right to believe in free will. Of course he believes in it; otherwise he would not be writing this passionate poem.

*Cairns:* It seems to me you are now shifting your ground.

*Tate:* Before you begin, Mr. Cairns—because I know you have an argument that will be hard to meet—I want to make this point . . .

*Cairns:* Don't you think you ought to save it for rebuttal, Mr. Tate?

*Tate:* No, because I want to see if I can sidetrack you first.

*Van Doren:* Yes, we are trying to prevent this point from being made.

*Cairns:* Well, I warn you that I am going to read this passage, whatever you say.

*Van Doren:* Perhaps we had better let him read it.

*Cairns:* Lucretius and Epicurus appreciated the points you are making. Lucretius said that there is no need of telling a man what to do unless he is free to do it, and Epicurus, of course, constructed an ethic which told men what to do. Lucretius had to work out in his atomic theory and his sensational theory a basis for free will. Otherwise, he would be in the dilemma that you gentlemen have presented. He therefore introduced into the movements of the atom what is known as the swerve. That is, the atoms moved unpredictably.

*Tate:* They moved in a straight line.

*Cairns:* Not altogether. They also at various times jumped out of line.

*Van Doren:* And why, Mr. Cairns?

*Cairns:* Just give me a moment. In the physical world they jumped because of chance—that is what Lucretius says. It may not be entirely satisfying, but it flows from his premise; more strictly, perhaps, his system requires it. The atoms jumped by chance in the physical world.

*Tate:* What other world is there for Lucretius than the physical world?

*Cairns:* Lucretius was also concerned with the world of human beings, and he was concerned expressly with free will.

*Van Doren:* Are you sure—I think it is important to ask this question—there is any other world than the physical world for him?

*Cairns:* The entire world is made up, in Lucretius' mind, of atoms, space and motion.

*Van Doren:* And nothing else whatever.

*Cairns:* Nothing else whatever except the gods who inhabit the interstellar spaces, and they are composed of peculiar atoms.

*Tate:* Mr. Cairns, isn't it true that in Lucretius' theory some atoms swerved off their straight course and then got mixed up and tied into knots and some of these knots were human beings?

*Cairns:* That is correct. A similar process occurred with respect to the universe itself, and this aspect of Lucretius' theory later suggested the nebular hypothesis to Immanuel Kant.

*Van Doren:* But I should like to know something. You say this swerve, for Epicurus and for Lucretius, is something that comes about through chance. The atoms do not decide to swerve. They were not free to swerve.

*Cairns:* I am talking about the world of matter outside the matter embraced in living creatures. The element of chance refers to the world of inorganic matter. Now what does Lucretius do with the world of living matter? This is what he says: "Whence, I ask, is it wrested from fate, this power whereby we move forward, where our will leads each one of us, and swerve likewise in our motions neither at determined times nor in a determined direction of place, but just where our mind has carried us? For without doubt it is his own will which gives to each one a start for this movement, and from the will the motions pass flooding through the limbs. Do you not see too how, when the barriers are flung open, yet for an instant of time the eager might of the horses cannot burst out so suddenly as their mind itself desires? For the whole store of matter throughout the whole body must be roused to movement, that then aroused through every limb it may be linked together and follow the eager longing of the mind; so that you see a start of movement is brought to pass from the heart, and comes forth first of all from the will of the mind, and then afterwards is spread through all the body and limbs." I am prepared to admit that this paragraph is controversial; but he seems to say that the atoms which inhabit the human being become in some way conscious, as distinguished from chance, and through that consciousness we have freedom of the will.

*Van Doren:* But once he does that, he puts himself in competition with another race of poets and another race of thinkers altogether than the one to which he belongs. That is to say, he releases us as readers into the great world of speculation where Plato and Aristotle and Dante and Shakespeare live. And compared with them, he has relatively little to say. It seems to me he has nothing to say if he abandons the very straight and narrow path of his materialism—where he has a good deal to say.

*Cairns:* That may be. All I am concerned to show is that materialism in his hands provides for free will.

*Tate:* It seems to me that in the very structure of the poem he implicitly abandons that materialistic basis. For example, the entire poem—the whole atomic theory, the atomic picture of the universe—is developed in a series of analogies. For example, in order to give us the picture of the way in which the atoms, which are below perception, may be behaving, he shows us a sunbeam coming into a dark room and the motes whirling and turning in that sunbeam. Now, as a matter of fact, is his theory based upon sense perception? Isn't it a logical picture which is merely presented by analogy through sense perception?

*Van Doren:* He has many such analogies.

*Tate:* It seems to me to be severely intellectualistic at bottom.

*Cairns:* It is a strictly logical system, based, I believe, on sensation.

*Tate:* Mr. Cairns, how can it be based on sensation if you cannot perceive the atoms? The whole structure of the system is atomic, and he cannot perceive them.

*Van Doren:* Mr. Cairns, how can logic be based on sensation? Sensations are not conscious of themselves—are not, surely, able to produce thought.

*Cairns:* That is correct. Lucretius did not have a scientific method in the sense that we have it today. The absence of that method causes him to fail to doubt some of his assumptions. Of course, he never saw the atoms; our modern physicists have never seen them either. To that extent his logic is faulty. He is reasoning from assumptions which have no relation to data. There is a connection, however, between the assumptions of the modern physicist and the data of the external world.

*Van Doren:* Now I wonder about our scientific method. Mr. Tate is quite right about these analogies—they are the glory of the poem.

*Tate:* They make the poem; they are developed with great cunning. So there is a tremendous amount of natural observation. He sees all nature. He is a great nature poet, as well as a so-called philosophical poet.

*Van Doren:* My point about modern scientific method is that it is substantially the same. The laboratory experiment is also an analogy. The physicist shows you that a certain thing now is happening in his laboratory. It is analogical to the truth which he claims to be proving.

*Cairns:* And he generalizes from that observation in the laboratory. The difficulty with Lucretius is that he did not go into the laboratory at all. He does in one place refer to having seen iron filings in a brass bowl under which a magnet was placed. But that is the only instance I know of in the whole poem.

*Van Doren:* And he has this elaborate psychology, this elaborate theory of sense perception, which indeed is quite fascinating. The air must be full of images that fly between the things seen and the persons seeing them.

*Tate:* To go back to the magnet picking up the iron filings, his explanation of it seems to me to be remarkably ingenious, from our point of view, but it is all wrong.

*Cairns:* On its face Lucretius' explanation of the magnet is illogical, and I cannot understand why he, with the acuteness of mind that he obviously had, made that error. You will recall that he said the magnet attracted iron filings because it exuded atoms at such a rate that a vacuum was created and therefore the iron rushed in to fill up that vacuum. Now if that were true, other matter would rush in to fill up that vacuum.

*Tate:* That is the question.

*Cairns:* I don't know why he did not see that.

*Tate:* The reason he attempted to explain the magnet was that he sets out to explain everything, so he has to explain that. This poem pretends to explain the whole nature of things.

*Van Doren:* I see here a possibility of explaining why it is that this poem is not a perfect philosophical poem. *Hamlet,* for instance, or the *Divine Comedy,* or *War and Peace* is a more perfect philosophical poem because the attempt is not made in them which you have just attributed to Lucretius—the attempt to explain literally everything. I should say that a philosophical poet can succeed only if he starts at some particular place in the universe and goes as far as he can from there.

*Cairns:* Let me ask you some questions, because I am not certain I grasp your full implications. You are not asserting that this is not a philosophical poem in the sense that it might be claimed it is the greatest poem that states a philosophy?

*Van Doren:* That is not the same thing as a philosophical poem, necessarily.

*Cairns:* One more point: Coleridge said, "Whatever in Lucretius is poetry is not philosophy and whatever is philosophical is not poetry." I cannot accept this assertion, but I would be curious to know what your position is.

*Tate:* I do not agree with it.

*Van Doren:* Lucretius, nevertheless, tends to separate them like oil and water. You remember, he begins by saying: "I am going to write a poem which is not recognizably a poem at all but a treatise on physics. It will be rather ugly and will be full of argument. Just to tease you into reading me, I will start off each section by writing pretty language. I will write poetically for a while, then I will plunge into my physics." Of course, he was ironic, but just insofar as a separation is possible of the two elements, poetry and truth, he is not a perfect philosophical poet.

*Tate:* When he is developing his analogies, the analogy contains the philosophical idea that he is setting forth. In that sense the two things are one. The great passages of poetry in this work are these wonderful natural descriptions: the thunder, the piling up of the clouds and then the flash of lightning. All that is analogy to set forth a phase of the atomic theory.

*Cairns:* That is undoubtedly the poetic side. But there is still a further question. Must poetry be what today is known as pure poetry, or can it state a philosophy; or in other words, is reason essentially unpoetic? I do not think so, myself. There have merely been bad attempts at it. There is also the moral side of the poem, which some modern critics would condemn as out of place in poetry.

*Tate:* The moral aspect of this poem will remain the most interesting thing about it. For example, it states a fundamental conflict in all men's minds. Shall we fear death or shall we be able to meet it bravely? One of the great interests of the poem lies in Lucretius' failure ever to make up his mind. Logically he had to believe that death was nothing, that it was just a re-combination of the atoms, and that it was nothing to be afraid of.

*Cairns:* He tries to prove that, as I remember, by twenty-eight arguments.

*Tate:* And this passage I am going to read to you comes right after those arguments.

*Cairns:* It weakens the arguments.

*Tate:* It is a little imaginary dialogue. " 'Now no more shall thy glad home welcome thee, nor thy good wife and sweet children run up to snatch the first kisses and touch thy heart with the silent thrill of joy. No more shalt thou have power to prosper in thy ways or to be a sure defense to thine own. Pitiful thou art, men say, and pitifully has one malignant day taken from thee all the many prizes of life.' Yet to this they add not: 'Nor does there abide with thee any longer any yearning of these things.' But if they saw this clearly in mind and followed it out in their words they would free themselves from great anguish and fear of mind. 'Thou indeed, even as thou art now fallen asleep in death, shalt so be for all time to come released from every pain and sorrow. But 'tis we who have wept with tears unquenchable for thee, as thou would turn to ashes hard by us on the awesome place of burning and that unending day no grief shall take from our hearts.' But of him who speaks thus we should ask: 'What is there so exceeding bitter if it comes at last to sleep and rest, that anyone should waste away in never-ending lamentation?' "

(1265-1321)

# DANTE

# *The Divine Comedy*

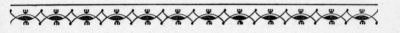

*DANTE is one of the three great poets of the world, and there are those who rank him above either Homer or Shakespeare. His* DIVINE COMEDY *is the narrative of a journey through Hell, Purgatory, and Heaven; it is a description of the universe in moral and metaphysical terms; it is a vindication of God's greatness; it is an ethical treatise; it is autobiography; it is political prophecy; it is medieval philosophy in verse. It is all these things and more. It is, simply, a great and complete poem which has as many meanings as we are capable of finding in it. Dante himself said that it was written so as to be comprehensible on three levels at once. But something like this is true of any great book, and if it is especially true of* THE DIVINE COMEDY *we have in effect another proof of its vast stature. On the merely narrative and descriptive level Dante succeeds from the first page; the journey he takes has a continuing fascination for the eye and*

*ear, and there are dozens of episodes which every reader remembers. On the more difficult levels his success requires the contribution of our understanding. This given, the poem mounts steadily in scope and intensity until at the Beatific Vision we are presented with "all the scattered leaves of the universe, bound by love into one volume." It is only then that the poem reveals its full intention. At that point we discover that his subject has been nothing less than the world in its manifold meanings. No literary project was ever grander, and no art more perfect.*

*Cairns:* In 1818 Karl Witte, the great nineteenth-century Dante scholar, was in Florence. He was seventeen or eighteen years of age, and he was studying Italian literature under the instruction of a Florentine woman. He had not read Dante, but he came one day to the house of his instructor with a handsome, two-volume edition of *The Divine Comedy.* His instructor advised him never to read the poem. She said: "We Italians sometimes persuade ourselves that we understand this extraordinary poem, but we do not. If a foreigner sets about it, one can scarcely repress a smile." I take it that the three of us do not share the opinion of Witte's instructor.

*Tate:* I am so far from sharing it that it seems to me that even a mere American has some chance of understanding a little of *The Divine Comedy.*

*Van Doren:* Don't you fear that this Italian lady did not understand it as well as she thought she did, if she talked that way about it?

*Tate:* Nobody can ever completely understand this poem. Any scholar could spend a lifetime, as many scholars have, in studying it, but there is a certain sense in which it can be generally understood better than any other great poem ever written.

*Cairns:* That is true, I assume, even for the non-Italian reader.

*Tate:* Even for the non-Italian reader. It has a structure which is absolutely universal, rational and communicable to everybody after a certain amount of study.

*Van Doren:* The style in which it is written is so plain and so economical, so practical, that any translation of it in English that I have ever examined seemed to me virtually as good as any other, whether in prose or in verse.

*Cairns:* I was just going to ask you if that applied to verse translations.

*Van Doren:* As a matter of fact, I prefer the prose translations of Dante.

*Tate:* The translations of Dante, of course, while some are good and others better, are none of them actually bad. It is almost impossible for a competent scholar to translate Dante badly.

*Van Doren:* Dante is a real poet. Therefore, anything that he says becomes poetry, no matter through what medium it arrives.

*Tate:* I am very much interested in this quality in the poem which makes it communicable even to people of our time. We are in the habit of thinking of the thirteenth century and the early fourteenth century as the Dark Ages. Yet while that age, like every age, was confused—there were all sorts of conflicting currents—and feudalism was coming to an end, and there was great violence and disorder, especially in Italy, reflected in philosophy, religion, and art—nevertheless, the age was also the climax of a great culture that had come before. It was one of the greatest cultures in history, and Dante is probably its spiritual climax.

*Cairns:* Dante, of course, summed up everything that had gone before him in the particular culture in which he lived. He did not sum up Greek thought because, for one reason, it is more than doubtful that he knew any Greek. He never quotes from Aeschylus or Sophocles, and his Euripides quotations are all from Horace. Aristotle, of course, was the infallible authority of the period, and Dante refers to him as the philosopher *par excellence.* Virgil reminds Dante how thoroughly he has absorbed the *Ethics* of Aristotle, but he knew Aristotle only in Latin translation. No one, however, has summed up the Middle Ages more perfectly than Dante.

*Tate:* He not only summed up the Middle Ages, he also gathered in the essence of antiquity. One of the nineteenth-century critics made a profound observation about Dante, that he has one thing that no other great poet seems to have, except perhaps

Shakespeare: that most poets, even great poets, can be allegorical and philosophical, but they do not succeed in combining those two things with history.

*Cairns:* At one level, however, the poem is purely historical—there is no allegory and no philosophy.

*Tate:* The ancient world is drawn into this too. The imagination is extended indefinitely in a vast historical perspective.

*Cairns:* And that puts together a picture of interest which no other poem yields, so far as I know.

*Van Doren:* And line by line this poem, which is an allegory, is unlike other allegories, in that it is more than a story under whose surface we have to look for a meaning. The meaning and the story are always one thing.

*Tate:* They are all the same thing. I have in mind here the magnificent passage in the Twelfth Canto where the troop of pagan centaurs wondrously appears in the Christian Hell. Here these strange creatures from classical mythology come, and they are fixed forever, they will live forever—these creatures are as permanent as anything in the universe. May I point out something about them that seems to me to make Dante about the greatest poet in the world?

*Cairns:* By all means.

*Tate:* The centaurs approach, and, Dante says, "Perceiving us, they all stood still." At that moment the centaurs are perfectly fixed. Dante and Virgil are standing apart looking at them, and it is one of the most dramatic moments in all literature. Then Chiron, the leading centaur, does this: "Chiron took an arrow and with the notch put back his beard upon his jaws." Only the greatest poets can do that sort of thing.

*Cairns:* Let me ask you to what extent you think the allegory is important. Can you read the poem directly as a fairy tale, or is the allegory essential to the understanding of the poem? Here is what I have in mind. In the very first Canto of the Inferno, Dante encounters a lion. Now, that lion can be regarded as a lion in the landscape; it can be taken as a symbol of pride or ambition in general; or a symbol of the power of the Royal House of France in particular, and there are various other interpretations that can be put upon it. In order to appreciate the poetry of the poem or the significance of it, to what extent is a knowledge of the allegory essential?

*Van Doren:* I do not distinguish, Mr. Cairns, between the poetry and the allegory. The poetry is the allegory; the allegory is the poetry. The lion you refer to I take to be one of Dante's failures because it is a symbol the meaning of which is not immediately clear. But in his first line, when he tells you that in the middle of a dark wood he had lost his way, the word "way" as he uses it immediately for us has two meanings. It still has two meanings for us—a way of life, a road. It is a path, but it is also the direction in which our life is moving. Now, Dante, when he is successful, and he is successful about ninety-nine per cent of the time, is not telling a story, as I said a moment ago, under which a meaning is hidden. The meaning is always as much on the surface as the story. I think of a passage at the beginning of the Purgatory where he suddenly meets Cato. Cato is standing with his back to the sun but his face is shining. That is because, Dante says, four stars never seen since the fall of man are shining upon his face. Those four stars also mean the four virtues, the four cardinal moral virtues of Aristotle. Now whereas an ordinary poet would say, "His face was as bright with his virtue as if stars were shining upon it," Dante means equally—I think he is equally successful in suggesting this—"the four stars that we have been looking at were as bright as if they had been the virtues of Cato." The meanings are always interchangeable.

*Tate:* I am not sure, Mr. Van Doren, that I agree with you about the lion, if you are willing to come back to him. Dante has a wonderful phrase for the lion; he is a real lion as well as an allegorical lion.

*Cairns:* Let me find out if I understand Mr. Van Doren correctly. Are you saying that the allegory is important and poetical when it is understood? When it is obscure the reader can just skip it without missing anything.

*Van Doren:* I must insist that you are misquoting me.

*Cairns:* I am merely trying to understand you.

*Van Doren:* I do not admit the existence of an allegory here which is separable from the story, from the poem.

*Cairns:* How do you regard the lion? Are you content to take the lion as being merely a lion in the landscape?

*Tate:* Now, if you will excuse me, I should like to shift the discussion from the lion to the centaurs we were talking about. There we have a more difficult case. The centaurs are pagan and fabulous creatures. They are not a part of the Christian tradition. Do they stand allegorically for anything or do they not? Are they something in excess, a rich, ornamental detail that Dante has put in in addition to the allegory? I do not think so. I think that their reality is just as great as the reality of any of the historical or allegorical figures in the poem.

*Van Doren:* The word "reality" is surely important there. The story is always real as an account of physical events taking place. These two men walk through the story as two men walk through many famous stories—Don Quixote and Sancho Panza, for instance—and have things happen to them, all of which are real. But the meaning of what happens to them is also real. It is not something that you can take or leave. You are not free to leave it.

*Cairns:* That answers my question, that it is possible to regard the story as a real description of the occurrence of actual events. The centaurs have given much trouble to Dante commentators because of their obscurity. One view is that they represent the three principal passions of man—Lust, Wrath and Ambition. Since they gallop about armed with arrows, they have also been compared to the Hungarians in Italy. I am content to take them merely as centaurs, part of the colorful furniture of Hell. If they have some additional meaning which is clear to us, then that is our gain. As centaurs alone, they are completely realized poetically.

*Tate:* But consider Farinata and Cavalcante lying in their burning coffin. They are literal men lying in a real, literal coffin and there is real, literal fire burning there. You see it. If you pause and separate the perception of that fire from what it is supposed to convey, I believe you lose the force of both the symbol and the reality.

*Cairns:* Perhaps we ought first to decide, if we can decide, what the subject of the poem is before we discuss its meaning. I should like to refresh your recollection by reading a sentence in which Dante, in a letter to his friend, Con Grande della Scala, described the subject of *The Divine Comedy*. He said, "The subject of the whole work, taken merely in its literal sense, is the state of souls after death, considered simply as a fact. But if the whole work is understood in its allegorical intention, the subject of it is man, according as, by his deserts and demerits in the use of his free will, he is justly open to rewards and punishments." That is Dante's description of the subject of the poem and it does not satisfy me, because I think there is much more to it than Dante has indicated. I do not know if it satisfies you.

*Van Doren:* It satisfies me, if you understand that these two meanings exist simultaneously in the poem. The story is the story of how two men went along a way. The word "way" can mean a road; a circuitous route, it turns out to be. It can also mean the thing that we vaguely indicate today when we use the phrase, "way of life." That is to say, the movement is both horizontal across the earth or through the earth. It is also vertical through understanding, with every step these men take. Now there again is a word which has two meanings. Every step they take is a step with their feet and with their minds. They understand more as they see more and do more.

*Cairns:* Let us compare Dante for a minute to the poet we last discussed—Lucretius. Lucretius was intent upon describing the material universe. It seems to me that Dante is just as intent upon describing an entirely different kind of universe.

*Tate:* But it is just as material. That is, it is just as much within the range of our perception, or even more so. It is more visible than Lucretius' universe because it has proportion and shape.

*Cairns:* Let us see if we agree what that universe is. To me it is the moral universe.

*Tate:* I think it is the whole universe.

*Van Doren:* The reason this is really a great poem, the reason we can learn so much from it—and we can learn everything from it—is that its world, to begin with, is the world that everyone can see, hear, touch, smell, and everything else. It is the whole material world.

*Cairns:* Have you ever touched a moral value?

*Van Doren:* No, I say that, to begin with, it is the world we touch. At the center of the poem, at the pivot so to speak, the whole structure seems to turn on a lecture which Virgil gives to Dante on gravitation, which is as physical as the gravitation of Einstein. It is also, for Dante, love.

*Cairns:* Both of those gravitations are intangible.

*Van Doren:* Gravitation for him is also attraction, or love.

*Tate:* Now I should like to bring up the question Mr. Cairns asked a minute ago. Can we touch a moral value? I would say yes—in Dante. You touch it in the sense that you visualize it. It is always there in terms of the action, the visible scene.

*Cairns:* That is what Dante has done for us. He has taken moral values and given them shapes, just as Plato gave apparently an objective existence to his ideas. Dante has done that with his moral values. But that does not mean moral values are material.

*Tate:* This is a whole universe that Dante gives us. I should like to explain what I meant by that.

*Cairns:* You might consider Milton at the same time.

*Tate:* Yes, we are going to consider Milton. I do not think Milton gives it to us the way Dante does.

*Cairns:* He gives you a much larger universe.

*Tate:* In terms of extended space the Miltonic universe is larger. But it does not include as much. That is the point involved here. We know—all of us know—today something about moral behavior, insofar as we continue to live. But we never see the parts of our behavior against a great ordering of all possible kinds of moral values. We tend to see our behavior in isolated segments. Dante orders the whole world, relates it all, brings it together; and every man's behavior can be related to the moral scale of *The Divine Comedy.*

*Cairns:* That is the point I am making: that it is a moral universe Dante is describing and not the material universe of Lucretius. Dante's world is entirely different from that of Lucretius.

*Tate:* It is not merely the physical universe.

*Cairns:* It is not merely or wholly the physical universe of Lucretius; it is both moral and physical.

*Van Doren:* Oh, no, of course not. Lucretius' universe is merely the material universe. This is the material universe to begin with, plus all its meanings, and it is rather interesting to remember how little space Lucretius needs to be disposed of in this poem. When Dante and Virgil enter the City of Dis among the burning tombs that Mr. Tate spoke of, one of them is occupied by Farinata, a Lucretian, who is still there and still scornful of Hell, although Hell is proving to him, or should be proving to him, that the soul does not die with the body, as he had insisted it did.

*Cairns:* I consider that one of the finest scenes in the Inferno.

*Van Doren:* One of the ironies.

*Cairns:* Yes, particularly in the haughtiness that Farinata exhibits. You will recall that Farinata's first sentence to Dante is: "Who were your ancestors?" Farinata speaks a few words and is then interrupted by Cavalcante dei Cavalcanti, the father of his own daughter's husband, the poet Guido Cavalcanti. After a few words with Dante, Cavalcante sinks back in despair, fearing that his son, Dante's friend, is dead. Farinata, who has taken no notice of the interruption, continues and says in effect: "As I was saying when I was interrupted."

*Van Doren:* We have spoken of the multiple meaning of this poem. That is why it is not easy to sum it up all at once. This multiple meaning can be seen if you think in terms of it in large units instead of small. Take the whole of the Inferno, which is a third of the poem. You might consider all the persons who are being punished in this Hell, and punished most cruelly, so that some people are shocked as they read. The punishments seem too great, or unjust. It is proper to understand as Dante's meaning that all these persons have punished themselves. They are getting what they wanted. They died in life. They are the only persons in the poem who are really dead.

*Tate:* Capaneus, one of the heroes of *The Seven Against Thebes,* says: "What I was living, that I am in Hell."

*Van Doren:* Exactly. The usurers are carrying great purses around their necks which bow them to the ground, just as they did in life. The carnal sinners are blown hither and thither on a wind which will never let them rest, as they were in life.

*Cairns:* And the punishment of the Misers and the Prodigals is the same because both misused their possessions. They both press forward with heavy burdens to a middle line which represents perhaps the moderation of Aristotle, but in any event moderation. They do not reach that middle point; but the important thing to notice is the Aristotelian doctrine that the virtue of liberality is the Golden Mean between the sins of Avarice and Prodigality. These considerations bring up what I think is the chief value of the poem, which is its intense human interest. Here is a poem describing an imaginary journey of Dante's in the year 1300, and it has been read ever since. Many scholars have attempted to account for its long life. The first man ever to occupy a professorial chair on Dante was Boccaccio, and he summed up the poem by saying that it was a gallows on which Dante gibbeted his political enemies. That is hardly the full story.

*Tate:* There is only a slight element of truth in it.

*Cairns:* He undoubtedly paid off some old scores, but that is not why we read the poem today.

*Tate:* It is quite possible that a critic with a psychological bias might say that that is what the whole poem means. Revenge would be Dante's motivation. The poem would be a "rationalization" of revenge. But that element is vastly complicated. We were talking about Farinata and his great scorn of Hell. Even in Hell he still has his pride. While Dante thinks that the punishment he is receiving is just, at the same time he admires and sympathizes with him. There is this dramatic complication running through the whole poem. Dante at one point is so fascinated by what he sees when the Malebranche are quarreling and fighting that Virgil reprimands him for displaying "vulgar" interest.

*Cairns:* I do not want to shock you, but I think, in my own opinion, that we read the poem for much the same reason that we read Balzac or Pepys or Rousseau—that is to say, for their human interest.

*Van Doren:* I should say that we read the poem for that reason among others; and then it is as richly rewarding as any of those authors. However, it has more in it.

*Cairns:* Oh, undoubtedly.

*Van Doren:* It has more understanding; it is more inclusive in its definition of man. It is all human, if you like, but the word "human" is a tremendous word.

*Cairns:* The poem sums up the whole world as Dante knew it, even the modern world, in the sense that when we read it we are taking the modern world into Dante's ancient and medieval universe.

*Van Doren:* It sums up the world of men whenever and wherever they live.

*Cairns:* When the modern reader reads the poem, however, there are certain things that must trouble him. For one thing, we find that all the best people are in Hell; for example, the men we have been admiring most in these discussions: Aristotle, Socrates and Plato.

*Tate:* But they are in Hell with a difference. The ancient philosophers who lived good moral lives create a theological difficulty to Dante. They could not get into Heaven because they were in the pre-Christian era. They had to be technically in Hell, but Dante spares them all punishment.

*Van Doren:* Dante is trying to say there that the truth is the truth and that it is important—which it was to him, of course, to an almost infinite degree. Even the best and wisest men who ever lived before the truth was discovered suffered because they did not know it.

*Cairns:* I realize that Dante's theology compelled him to put such fine people in Hell, but that merely means that perhaps something is wrong with his theology. Let me give you a case that is even more difficult for the modern reader. When Dante was crossing the river Styx in a vessel, and the river Styx was slimy and unpleasant, a spirit, Filippo Argenti, approached the vessel. Filippo Argenti stretched out his hands to the boat and Virgil explained to Dante that this one who was trying to get in the vessel was an arrogant person in the world, and Dante replied: "Master, I should like much to see him ducked in this broth before we depart from the lake." Well, Virgil proceeded to do that, and Filippo Argenti was not only ducked, but the other spirits in the river Styx began to tear him apart, so that in his frenzy he turned with his teeth upon his own self. Dante said: "Even now I still praise God therefor, and thank him for it." That seems to me to be a concrete expression of the saying, "Kick him again. He is down."

*Tate:* Dante breaks off a branch of the living trees, the men who committed suicide, for the suicides turn into trees and the branches are alive. Dante breaks one off, and Virgil very curiously justifies it when he says: "I knew that if you broke that branch off you would cause Pier delle Vigne a lot of pain, but I let you do it because you wouldn't believe that these trees are living men unless you saw them suffer." It seems an almost frivolous excuse at the moment, but I think it has great dramatic power. Even Virgil is human.

*Cairns:* It has great power. But Dante is violating an injunction of Virgil's when he feels sorry for the souls in Hell. You will remember that he wept when he saw Francesca. Virgil tells him: "Who is more wicked than he who feels compassion at the divine judgment?"

*Tate:* But Dante himself is not capable of divine judgment because he remains a human being. He is on the human level the whole time.

*Cairns:* But he can recognize divine judgment when he sees it.

*Tate:* Yes, but he cannot act upon it.

*Van Doren:* The corporeality of Dante is always being emphasized. He casts a shadow.

*Tate:* And the boat gets heavier when he gets into it.

*Van Doren:* The boat gets heavy; and they see him breathing. He is not a shade. We speak of the cruelties of Dante, which are real and not to be apologized for, if you like. But the man has almost everything. He has also, in the story of his relations between himself and Virgil as they walk through the two parts of the world, and later in the story of his relations with Beatrice, the lady whom he sees again after so many years in which he has not seen her—and if you like, that is after many years in which he has neglected philosophy and theology—

*Cairns:* She is, I take it, a symbol of theology.

*Van Doren:* I think she is a woman.

*Cairns:* But she is also a symbol of theology, just as Virgil is a symbol of philosophy and is also a man.

*Van Doren:* But his story of his relationships between himself and these persons involves, I should say, a display of the most beautiful courtesies that exist anywhere in literature. The mutual love and respect between him and Virgil—student and teacher, teacher and student—has no parallel anywhere else in literature.

*Tate:* That same courtesy holds in Dante's relations with most of the people in Hell. The vindictiveness is only occasional. Think of the magnificent conversation with Brunetto Latini, in which they renew the friendship they had before Brunetto died.

*Cairns:* Even if his venom and his cruelty are defects of the poem, from the modern point of view, they nevertheless are defects that hold our attention. There has always been the problem why Dante wished to destroy Brunetto's reputation by revealing his crime and punishment in Hell. The old theory that it was because Brunetto was a Guelph and Dante a Ghibelline does not hold water, inasmuch as many Ghibellines are in Hell and some Guelphs are in Purgatory. Whatever the explanation may be, Dante's affection for Brunetto is clearly evident. He would have embraced him had he been able to descend on to the sand. And, to go back to the point of courtesy, one of the great scenes in the poem is the opening canto of the Purgatory, where Virgil takes the dew from the grass and wipes the grime of Hell from Dante's face.

*Van Doren:* As far as Brunetto Latini is concerned, consider the magnificent charity with which Dante leaves him. Of this great sinner, to be sure, but also a teacher of Dante whom Dante had loved, at the end of the Fifteenth Canto we read: "Then he turned back" [that is to say, Brunetto] "and seemed like one of those who run for the green cloth of Verona through the open field, and of them seemed he one who gains, not one who loses."

*Tate:* There is a man whose nature is so complicated with good that, although he is justly condemned, there is something so magnificent in him that he perhaps ought not to be in Hell.

*Van Doren:* The last view we have of him is of one graceful and fortunate.

*Tate:* Dante says of Brunetto that Brunetto is "the man who taught men how to be eternal."

*Cairns:* He does. One of the interesting points about Dante's method is the parallel that can be drawn with Aristotle: the compression, the hard objectivity, the precise naming of names, the habit of using few words and proceeding straight to the heart of the subject.

*Tate:* Do you think that he got his power of poetic detail from Aristotle? You remember the people who were under the ice down in the very lowest circle of Hell? He says they look like straw through glass.

*Cairns:* His poetry is all his own. He would not have had that from Aristotle. That is too poetic. You will recall Plato's description of Aristotle as "one not a poet, but a friend of poetry."

*Van Doren:* Aristotle, nevertheless, is some kind of poet. I have always been convinced that his imagination was very rich, though he never calls attention to it or boasts of it. At the end of *The Divine Comedy*—we have perhaps dwelt for so long on the ugliness of the Inferno that we are inclined to forget the beauty of Paradise—Dante has his famous vision as he looks into the face of God. A few lines from there might redress the balance. "Oh, grace abounding wherein I presumed to fix my look on the eternal light so long that I consumed my sight thereon. Within its depths I saw ingathered, bound by love in one volume, the scattered leaves of all the universe. Substance and accident and their relations, as though together fused after such fashion that what I tell of is one single flame. Now shall my speech fall farther short, even of what I can remember, than an infant's who still bathes his tongue at breast. To the high fantasy here power fails, but already my desire and will were rolled even as a wheel that moveth equally by the love that moves the sun and the other stars."

*(1608-1674)*

# MILTON

# *Paradise Lost*

*THE greatest narrative poem in the English language has suffered in recent years from the emphasis we have placed upon its style. Milton in his* PARADISE LOST *was master of so rich a harmony that we have been content to listen rather than to understand, to read the first two books and let them go as representative of the poet's unsurpassable way with words. But the whole of* PARADISE LOST *is an important and exciting story, and the work gains immeasurably if we give ourselves to its meaning. Milton, a political and ecclesiastical rebel, a hater of authority and a person of inordinate personal pride—in other words, an arch-Puritan—sat down in his old age to justify the ways of God in punishing Satan for his rebellion, his resentment against authority and his pride. He took the theme of Aeschylus and Job, giving it Eden for its setting and localizing it in the characters of Satan, Adam and Eve. But the entire universe is here for an environment, and Milton's own character shows through every line. He is arguing with himself as he vindicates God's punishment of man for disobedience. The sin of Adam and Eve was the sin of desiring knowledge; and Milton was one of the most learned men of whom we have a record. Satan reasons not only cleverly but nobly in favor of eating the forbidden fruit; his processes are those of Milton himself. Yet Satan must fail in God's ultimate economy, and Milton as a poet has no mercy on him. The result is the most moving and complexly beautiful of modern epics.*

*Cairns:* John Dryden, who was Milton's friend and first critic, observed that Milton combined the "loftiness of mind" exhibited by Homer with the "majesty" of expression exhibited by Virgil. It has always seemed to me that subsequent criticism has not improved upon that judgment.

*Van Doren:* I am not sure that Dryden was a friend of Milton. Or rather, I am not sure that Milton was a friend of Dryden. Milton had contempt for Dryden as a poet of another generation; he considered him just a rhymer.

*Cairns:* But Dryden used to call upon him as an act of kindness at his home after he became blind. It was in that customary sense that I used the term "friend."

*Van Doren:* They had relations of one sort or another, but the legend is that when Dryden asked Milton's permission to make an opera out of *Paradise Lost,* which he eventually did, Milton said: "You may tag my verses if you please." But Dryden's epithets—loftiness and majesty—do fit Milton. These epithets seem to refer chiefly, however, to the manner of Milton and to the quality of his mind. I am not at all convinced that the poem we have before us this evening is—well, let me put it this way—more than lofty and majestic.

*Cairns:* Mr. Tate, would you say that he had any rival in those two characteristics except Dante?

*Tate:* He is almost wholly unlike Dante in that respect. The loftiness that Dryden attributed to Milton is what Matthew Arnold meant by "high seriousness." It is all on one level. There is no letdown; the tone is the same throughout.

*Cairns:* It is what Matthew Arnold called the "grand style."

*Van Doren:* The great style. And that great style in Milton is something which he must write or else fall from poetry altogether. We agreed in an earlier discussion that the difference between him and a poet like Shakespeare, if there is a poet like Shakespeare—or one like Dante, or one like Homer—is that those men have no style which they must pursue at peril of complete failure otherwise.

*Cairns:* Shakespeare's style was absolutely free; he used all the forms of blank verse and employed other metres as well. Milton as an extremely self-conscious artist—something Shakespeare was not—was much more on the side of strictness, although, of course, both his verse and his style vary.

*Tate:* In Books X and XI of *Paradise Lost,* in which there is so much description of the physical universe, in which there are prophecies of the future after the Fall of Man—in those passages we get Milton thinking, and his language loses its elevation. In fact, it seems to me to become dull. Milton has not been able to think and to imagine at the same time.

*Van Doren:* The old epigram to the effect that Milton wrote English as if it were a dead language applies there. You cannot think in a dead language. When Milton needs to think, his style shows the strain.

*Cairns:* He apparently thought in Latin just as easily as he thought in English; but I believe we ought to recognize what he attempted to do. He attempted the greatest undertaking in poetry ever ventured by an English poet. In doing that he teaches us that poetry is no trivial matter. He shows us also how important a thing form is.

*Tate:* Now, Mr. Cairns, don't you think we ought to get that undertaking clearly in mind? The fundamental subject in *Paradise Lost* is the dramatization of the origin of evil.

*Van Doren:* Let me interrupt you just a minute, Mr. Tate; please go on with the point later. I should like to quarrel with Mr. Cairns' use of the word "great." I do not see that this is the "greatest" undertaking, judging at any rate by the success achieved. If you judge by success rather than ambition in a poet, any one of a dozen plays by Shakespeare was a greater undertaking. *King Lear* is a greater undertaking.

*Cairns:* Let me explain what I meant. I expressly used the word "attempted" in referring to Milton's undertaking so as to negate the notion that the enterprise was necessarily successful. I meant a number of things by the phrase "greatest undertaking": first, that, at the time Milton wrote, the epic was generally regarded as the highest form of poetry; Milton therefore resolved he would write an epic.

*Van Doren:* Or, as they said in those days, heroic.

*Cairns:* Sometimes called the heroic poem. Since we are still without a satisfactory epic, it might be possible to draw the conclusion that an epic is the most difficult of all verse to write successfully and that Milton therefore undertook the poet's most difficult task. Second, the language in which Milton wrote is the most dangerous language that a poet can employ, I believe.

*Tate:* What do you mean by that?

*Cairns:* Because he must maintain at its full intensity the poetic note, or the language becomes absolutely flat. A poet could not possibly utilize a language more full of pitfalls than that in which Milton wrote.

*Tate:* What you say may be very true, but I do not see exactly what you mean by it. Dante's purpose in the *Divine Comedy* was certainly just as lofty, but Dante varies his language; he does not need to maintain the grand style.

*Cairns:* But Milton, in writing his kind of blank verse, had to maintain the grand style. He undertook that risk. He said: "I will write an heroic poem in twelve books in blank verse of the most difficult kind. I am certain I will be successful. At least I will undertake that risk." I can think of no other poem to put beside *Paradise Lost* in its kind of greatness.

*Tate:* There is another kind of blank verse altogether which Shakespeare used. Shakespeare's blank verse varies. It is not the same from play to play, but it shows that blank verse is a very flexible instrument. There is no reason why it cannot be varied.

*Van Doren:* You did not mean blank verse alone, did you, Mr. Cairns, when you referred to his style?

*Cairns:* I was thinking specifically of blank verse. It was created by Marlowe and the other dramatists. Of course, Milton's verse is quite varied. By dropping or doubling stresses he can achieve effects of grace or solidity and emphasis.

*Van Doren:* But the blank verse of Shakespeare comes between Marlowe and Milton. The style we are talking about in Milton's case is not necessarily wedded to the measure that he uses. Style, I should say, is his way of thinking about his material. If we can interpret a man's style as meaning something about his whole mind and his whole intention, as I am sure we can, then we discover that Milton's style, since it is as artificial as it is (of course, only at its worst is it stilted; at its best it is magnificent), means that his subject was in his own mind somehow above him, somehow out of reach. There is always the effort to reach up, to put himself on a level with subject matter which he assumes to be almost beyond human grasp.

*Cairns:* I was not speaking of the importance of the subject. That is a different matter. I was emphasizing the risk Milton ran in using his kind of blank verse which did not possess the freedom of Shakespeare's. His subject, like all subjects, was dictated to him by the age he lived in.

*Tate:* It seems to me that he never embodies the subject in the language. Now doesn't that bring us back to the theme of the poem?

*Cairns:* Tell us what you think the theme is.

*Tate:* The theme is the dramatization of the origin of evil in the world. If you look at the story of the Fall of Man, it is a very limited thing within this poem. The simple narrative running through the poem is concerned with that story, and Milton is at his best while he is telling that story, or leading up to it. Satan's escape from Hell, the temptation and the fall—all that is beautifully done.

*Cairns:* He is at his best, in my opinion, when he is most similar to Dante. That is to say, when he is concrete, as in his description of Pandemonium, the capital of Hell, or in his description of Satan's conversation with Sin and Death at the gates of Hell. When he is misty and unsubstantial, when he deals in images that are difficult or impossible to visualize, then he is least satisfactory.

*Tate:* But isn't he weakest in the description of this universe in which these events take place? Then his language becomes stilted, as Mr. Van Doren says; it becomes inflated and vague. Don't you think that is due to the fact that Milton never successfully imagined his universe? You might even call it a jerry-built universe. It is arbitrary and magical. For example, the bridge built from the gates of Hell to the Earth after the fall of man is an arbitrary trick incomprehensible in any real mathematical universe. It was arbitrary and almost perverse on Milton's part.

*Van Doren:* That bridge is something you cannot believe in. It does not seem any more substantial than a rainbow. Now your use of the word "imagination" interested me. Might it not be true that the trouble with Milton's universe—if there is any trouble with it, and there must be for us from the way we are talking—is that it is not as solid and convincing as Dante's. The trouble with it is that for Milton himself it was something that had to be imagined. It was not something that he believed, that he knew. Dante can be understood as making his universe out of all that he knew, out of all that he could think in any capacity at all—as a scientist, as a theologian, as a poet—whereas Milton, who was a Puritan, had a special view of the spirit. It is something much less substantial than it was for Dante; so he has to make his poetry out of something unsubstantial too, and imagined. Perhaps when we have to imagine a world, we are bound to fail. No man can imagine a world.

*Tate:* But don't you think that the structure of Dante's world was recognizable to men at that time and is still recognizable to us?

*Cairns:* I think so. The features of Dante's world are recognizable because Dante visualized them precisely and was artist enough to put that visualization on paper. There is a technical term applicable to the point you are making, the so-called "Miltonic vague." It describes those vast but indeterminate pictures that Milton drew. I don't think anyone, even of Milton's own time, saw concretely the whole of what Milton had in mind, as they saw concretely what was in Dante's imagination.

*Tate:* Now, in the first place, Mr. Cairns, I agree with you when you say that he is at his best when he is most concrete, most Dantesque, let us say. But at the same time, there are certain passages in Milton—for example, the description of Satan that you get in Book I which he develops through elaborate Homeric similes. He always begins with *As* and he goes on for eight or ten, sometimes twenty, lines. They are like great Renaissance frescoes. It is word-painting. It is what Lessing would call descriptive poetry, and it is magnificent in its kind, but those fine passages tend to be just thrown into the poem. Then the narrative is resumed. The texture of the poem is not all of a piece.

*Van Doren:* He surely is a descriptive poet. The architecture of this poem is something like a veneer, something applied, the structure being invisible behind it and perhaps not so certain. I find myself more and more uncertain as I read *Paradise Lost* as to what its structure is, and I can doubt that this structure is sound, in view of the fact that Milton must borrow so many things for it. For instance, his God is not like the God of Dante, whom Dante is satisfied to speak of briefly from time to time as king of the universe or Him whose will cannot be withstood. Milton does not believe in God in that simple and complete way. He must give us a Charlemagne, a military leader, a stuffed shirt.

*Cairns:* He also gives you the colonel of a British regiment.

*Van Doren:* This God, incidentally, is a synthetic God. He hangs out scales in the sky, the way the Zeus of Homer does, or he nods and thunder shakes the world.

*Tate:* He laughs too, occasionally, but there is no humor in the laughter.

*Cairns:* Milton is absolutely humorless. At least, I do not find any humor in him.

*Tate:* None whatever.

*Van Doren:* The very synthetic nature of his God and of his Christ, and of his whole universe, for that matter, leads me to suspect that somehow his conception of what he wanted to do, his conception of his subject, has not that clarity and that substantiality which we find in Homer, Dante and Shakespeare.

*Cairns:* We must not forget that Milton has survived for a long time and many fine judges have praised him. We have dwelt upon his defects, which is proper. But I should like to consider his good qualities also. To begin with, he has an exactness of expression which is admirable; also the associations he employs when he wishes to suggest images leave him few rivals in English. I have two stanzas here which may illustrate my point; one describing the gates of Heaven and the other the gates of Hell. You will notice how the character of the words changes when he switches from Heaven to Hell. His words are sweet and harmonious in describing the gates of Heaven; for the gates of Hell they are rasping and rough. This is the description of the gates of Heaven:

> *"Heaven opened wide*
> *Her ever-during gates, harmonious sound*
> *On golden hinges moving."*

He describes the other gates:

> *"On a sudden open fly,*
> *With impetuous recoil and jarring sound,*
> *The infernal doors, and on their hinges grate*
> *Harsh thunder that the lowest bottom shook*
> *Of Erebus."*

The point can be illustrated another way. Here is a line of Wordsworth, in which Wordsworth is perhaps attempting to say the same thing that Milton had said before him. Wordsworth says, "Negro ladies in white muslin gowns." Milton says, "Dusk faces with white silken turbans wreathed."

*Tate:* I prefer Wordsworth.

*Cairns:* I was afraid of that. Why do you prefer Wordsworth?

*Tate:* Because it is sharp and direct, and Wordsworth's words denote objects which are brought before you.

*Cairns:* I prefer Milton because his line is more poetic and because of his suggestion of mystery.

*Van Doren:* Well, here is another passage from Milton which magnificently explores in words—note the sheer weight of the words it uses, and their quality—the mysterious realm, the no-man's realm, between Hell and what is above it. Satan is asking who shall be sent on that first exploratory flight toward Earth.

> *"Who shall tempt with wandering feet*
> *The dark, unbottomed, infinite abyss,*
> *And through the palpable obscure find out*
> *His uncouth way, or spread his aery flight*
> *Upborne with indefatigable wings*
> *Over the vast abrupt ere he arrive*
> *The happy isle?"*

Now that suggests to me Milton's greatest quality as poet, and anyone who knows the capacities of the English language for verse knows that Milton has no competitor. He explores these capacities, however, chiefly in musical terms. Milton is the greatest of all our versifiers on the musical side, not merely for the sonorousness that you so often hear about, not merely for the organ tones, but also for the really very precise fitting of the movement of a line, as here where the movement suggests effort, suggests titanic effort, to its subject. We all, I am sure, recognize his mastery of these verbal arts. Our only point—and it is one that should be made—is that the English-speaking people still have no first-rate epic poem. This poem does not compare for a moment with the *Iliad.*

*Tate:* I agree. Bearing that in mind, I think we can say it is a great poem. It seems to me that the musical quality that you . . .

*Van Doren:* I beg your pardon, Mr. Tate. I should say it was a great piece of writing. I should not call it a great poem; its structure and its conception are not first rate.

*Cairns:* May I add one thing to that? I should like to suggest that the chief interest that the modern reader has in Milton today is in his craftsmanship as a poet and, secondly, in the moral personality that is reflected in this poem.

*Tate:* I should like to say something about those two points if you are finished.

*Cairns:* Let me explain what I mean by the second point. The *Divine Comedy* has a human interest in the story itself. There is also a human interest in *Paradise Lost,* but of an entirely different kind. Its human interest is to be found in Milton's moral personality, which comes out in nearly every line.

*Tate:* In the personal passages about himself, and, of course, in the domestic relations of Adam and Eve which are in their way very charming. I must confess that if Milton had faced the humorous possibilities of that situation, it would be still more charming. The humor is largely unconscious.

*Cairns:* Of course, I am criticizing Milton when I say that we read him just for his craftsmanship, because the poem is too long to read for its craftsmanship alone; and Milton's personality can be found as easily, even more attractively sometimes, in his prose.

*Tate:* I don't know about that, Mr. Cairns. A point Mr. Van Doren made just a minute ago about the musical qualities of Milton's verse ought to be elaborated a little. Nobody can read Milton very long without realizing the masterly way in which he organizes what has been called by the critics the "verse paragraph." Now another poet, using the same material and having Milton's ability line by line, could write a magnificent line the way Milton does, but might cease to interest us because he lacks Milton's power of organization. The poem is actually broken up into units—the books—and the books are broken up into small units of attention which are managed very cunningly. Our attention is not exhausted over too long a stretch. And that is all a part of this musical quality. The units of thought are expressed in units of rhythm.

*Van Doren:* Would you agree that here Milton has no competitor?

*Tate:* None whatever.

*Van Doren:* In English verse, or possibly anywhere at all?

*Tate:* None whatever. For example, Tennyson's blank verse,

which, of course, is inferior to Milton's on many counts. But just on that count alone it is inferior. Tennyson does not know how to make the verse paragraph in the blank verse structure a unit of attention. It tends to be diffuse. In other words, Tennyson merely holds our attention line by line. Milton is far too cunning for that.

*Cairns:* I take it that you agree that we read him for his craftsmanship, but, at the same time, you do not want the poem any shorter. I cannot help thinking of Samuel Johnson's remark: "No one ever wished it longer than it is." It is only fair to say that he also said: "I cannot wish Milton's work other than it is." That is to say, I assume, he did not want it any shorter either.

*Van Doren:* We continue to read *Paradise Lost,* and I hope we shall do so for a long time. But the English-speaking peoples read *Paradise Lost* chiefly for its style. Here is our epic, if you will, but an epic which we can praise most for its language. We have said in the past that the greatest poets can be translated. That is to say, there is more in them than their language, important as language is. And one sign of this is that Homer and Dante and Shakespeare translate easily, translate well. They seem to keep their important qualities in whatever language they adopt. It is difficult to imagine Milton succeeding in Hungarian.

*Cairns:* It is their substance that is translated, not their craftsmanship. Take away Milton's craftsmanship and there is little left to interest the modern reader. Altogether apart from his style, his theme would baffle most people. I recall that Voltaire said that the French laugh when they are told that in the great English epic Satan struggles against God and a serpent persuades a woman to eat an apple. He said that is a subject that should be treated in a farce. The French just cannot get interested in it.

*Tate:* That brings us back to Milton's myth, and I have a great deal of respect for it, I must say.

*Van Doren:* But let me ask you whether that myth is not something which almost necessarily is to be treated briefly—treated as most myths are, in a few sentences, a few lines.

*Cairns:* The myth cannot support the burden it is designed to carry. No matter what the apple signifies, it is not convincing to have Adam and Eve behave the way they do after Eve eats the apple. Why should their love be less innocent? The modern reader merely smiles and flips the pages.

*Tate:* But what about the myth of Prometheus? Now, of course, the *Prometheus Bound,* which we have discussed, is relatively short.

*Cairns:* Prometheus is in this poem in the person of Satan.

*Tate:* That is what I am getting around to. He is Lucifer.

*Cairns:* In the Greek tradition he is Prometheus, and like Prometheus, Lucifer is rebelling against Omnipotence.

*Tate:* It seems to me that the symbolism of the Tree of Knowledge brings us very close to the Promethean myth. But I grant you that Milton's way of doing it is much longer than it should be.

*Van Doren:* We might put it this way: The myth is perfectly handled in a few verses of the Book of Genesis. It is also, if you like, treated at length by two poets, Aeschylus and Milton. Aeschylus chose the wiser way, as a poet, and this is where we can test his true greatness. He did not attempt the impossible. He made his drama into nothing more than a series of conversations. Prometheus is stationary, and to him come certain significant persons whose conversation with him reveals the depth and the sources of the myth. Milton makes the mistake, the technical error, of trying to set the whole universe in motion in order to elucidate his myth, and the universe he constructs for the purpose, of course, does not move simply and quietly enough to do the job. His universe, rather, gets in our way.

*Cairns:* That is an important point that can be extended: Milton in taking in the whole universe for his field of operation leaves out too much that is familiar and therefore necessary for the modern mind, if it is to feel at home in the poem. There is no love in the poem; there is no child in the poem; his description of the Garden of Eden is a place that we just do not recognize if we have ever been in the country.

*Tate:* That is a revival of Saturn's reign, the myth of the

Golden Age again. I should put that same notion in slightly different terms. There is too great a discrepancy between this enormous universe and this central event which occurs in it. There is only one sin. There is not enough moral discrimination. In Dante you get a wonderful gradation of sins in which they are all related, in which all human experience is comprehended. The whole human experience in Milton is merely implied. You are given this one thing, the Fall of Man, and you are asked to arrange the rest for yourself.

*Van Doren:* Adam and Eve in the Garden of Eden have nothing to do except prune a few vines.

*Cairns:* There are no ice ponds or hay stacks; no barns or smoke from chimneys. They just ate nuts. They did not even drink wine, although Milton himself loved it.

*Van Doren:* And of course, this question is never really answered by the poem: Why should they not have plucked the fruit of the Tree of Knowledge? Why was knowledge so dreadful a thing for them to have? We never learn.

*Tate:* If we consider what he meant by knowledge, though, we have to concede the point. Isn't the state of Adam and Eve in the Garden a unity of being? This rational knowledge of the forbidden tree brings disunity of being.

*Cairns:* Not only does his argument fail there, but I think his whole theme fails when he attempts to justify the ways of God to man. If he had reversed his theme and tried to justify the ways of man to God, he would have been more interesting. He lacks the modernity of Shakespeare and Dante.

*Tate:* Gentlemen, we have talked about Milton's narrative powers and how good he is when he is actually giving us a piece of action. At the end of Book II, Satan has been appointed by the Congress of Hell to go up to the world and to corrupt this new race, Man.

> *"But now at last the sacred influence*
> *Of light appears, and from the walls of heav'n*
> *Shoots far into the bosom of dim Night*
> *A glimmering dawn: here nature first begins*

*Her farthest verge, and Chaos to retire*
*As from her outmost works, a broken foe,*
*With tumult less and with less hostile din,*
*That Satan with less toil and now with ease*
*Wafts on the calmer wave by dubious light,*
*And like a weather-beaten vessel holds*
*Gladly to port, though shrouds and tackle torn;*
*Or in the empty waste resembling air,*
*Weighs his spread wings, at leisure to behold*
*Far off th' empyreal heav'n, extended wide*
*In circuit, undetermin'd square or round,*
*With opal tow'rs and battlements adorn'd*
*Of living sapphire, once his native seat;*
*And fast by hanging in a golden chain*
*This pendant world, in bigness as a star*
*Of smallest magnitude close by the moon.*
*Thither full-fraught with mischievous revenge,*
*Accursed, and in a cursed hour, he hides."*

# RELIGION

# THE HOLY BIBLE

# *The Book of Job*

*THE Old Testament of the Hebrews is a great work of history, biography, theology, prophecy, law and lyric poetry. It is also, in the* BOOK OF JOB, *a work of exalted tragedy, for the form of that book is essentially dramatic. At its critical points it proceeds through dialogue: between Job and his friends; between Job and his Redeemer. The theme once more is Aeschylean in its nature and its proportions. Job, a man of God, has suddenly been visited by calamities; he loses his wealth, his family and his physical well-being. Why have these things happened to a good man? Is it punishment from above for sins of which he was not aware? Friends come to discuss the question with him, and are more or less superficial in their counsels. They say the easy things; they offer the conventional comforts; they draw the trite conclusions. But Job is not satisfied in his profounder mind. It is a problem which he must solve by himself. The climax of the book is a series of illuminations which a vision of God's awful greatness inspires in him. The things which happen to man are not always or easily to be understood by man alone. His explanations are those of a little creature trying to make the best of his size. The greatness of God is in another dimension which human wit may scarcely penetrate. The language of the King James version rises to a unique height at the close, supplying harmonies such as few books in the world's literature contain.*

*Cairns:* There is, of course, a striking parallel between the myth of Prometheus, which we have previously discussed, and the *Book of Job.* For one thing, both characters are stationary. Prometheus is riveted to a mountain; and Job, afflicted with elephantiasis, sits upon a large rubbish heap outside a Near-Eastern city. What interests me, however, is the difference between the two figures. Prometheus is guilty. He is punished for stealing fire from the gods which he intended as a gift for man. Job, however, is essentially innocent.

*Tate:* He is innocent from the point of view of the ancient Hebrew ethics. Is that the question you are raising?

*Cairns:* In the ancient Hebrew tradition Job must be guilty or he would not be afflicted. That is the argument of his three friends. We know, however, and Job knows, that he is innocent. That is the basis of the drama.

*Van Doren:* He might have been guilty in a sense which transcended the understanding of the three friends.

*Tate:* He had not committed a sin, strictly speaking. He had not committed an obvious wrong. Isn't what is wrong with Job simply that he does not have the proper humility toward God in his heart? That is something that man cannot see and measure.

*Van Doren:* No man, perhaps, has that humility until he is taught to have it.

*Cairns:* I think the essential point of this book is that an innocent man is afflicted with all kinds of calamities. He has lost his children, his money, and he is afflicted with a loathsome disease. Is he being punished, and if so, for what? Or, more generally, what is the explanation of the fact that in a world created by a God of infinite love and mercy, the innocent suffer with the guilty?

*Tate:* Job himself asks that question. He states a dilemma. He says in Chapter X, verse 15: "If I be wicked, woe unto me, and if I be righteous, yet will I not lift up my head. I am full of confusion." Then he says further to God: "Therefore, see Thou mine affliction." If he is righteous he is still not arrogant about it. At the same time, if he is guilty of some wickedness he accepts his woe.

*Van Doren:* One of the commonest experiences in the world, I take it, is the experience of suffering calamity for reasons which we do not know. It is common for someone to say: "Why has this been done to me? Why in this world which I assumed was friendly to me has suddenly the spirit of enmity appeared?"

*Tate:* Isn't that the theme of the *Book of Job* then? The great mystery of human experience is why people should suddenly suffer calamity without any apparent reason.

*Van Doren:* Why should they be *elected* to suffer calamity? The theological term almost necessarily comes in here. And that reminds me that there are two modern novels which deal with the theme. One is a German novel by Franz Kafka, in which a young bank clerk suddenly becomes aware that he has been elected to be condemned for reasons which he never discovers. And there is the novel by H. G. Wells, written during the first World War, in which a man who has lost his son and suffered many other calamities speculates as to why they should have happened to him.

*Tate:* Isn't the same theme in a great many of Dostoyevsky's stories? What is the very nature of human frailty? What is it in human nature that makes it imperfect and susceptible to calamity?

*Van Doren:* The thing is stated this way by a Spanish proverb: Beware of the unlucky man. There are men to whom terrible things seem to happen.

*Cairns:* Prior to the *Book of Job* in the Bible, particularly in *Deuteronomy,* it is apparent that the Hebrews believed that man's life and his lot must correspond; otherwise God would be unjust. They had, therefore, formulated the doctrine of retributive justice. The *Book of Job* raises that problem in an acute form and makes an advance beyond the ancient idea of retribution.

*Van Doren:* Yes, but a question of logic arises there. If it is true that all those who sin must suffer, does it follow that all those who suffer have sinned?

*Cairns:* No, it does not.

*Tate:* That is the problem in the *Book of Job.*

*Cairns:* There are also other objections to the position of retributive justice in the earlier books of the Bible. Aside from logical objections, there are also ethical objections. One is that if virtue is practiced for the sake of its results, men could object if they were not rewarded. Still another objection is that if the doctrine were true—namely, that man's life and lot must correspond—religion would then become the possession of the rich and the wealthy. A man who is poor or sick would hardly be welcome at the altars on feast days.

*Van Doren:* So the three friends of Job who come to him seem to think.

*Cairns:* Their point of view is the older point of view: they believe that man suffers only if he has sinned; they are convinced that Job is a sinner, that he has committed some sin and won't confess it.

*Tate:* They cannot see the sin precisely, but they assume that it must be there, because any man who does not prosper must be sinful.

*Van Doren:* They are quite cynical, aren't they, when they say to him in effect: If you will only admit that you have sinned, you will get all your herds back and the boils will disappear from your body?

*Cairns:* That also is the doctrine of retributive justice—be good and good will be done unto you. Nevertheless, those three men are, I think, distinctly realized. Their characters are entirely different. Eliphaz is apparently an old man and certainly an oracle. He looks into the future and he has visions. The second man, Bildad, is a fundamentalist. He argues for what is essentially the ancient Hebrew tradition. The last man, Zophar, has also a distinct personality: he is a zealot. All three of them are arguing for the ancient Hebrew tradition, but Bildad argues for it most vehemently. All three of them are sure of the ideal justice of God.

*Tate:* What about Elihu? This young man steps up and accuses the three elders of lack of wisdom. He says these older men have not really got at the truth of this matter about Job. It seems to me that Elihu is the most interesting figure dramatically—in terms of character—in the entire story.

*Cairns:* The theory is that Elihu's statement is a later interpolation by a scribe who was dissatisfied with the arguments advanced by Job's three friends.

*Tate:* An attempt to make the structure of the plot, let us say, more logical.

*Van Doren:* Also to improve the morality of the book.

*Tate:* Exactly. To put it on a higher level. That is, even if Job has not committed a visible wrong, there must be something secret in his nature which has not been "right with God."

*Van Doren:* There must be something more general about this situation than the three friends can understand.

*Tate:* It is not a simple matter of committing a sin and being punished for it in proportion to the sin. There is something mysterious about this: that although man is punished and often undeservedly, nevertheless it behooves man to inquire more deeply into his own nature. And I think that is the real profundity of this book.

*Cairns:* I am not sure that it is profound. As I understand Elihu's position, he makes the point that suffering is a discipline intended to purify and mold the character, and that is why Job is suffering, even though he may be innocent.

*Van Doren:* I am not sure that that is Elihu's point of view. Would you say it was?

*Cairns:* I think it is. What do you think his position is?

*Van Doren:* My interest in him in the first place is an interest in a man who, as Mr. Tate says, makes a very dramatic entrance.

*Cairns:* Oh, he does that.

*Van Doren:* But also as a man who introduces into the problem a theological dimension which it did not have before.

*Tate:* Perhaps the later scribe, if there was a later scribe, who introduced Elihu, had that in mind. Elihu in a sense prepares dramatically for the entrance of God, and God's entrance is the most dramatic of all characters in the story.

*Van Doren:* That is as it should be.

*Cairns:* I should like to find out from Mr. Van Doren what theological element he thinks Elihu brings in, other than the ethical element I suggested.

*Van Doren:* This is what I meant. I am not sure that it is the proper way in which to use the word "theological," but I am reminded by this part of *Job* of all Hebrew thought, and, for that matter, of all Christian thought, which has to do with the question of original sin. According to the doctrine of original sin, which is, of course, in the *Book of Genesis* as well as in any Christian theologian, all men are guilty. There is no man who by definition is innocent, and that being the case, the guilt of Job, if any, is simply the guilt he possesses as man.

*Tate:* I was just going to say that perhaps Elihu's point of view can be expressed in another way. At one point he says: "Surely God will not hear vanity. Neither will the Almighty regard it." And it seems to me that that point of view tends to link Job with Prometheus more than almost any other thing in the book. In other words, the real trouble with Job is not that he has committed a definite sin, but that, not being sufficiently aware of his relation to God, he has been guilty of arrogance in his heart, and arrogance is probably the greatest sin of all, from the religious point of view.

*Van Doren:* For a Greek as well as for a Hebrew.

*Cairns:* Are you asserting that that is Elihu's position?

*Tate:* Not wholly his position; only partly.

*Cairns:* If Mr. Van Doren is right, if all men are guilty, then a man's lot in life is irrelevant, is it not?

*Van Doren:* I think it is.

*Cairns:* Then that argument, it seems to me, ignores the point of this book, or rather, the conversation of Job and his three friends—namely, is the doctrine of retributive justice sound? If Mr. Van Doren's argument is correct, that conversation seems to be meaningless.

*Van Doren:* I should say—somewhat arrogantly—that it is the point of the book, but that it takes the whole book to make the point. That is to say, the three friends who take the cynical position, the naive position, with reference to Job's alleged guilt, are slowly but finally disposed of. They are wiped away by Elihu; and then they are completely swallowed up in the final appearance of God. God is not interested in the crimes committed by Job. God is interested in Job as a man.

*Tate:* Don't you think, however, that the point of view of the three accusers is emphasized—in fact, it dominates the plot of this story—because after Job satisfies God, or God relents toward him, Job gets all his property back again? He gets his oxen and his she asses and his sheep all back again, and we have a nice happy ending. The ending is a little disappointing.

*Cairns:* Aristotle would not have approved of that ending, would he?

*Tate:* No. Contrast it with the end of Oedipus. Yet we do have tragic material in this story.

*Cairns:* But it would not be a tragedy in Aristotle's sense.

*Tate:* The tragic problem seems to be dissipated in a sort of narrative solution to the story. Job is prosperous first and last.

*Van Doren:* Job seems to be rewarded for taking that position with reference to himself and God which he should have taken anyway, which it had been his guilt not to take.

*Cairns:* Don't you think that the error of Eliphaz, Bildad and Zophar lay in sacrificing their friend to a creed? They were firmly wedded to the ancient Hebrew belief that suffering is the result of sin.

*Tate:* But Job would not admit it.

*Cairns:* But isn't the error, the fundamental ethical error, of their position that they were willing to sacrifice their friend to this creed? That is to say, they put their *a priori* beliefs ahead of the realities that confronted Job.

*Van Doren:* Also, Job suggests that they are "magnifying" themselves at his expense. They feel superior to him because they have not lost their flocks and their wives. He has lost his flocks and his wife and therefore must be inferior. I think there is some gloating.

*Cairns:* Oh, I think there is quite a lot of gloating.

*Van Doren:* One of the most interesting parts of the book for me lies between the visit to Job by his three friends and the appearance of Elihu—that central and pivotal portion in which Job delivers a monologue concerning his innocence. Now I take it that all through this portion of the book, Job—and I admire him there very greatly—is taking the following position. I wonder, Mr. Cairns, if you would agree with my statement, because curiously enough, this book is brief and apparently simple, and yet it is not too easy to agree about. I should say his position is this: To my knowledge and on the evidence that exists, I have not sinned; I am being punished nevertheless; or, at any rate, calamities are being visited upon me; all I want to say is—and he says this over and over again—I do love God and trust in Him; I do accept anything that God wishes to do to me; but I will not commit the sin against God of telling a lie, of admitting guilt which I do not believe.

*Cairns:* I agree with that; but I would state it a little differently. It might be summed up by saying that Job is true to himself in this sense, that he is more conscious of his own innocence than he is of the goodness of God, and one of the great tragic elements in this book is that he stands alone not only against the world as represented by Elihu and the three friends, but he also stands against God.

*Tate:* Mr. Cairns, you have hit on a fundamental point in speaking of the tragic element. I believe that practically the only thing in the whole *Book of Job* which would fit Aristotle's classical formula for tragedy is Job's strength and courage. In this intermediate section that Mr. Van Doren has discussed, Job is telling us that he is innocent and yet he has suffered. He is accepting for the moment the point of view of his three friends. Suddenly God enters. He comes out of the whirlwind and He says: "Who is this that darkeneth counsel by words without knowledge?" In other words, God shifts the whole plane of the discussion. Job's position is altered. He is made to realize that there is an extension of this problem that he has never been aware of at all.

*Cairns:* If the doctrine of retribution is true, then it seems to me that it must follow that Job's good conscience is incompatible with the goodness of God and that that is the dilemma that Job is in.

*Van Doren:* But Job—and I think this is why we admire him, for I agree with both of you gentlemen that he is a tragic hero, and a tragic hero must be one whom we can admire as well as see error in—insists, as he says, "on maintaining mine own ways before him." That is to say: I am willing to admit anything that God will charge me with, and yet I will not commit the outrage against Him of saying what I do not believe; I will maintain my integrity, I will be the man He has always known me to be.

*Tate:* But does God say that in the long run the real question is Job's integrity? Isn't the point involved, when God shifts the discussion, rather, that some lack of insight on Job's part, some lack of knowledge, is his real fault? Consider the magnificent speech that God utters describing the foundations of the world and the mysteries of the universe. In other words, Job has been, in spite of his lack of sin, a selfish man, a man lacking in humility.

*Cairns:* I don't see where you get that.

*Van Doren:* Well, I agree that Job finally turns out to be a man who has not looked at himself from a universal point of view. I quite agree that he is then thrown into relief as a man of imperfect humility. I was only trying to point out that the arrogant man in the middle portion of the book—if we must call him arrogant, he is also magnificent, completely human—is admirable within the limits of human nature.

*Cairns:* He is combatting the doctrine that was summarized in a line of Schiller's: "The history of the world is the judgment of the world." (*"Die Weltgeschichte ist das Weltgericht."*) That is the ancient Hebrew tradition. Let us see if we can agree upon what Job's position is. Job is, it seems to me, aware both of the meanness and the dignity of man. He accepts without any question the greatness of God, but he protests against the thought of the worthlessness of man.

*Tate:* He accepts the greatness of God—there is no question about that—but is his acceptance sufficiently conscious and deep? Does he know the full extent of the greatness of God? That is the chief point that God makes. He reproaches Job for the narrowness of his knowledge of the world and his relation to the world.

*Van Doren:* And surely the magnificent thing about God's entrance is that He does suddenly expand the field of the book until it is the universe.

*Tate:* God is really saying that from one point of view Job and his friends have been magnifying his plight, which has another dimension that these people have ignored.

*Cairns:* Very true, but isn't God's position when He comes in the whirlwind utterly irrelevant to the point that Job, Elihu and the three friends have been making? They have been questioning God's justice. But God says: "I am not going to talk about my justice. I am going to talk about my power." And He develops the wonderful description of the animals that He created, how the calves were born and how the clouds appeared in the sky. But it is all irrelevant to the argument of Job and his friends. It is not irrelevant to the book as a whole. In fact, I should say that the speech is not only one of the greatest things in the poem as art, but philosophically it is just as important.

*Tate:* But doesn't Prometheus make exactly that same point? Prometheus was doing a noble thing for man and Zeus is arbitrary power, punishing Prometheus arbitrarily, even irrelevantly.

*Van Doren:* On the level of God's existence, can we distinguish between justice and power? The power of God is His justice.

*Cairns:* Would not Plato and Aristotle have distinguished between the two? They would have been shocked by God's answer.

*Van Doren:* I think not. The power of truth for Plato, the power of ideas, is also their justice.

*Cairns:* It seems to me that God's position is essentially the position of Nietzsche; He is beyond good and evil, at least in the sense that a total understanding of the universe may be possible to God (I am not speaking of Nietzsche) alone. Do you think that is Plato's position?

*Van Doren:* No. I would turn the word "irrelevant" against you there. I should say that man's ideas of justice are irrelevant to the truth of the matter, which is possessed only by God. Of course, I am talking to a lawyer now, but men argue about what justice is and apparently never agree. The reason they don't agree is that there is no way of their knowing.

*Tate:* I would agree with Mr. Cairns that Plato and Aristotle would not accept this God, because I think both—particularly Plato—would say that the Hebrew God is an anthropomorphic God. He is like Zeus the Thunderer on Olympus.

*Cairns:* They would have insisted upon an ideal element being present in that God.

*Van Doren:* But remember what Aristotle is saying in the tenth book of the *Ethics*. He says: "Now I free the subject of my discussion, namely, the man who is trying to be good, from his own concerns. I free him from the necessity of considering his own acts, which he can more or less control, in order to contemplate those things in the world which he cannot control." Those are assumed, I take it, by Aristotle to be the final things, the great things, and they are non-human, or super-human.

*Tate:* One of the great things about the *Book of Job* is that paradoxically this problem of justice is not solved. We get a statement of the problem dramatically in human terms, as Job's plight and his misery and his confusion. At the same time, we get a sudden lift at the end in which we see God's attitude toward it and we are convinced that final justice is beyond human comprehension.

*Van Doren:* That is something like a myth in Plato. It has something like the same rhetorical or literary significance.

*Cairns:* It certainly leaves the problem unsolved. However, I think that God's position is the position that Lucretius might have taken; for all we know, it may be the correct position.

*Van Doren:* That is a terrible thing to say, Mr. Cairns, isn't it? Can God agree with Lucretius?

*Cairns:* Perhaps Lucretius is agreeing with God. Renan, who translated the *Book of Job* into French, tried to solve the problem from the position of Jehovah in the whirlwind and also from the position of Lucretius, and he concluded that what happens is a result of blind effort tending on the whole toward good. I would say merely that what happens is the result of a blind effort, so far as man's comprehension is concerned, and speaking from the position of Jehovah in the whirlwind. Job just cannot grasp the activities of the universe.

*Van Doren:* I wonder if any light is thrown on them by another parallel work, namely, the *Samson Agonistes* of Milton, which is a drama (this book is a drama too). It is a drama in which the hero, Samson, has lost his vision, has suffered many calamities and is now a prisoner in a mill with slaves. He is visited, as Prometheus is visited and as Job is, by a series of persons or groups of persons who consider with him the meaning of his calamities. He, to be sure, is in the end, well, perhaps not justified, but rendered happy through being permitted by God to triumph over the Philistines.

*Cairns:* Why do you think—speaking of these three characters placed in such similar positions—that the thought of suicide does not occur to them?

*Van Doren:* Samson in a way commits suicide because, when he destroys the temple, it falls on him and kills him with all his enemies.

*Tate:* But the notion of suicide, if we can answer that question at all, is entirely alien to the Hebrew tradition.

*Cairns:* A Roman, of course, would have thought of it immediately. I should like to return to Jehovah a minute. I think that we agree that no attempt is made to refute Job, at least on the level of the argument conducted by Job and his friends.

*Tate:* Yes. The *Book of Job* is not a treatise. In other words, it seems to me that this book is really a work of the creative imagination. It is not an attempt to equate the experience of man with a theologically and rationally conceived God.

*Van Doren:* Would you call it, Mr. Tate, a work of the dramatic imagination primarily, or is it lyric?

*Tate:* I would say it is primarily lyrical. There is not even as much action implied here as in the *Prometheus Bound* of Aeschylus.

*Cairns:* It is also, of course, gnomic. I doubt if any of the other scriptural books exhibit its elaborate art; and while what it has to say is profoundly true, we are under no obligation to accept its drama as historical fact, any more than we are required to accept the legends of the Greek dramatists.

*Van Doren:* We have not said anything—and I think this is proper because the subject matter is so interesting and important—about the way the book is written.

*Tate:* It is written magnificently.

*Van Doren:* According to a lyric method which can easily fail but which in this case does not. It is the method of elaboration and extension, is it not? An image once offered is given us in an endless number of variations. There is an example of this in the 39th chapter, which I wish to read, chiefly because I like it. God is speaking, and He is asking Job whether Job has the power to create such a thing as the horse. Here is the horse: "Hast thou given the horse strength? Hast thou clothed his neck with thunder? Canst thou make him afraid as a grasshopper? The glory of his nostrils is terrible. He paweth in the valley, and rejoiceth in his strength: he goeth on to meet the armed men. He mocketh at fear, and is not affrighted; neither turneth he back from the sword. The quiver rattleth against him, the glittering spear and the shield. He swalloweth the ground with fierceness and rage: neither believeth he that it is the sound of the trumpet. He saith among the trumpets, Ha, Ha! and he smelleth the battle afar off, the thunder of the captains, and the shouting."

*(1628-1688)*

# BUNYAN

## *The Pilgrim's Progress*

*T*HE PILGRIM'S PROGRESS *was written for the very practical purpose of pointing out to men the way they must go through the world if they wish to be saved. Its author was an extreme sectarian, revolted from the established church of seventeenth-century England, and he wrote for other sectarians. He was without literary consciousness or ambition, nor did he hesitate to appropriate a form—the allegory of a spiritual journey—which many before him had used in his time, not to speak of Dante who had used it centuries before them. But the poor tinker, persecuted and imprisoned for his zeal, was a better artist than he knew, and the reputation of his masterpiece rapidly outgrew the class to which it had been addressed. It alone of all such books in its century survives. And its power is only in part impaired. John Bunyan has few equals in allegory; he possesses, that is, the secret of clear and shining symbols, and he knows how to give them the power* *to move in narrative. The adventures of Christian are as specific as they ever were; the scene, upon which so few words are lavished, remains as vivid as a landscape in a dream; and the personages we meet with on the journey still have their sinister or their benign force. The motive energy is somewhere in Bunyan's imagination, which here worked simply and rightly toward an end which he believed.*

(MR. LYMAN BRYSON, GUEST)

*Cairns:* Mr. Bryson, as you know, *Pilgrim's Progress* has had a vogue second only to that of the Bible. It has been translated into more than a hundred languages. Would you object to venturing an answer to the question: What is the secret of its popularity?

*Bryson:* I will make a guess. I should say that the fact that the Bible and *Pilgrim's Progress* are the two books of greatest circulation has some meaning in it, because the reasons behind the popularity of both, if you compare the works, are very much alike. *Pilgrim's Progress* has a basic interest for anybody who believes in revealed religion, who believes that there is a single path to heaven and that God has revealed that path to men. There are always people who hold that point of view. *Pilgrim's Progress* emphasizes that particular point of view with more vividness and directness and persuasiveness than almost any other book that anybody ever wrote.

*Cairns:* Mr. Van Doren has an expression of dissent, perhaps, on his face.

*Van Doren:* No, one reason surely for the success of the book is the importance of its subject. Mr. Bryson was more tentative in saying the the subject was important than I should be. The subject is that which Dante had for his *Divine Comedy.* It is one of the most absorbing subjects a man could think of.

*Tate:* How would you phrase that subject?

*Van Doren:* Bunyan has phrased it. I happen to be looking at a sentence in which Christian is talking, and he says: "When I was come to years" [Dante puts that, incidentally, "When I had reached the middle of our life"] "I did as other considerate persons do, I looked out if perhaps I might mend myself." This book is addressed to all those persons who in middle life—that is to say, in their prime—find that they don't understand the universe quite as well as they once thought they did.

*Tate:* Isn't the subject of the book a little more specific than that? Doesn't Bunyan ask the special Christian question: how shall I be saved? Isn't the way you state it just a general moral question? That is: how shall we reform our lives?

*Bryson:* I think that is very important, Mr. Tate. It is not: how shall I be a better man? It is: how shall I get to heaven?

*Van Doren:* Of course, I assumed "mend myself" to mean all that.

*Bryson:* But it does not for all people.

*Van Doren:* Oh, no, but the book as a whole means this.

*Cairns:* I should like to suggest that if there is an answer to the question I put to Mr. Bryson, it is on several levels. The main idea of the book is that the life of man is a pilgrimage to a better world when he has been redeemed by the grace of God. That is the specific Puritan point of view that Bunyan is expressing, but the book is not read necessarily for instruction in that doctrine. The appeal of the book seems to me to be on a number of levels. It appeals to children, to adults and to all nationalities. The scheme of the book is very old, and the book has been used as a fundamental pattern all over the world. There is *The Hindu Pilgrim's Progress, The Hebrew Pilgrim's Progress, The Chinese Pilgrim's Progress,* and so on. The idea of a pilgrimage is, of course, as the basis of a story, much older than *Pilgrim's Progress.*

*Tate:* Yes, the journey is one of the oldest literary forms.

*Cairns:* As a matter of fact, it was probably a circumstance particularly favorable to the success of Bunyan's book that he employed an idea which his readers would not find novel. The idea of a pilgrimage was too much in the air for anyone to claim it as his own. I don't think we need look much beyond the Bible for Bunyan's influences. What I am suggesting here is that the book has several appeals. One is the large element of romance that it contains. This is probably the level of its appeal to children.

*Bryson:* It is an adventure story.

*Cairns:* Another appeal is the religious element that Mr. Bryson indicated.

*Tate:* In what sense do you consider this to be an adventure story?

*Van Doren:* I would introduce this modification of the word "adventure." The adventure which Christian is recommending and which he is able to make, finally, is in his opinion not an adventure at all. It is a journey in which he foregoes all adventure. Adventure would consist of wandering through the bypaths which he thinks are wrong. Remember, Good Will points out the road that he must take, and says: "That is the way thou must go. It was cast up by the patriarchs, prophets, Christ and his apostles, and it is as straight as a rule can make it."

*Bryson:* But there were monsters in the way.

*Tate:* While the way is straight and prescribed which every Christian must take if he is going to reach the Celestial City, nevertheless the characters come in very suddenly and so the effect is largely the effect of the adventure story, even though it was all fixed in advance.

*Cairns:* Mr. Bryson, when he used the word "adventure," had in mind the point that the book is full of giants, highwaymen, enchanted places.

*Van Doren:* And devils.

*Cairns:* And devils. That is one element of appeal which is almost universal. It is to be distinguished altogether from what Christian thought of his journey. What he thought, and the symbols in which he thought, is important for adults; the child sees only the goblin.

*Bryson:* I would not believe that for the mature person—the adult person—the adventure element in this has been very important.

*Tate:* I find, Mr. Bryson, that it is the least convincing element to me, in rereading this book.

*Bryson:* The adventure scenes are dull, that is, nothing really stirs your blood when Christian meets Apollyon; it is just a fight soon over.

*Cairns:* But is it the same when he meets the Giant Despair?

*Bryson:* That is quite different, because that is not mere adventure, that is psychological adventure. Then you are dealing with something else. And may I add a point to this business of trying to decide why it is a great book? If you take the characterizations very seriously, you begin to identify yourself and your friends in people. I know the character in *Pilgrim's Progress* that I am myself. I am Ignorance.

*Tate:* We are all Ignorance, Mr. Bryson.

*Bryson:* None of you can be Ignorance to the extent that I am, Mr. Tate.

*Tate:* Mr. Bryson, you are claiming a little knowledge when you say with certainty that you are Ignorance.

*Bryson:* But Ignorance talks the way I do. He has very much the same ideas, and you know that Ignorance is damned, so that when I say that I am Ignorance, I say it with a good deal of regret.

*Van Doren:* I doubt that, Mr. Bryson. I detect some pride in your voice.

*Bryson:* Of course, I may be one of these devils who is proud of his damnation. But I do not think I am at all. I am just a reasonably virtuous man who does not believe in the revelation that Christian believes in.

*Van Doren:* Whereas, of course, Bunyan is interested in nothing but revelation.

*Bryson:* Nothing but revelation—there is one straight road to heaven, and if you do not follow that road, you do not get there.

*Tate:* Can we not state it another way? The morality in *Pilgrim's Progress* is a morality that depends upon revealed religion. Bunyan believes that morality in itself is nothing.

*Cairns:* That is not the point that Mr. Bryson is making. It is that this book reveals the secrets of the solitary heart; that is its appeal. Bunyan has started from his own personal experience, something that Milton did not do. It is for that reason that Milton's appeal is limited. He is not translated, as Mr. Van Doren has said in a previous discussion, into the Hungarian. But Bunyan is. The point can be summed up by saying that a writer who generalizes his own personal experiences, provided he probes deeply enough, will find an audience everywhere; for many people will recognize a portrait of themselves in what he says.

*Van Doren:* But we have to add this to it. Bunyan, to be sure, starts from a personal crisis, as Dante did and as Milton did not do, perhaps; but it is very important for Bunyan, as for Dante, that he does not think he can save himself. Bunyan needs the help of the straight way, the help of a vision or of a revelation. If this is not a straight way, it is no way at all for Bunyan.

*Cairns:* I agree with you; but I am making the point that Bunyan's appeal ultimately is the appeal of Rousseau—the faithful recording of an intense personal experience.

*Tate:* I cannot agree with that. I do not believe that Bunyan's interest in introspection or the analysis of feeling is as great as Rousseau's. It seems to me that what he is interested in is that part of private experience which can be externalized in allegory.

*Cairns:* That is right. He is limited by his Puritan world. But don't forget that in *Grace Abounding* he wrote an analysis of his personal experience, of his inner life, that is overtopped only by the two or three books which can be ranked with Saint Augustine's *Confessions.* It is true that his ideas represent the experience of every Puritan; but in that lies his appeal. It is for that reason that the Hindu Puritan enjoys Bunyan.

*Tate:* That brings up another question I should like to ask you. Suppose you don't believe in the Puritan assumptions. What appeal does this book have? Suppose you also do not believe in all the dogmas underlying *The Divine Comedy,* what do you do about *The Divine Comedy?* I find that the obstacle of belief does not keep me from enjoying *The Divine Comedy.* It somewhat does keep me from enjoying *Pilgrim's Progress.*

*Bryson:* Let me answer that question for myself. If that is true, it is because the drama of the *Pilgrim's Progress* does not affect you quite as deeply as the drama of *The Divine Comedy,* and because the characters in *The Divine Comedy* interest you more. Nevertheless, a great deal of the appeal that there is in *Pilgrim's Progress* is in the depiction of yourself and of your friends. It is not only that I find myself in Ignorance—that is, that the person Ignorance is I—it is not only that, but that I know several people who might very well be Mr. Talkative.

*Van Doren:* I am Talkative. Is none of us Mr. Worldly Wiseman?

*Bryson:* You would hardly admit it if you were, would you? You can boast about being damned, if you want, but not about being worldly wise.

*Tate:* This question about Dante seems to be of great interest. Mr. Bryson was right about that point. I can accept Dante's people, regardless of what they symbolize.

*Bryson:* You can get excited about them.

*Tate:* It does not make any difference what they mean; they are people in themselves.

*Cairns:* Do you have the same attitude that Poe had? He thought that *Pilgrim's Progress* was a ludicrously overrated book.

*Tate:* Oh, I do not feel that.

*Cairns:* You do not go as far as Poe did, but it appears to me that you have the same reasons he had for his conclusion.

*Van Doren:* There is a very important consideration to add with respect to Dante. The reason we can believe him, even if we are not Christian, is that we perceive from the beginning of his book that he is talking about the world we know. Dante never has to invent a geography or a climate for his poem; whereas we can easily suspect Bunyan of inventing.

*Tate:* May I ask whether this defect in Bunyan, if it is a defect, is somewhat related to Milton's deficiency which we discussed some time ago? You cannot find your way about in Bunyan's world and you cannot find your way about in Milton's world. In Dante's world you know where you are all the time.

*Cairns:* But the historians of the seventeenth century insist that Bunyan's world is an absolutely faithful description of England in the seventeenth century.

*Van Doren:* But that England no longer lives. People today

do not think precisely the way Bunyan's audience thought, and so Bunyan has suffered; whereas Dante has not suffered from even greater changes.

*Cairns:* That is a very important point. It may mean that this book, as time passes, may become nothing more than a pretty allegory.

*Bryson:* But are you not leaving out of account, Mr. Cairns, the fact that you are talking about a prose writer as against a writer of poetry? That seeems to me of some importance.

*Van Doren:* No, none at all. You can read *The Divine Comedy* in a prose translation and never, perhaps, be aware of the power of Dante as a writer of verse. In a prose translation where it competes with this . . .

*Bryson:* Of course, it does not compete with this, because it is translated poetry and has a good deal of the color and a good deal of the kind of surcharged emotion which great poetry may have even in the prose translation.

*Van Doren:* Why should we not say that this is trying to be a poem too? Any book that is trying to be good is trying to be a poem.

*Tate:* It is a poem because it deals with action conveyed through fictions of the imagination.

*Van Doren:* This would satisfy Aristotle's definition of a poem.

*Cairns:* But it would qualify as a novel unless an arbitrary definition of the novel is adopted. It was denied in the early nineteenth century that it was a novel, first because it is religious, and, secondly, because it is allegorical. To me those reasons are not convincing. If we look at the elements present in all novels—character, plot, action, description, dialogue—this may properly be regarded as a novel.

*Van Doren:* I do not want to class it as a novel for the simple reason that it is not free, as a novel must be by definition, to follow the wandering path of its own unpremeditated action in the world. This poem—I insist that it is trying to be a poem—is rigorously ruled by the desire of the author to draw a straight line. A novel never draws a straight line.

*Cairns:* We have agreed that it is a poem, but suppose that you, as a professor of literature, were writing a history of the English novel, would you include a description of the *Pilgrim's Progress?*

*Van Doren:* I should completely ignore it, for the reasons I gave. I find that its responsibility is not to this world but to another world. A novel is strictly responsible to this world.

*Cairns:* Whether Bunyan's book falls under that definition depends upon the attitude with which you approach it. If you read it as a work of art, then its responsibility is to this world; if you read it as a Puritan tract, then its responsibility is religious. Read as a work of fiction, I can see no elements missing that a novel must necessarily possess.

*Tate:* Could we not put it in still another way? In a work of fiction—that is, a novel—the action is not determined by abstract ideas primarily. The character of the individual determines the action. We have here just the reverse: the action is determined by a pattern external to the characters.

*Van Doren:* Yes, and the characters can have abstract names here, as they never may in novels.

*Cairns:* Possibly not today but in eighteenth-century works: Mr. Allworthy in *Tom Jones.* For that matter, even in nineteenth-century works.

*Bryson:* As somewhat more of a layman in this business, it seems to me to make very little difference. But is it not true that the reader of today would not read it for the same reason that he would read a novel? What he would want to find in it would be something different. And that is the thing that puzzles me about it. Now, I suspect a very large part of the reading that it gets is from people who share its point of view. There are a great many people who believe that this is the answer to the most profound questions that a man can ask of the world.

*Tate:* I am inclined to agree with that, Mr. Bryson. I do not see how people can read it as they would read a novel. The ordinary human element is lacking. Take such characters as Mr. Wordly Wiseman, Faithful, Hopeful. We have to accept the substance of those names almost as an act of faith, because the characters as men are not sufficiently developed to exemplify those qualities.

*Cairns:* That is a problem you are confronted with in all fiction. It is not customary today to label the characters with allegorical names; but are we not being a little over-sophisticated? It is not conventional now to call characters Mr. Clever or Miss Designing; but would we lose much if we did? In so far as characters are types, they are bound to be allegorical. It seems to me there is a stage in the development of the novel in which you do get something like Bunyan's allegorical characters in the eighteenth- and nineteenth-century novel. Becky Sharp is another example. In the Restoration drama, you have characters who possess names which more or less stand for their qualities.

*Bryson:* I am surprised when Mr. Cairns says that in a novel the characters are always allegorical. They may be in some slight degree, but certainly even in this book, which is primarily allegory—primarily a fable—it is the actual individuality, the realness of some of these people that carries the interest to the book. Christian is very much more than a typical Christian. Christian, in so far as he interests you, is a person.

*Cairns:* Of course, the allegory is always a matter of degree. It has always seemed to me that characters in fiction tend, more or less, to represent virtues and vices.

*Van Doren:* But let us consider the book as an allegory; it surely competes with other allegories. I should call it a second-rate one.

*Bryson:* But a first-rate story?

*Van Doren:* No, I do not think it is a first-rate story, or a first-rate book.

*Bryson:* Then why do people read it?

*Van Doren:* People do not read it as they read it in the seventeenth century, or the eighteenth, or the nineteenth.

*Bryson:* We just had a statement from Mr. Cairns that it had been over a long period a very popular book.

*Tate:* Do we have any figures on the circulation of the book now?

*Cairns:* I do not. I was in the Library of Congress the other day, looking at the copies of *Pilgrim's Progress* in the stacks, and I have never seen so many editions of one book in one place, except Shakespeare and the Bible. Whether it is read today or not I do not know. When I was a child it was read aloud to me by my grandmother, but I suspect that is an experience few children have today.

*Van Doren:* We can explain that by the evaporation from the world, so to speak, of the particular point of view which the book first capitalized. *Pilgrim's Progress* does not move under its own power as Dante's *Divine Comedy* does. Let us consider the allegory and see how unsatisfactory many of the symbols are. For instance, you remember Doubting Castle, where the Giant Despair has thrown our heroes into a dungeon. Suddenly one of them realizes that he has a key in his pocket with which he can unlock the dungeon gate, so he takes it out and the gate swings open and they leave.

*Tate:* Why didn't they do that sooner?

*Van Doren:* No reason is given, but I am interested in the fact that that key has a name. The key is Promise. Now that word "Promise" was completely opaque to me as I read; it meant nothing.

*Bryson:* Didn't you find that an interesting incident?

*Van Doren*: Yes, as an incident; and there the book tends to be an adventure story, if you like; the giant is something like the ogre of the fairy tales. But the word "Promise" conveyed no more meaning to me than the burden that Christian bears on his back. I do not know what that burden is.

*Cairns:* The burden, I think, is sin.

*Tate:* It is not dramatized; it is just a symbol in the book.

*Van Doren:* And then those really quite frightful peep-shows which you see one after another at the house of Interpreter.

Surely one of the most unsatisfactory bits of allegory anywhere in the literature of the world is that in which we find Christ maintaining a flame by pouring oil on it out of a vessel while the Devil in front pours water on it and tries to put it out. Behind the flame, unknown to him, is Christ—not with an oil-can, that is unfair; in the seventeenth century oil did not have a mechanical connotation, but at any rate with his vessel of oil—always feeding the flame. That little tableau is without moral or theological value because its symbolism is elementary and literal-minded.

*Cairns:* There is no question that much of the allegory fails, at least for modern tastes; some of the allegory, however, is quite successful.

*Bryson:* Does this not add up to the statement that it is not for allegory that people read it? If the allegory is bad, then the thing to do is not to worry about the allegory.

*Tate:* But we cannot separate the allegory from the story. Now, let us take another aspect of the allegory: the order in which the different people appear. Mr. Worldly Wiseman appears fairly early; Faithful comes on the scene, and then he is put to death in Vanity Fair; Hopeful takes his place. Then, at the very end of the story, Ignorance appears. There is no dramatic sequence. There is no reason why Ignorance should not have appeared much earlier. In fact, I think he probably should. There is no reason why Ignorance should be at the end of the story when the Pilgrims are entering the Celestial City.

*Cairns:* You are being too hard on the book. All I can say is that I read it with pleasure. A more fruitful subject might be the comparison of Bunyan with Pascal, who was his contemporary. Perhaps in that comparison we can find Bunyan's strength and weakness.

*Tate:* It is a difficult comparison.

*Cairns:* I think it is an obvious comparison. They are both in the same religious tradition. Bunyan seems to be losing his force in the modern world, and Pascal's force seems to be increasing. Why is that? There must be a good reason.

*Tate:* Pascal's doctrine, if you admit that it is very similar to Bunyan's, and I am not sure that it is . . .

*Cairns:* Puritanism and Jansenism both were attempts to restore the dogmas of Saint Augustine.

*Tate:* Suppose we say that they are similar. Nevertheless, Pascal's *Pensées* are based upon a very closely observed psychological experience, which is relevant and is valid at any time, and I do not think that the allegory in Bunyan has that psychological basis for spiritual experience which all men can recognize.

*Van Doren:* Bunyan has not built his faith from the ground up, as Pascal did.

*Cairns:* I cannot agree with that. Bunyan's faith represents one aspect or one way of looking at the universe, which is universal—that is, the separation of the spiritual and the unspiritual.

*Tate:* Mr. Cairns, as you state abstractly the relation of Bunyan and Pascal, it may be true. But isn't the main question whether Bunyan realizes the abstract idea imaginatively in the body of the story?

*Cairns:* That is part of the problem, but I had not quite finished. Pascal looks at the universe from the other point of view. He puts the visible and the invisible together, and that also is universal. There are those two ways of regarding Reality and both have their adherents.

*Van Doren*: But there is this great difference. We are talking about the books the two men wrote. Whatever Bunyan thought, nobody will ever know; what he wrote is in this book, where he has dressed his faith up in a lot of rags—many of them pretty but most of them childish; they are the rag-tags of faith.

*Bryson:* But I think you are using "childish," Mr. Van Doren, in exactly the wrong way here. I should say that Pascal, although he will be read perhaps when Bunyan is forgotten, is a profound mind examining his own psychology with great insight and great learning and great genius.

*Van Doren:* Certainly.

*Bryson:* Bunyan has a genius, but it is not the genius for self-examination psychologically; it is for putting into the very simple and, to the general reader, very impressive machinery of the story, a spiritual experience.

*Cairns:* I cannot agree that he has no genius for self-examination. Everything he wrote was psychological self-examination of the most intense kind. In little of it was he successful; but in *Grace Abounding* he reached the highest point of self-searching that any Puritan ever reached. It falls far short of the imaginative insight of Pascal, but that may be because of a defect inherent in Puritanism itself. Puritanism tends to realize itself in conduct and not in art. You should remember, furthermore, that Bunyan has had a wider appeal than Pascal.

*Bryson:* There will always be more people who can see a spiritual adventure in a story than can see it in psychological truth.

*Van Doren:* My objection is that *Pilgrim's Progress* is not simple. It seemed simple once when it did not have to be understood; now it is much too complicated.

*Tate:* That is the point I was making a minute ago, that the lack of order in the development of the action does not indicate simplicity; it indicates a certain complexity, the secret of which we have lost.

*Bryson:* It takes, Mr. Tate, a mind of considerable development and learning to see the difficulty in *Pilgrim's Progress.* The simple mind approaches *Pilgrim's Progress* in this manner: Here is a good man; he gets into trouble and he gets out again. It is not "boy meets girl"; it is "man meets sin" and overcomes it. And it is just as fundamental a story pattern as "boy meets girl."

*Tate:* I agree with you about the intention of the pattern, but the question sticks in my mind as to whether the pattern is imaginatively developed and embodied.

*Bryson:* It probably is not, but it is enough for the reader who wants the fundamental story pattern I have indicated.

*Cairns:* Our clue to the increasing influence of Pascal and the decreasing popularity of Bunyan may lie in the fact that the Puritan attitude is perhaps disappearing from the world.

*Tate:* It is, and that may explain our interest in the book's defects.

*Van Doren:* In speaking of something as having disappeared from the world, I myself mean not so much an attitude, perhaps, as a collection of symbols, a collection of terms, which Bunyan's colleagues in his particular sect understood with him. Now those colleagues are dead and so is he. Those terms, many of them, are dead. He used them without having examined their depth.

*Tate:* We have a fine passage near the end of *Pilgrim's Progress.* Christian and Hopeful have just come through the menace of death, and allegorically we should have to interpret it as meaning that Christian has died and is now proceeding to heaven. It is one of the very finest passages in the whole book, a magnificent piece of prose in itself, regardless of its position in the imaginative structure of the story. "Then they both took courage, and the enemy that was after them was after that as still as a stone, until they were gone over. Christian, therefore, presently found ground to stand upon, and so it followed that the rest of the river was but shallow. Thus they got over. Now upon the bank of the river on the other side they saw the two shining men again, and they waited for them. Wherefore, being come out of the river, they saluted them, saying: We are ministering spirits sent forth to minister for those that shall be heirs of salvation. Thus they went along toward the gate. Now you must note that the city stood upon a mighty hill, that the Pilgrims went up that hill with ease, because they had these two men to lead them up by their arms. Also, they had left their mortal garments behind them in the river, for though they went in with them, they came out without them. They, therefore, went uphill with much agility and speed, though the foundation upon which the city was framed was higher than the clouds. They, therefore, went up through the regions of the air, sweetly talking as they went, being comforted, because they safely got over the river and had such glorious companions to attend them."

# SCIENCE

(1452-1519)

# LEONARDO DA VINCI

## *Notebooks*

*THE creator of Mona Lisa and the Last Supper was not only one of the greatest of painters; he was a great sculptor, architect, musician, engineer, and scientist as well. He has been called the universal genius, and those who study him in any of his phases come away convinced that he is without his peer. His drawings, which survive in profusion among the libraries of the world, are the despair of anyone who has tried to explain their inexhaustible variety and their impeccable skill. Leonardo was that rare if not unique thing, a man equally gifted in art and in science. The two for him were not opposed or unrelated; his curiosity concerning the secrets of life, being unlimited, took him without prejudice into both precincts, where in the solitude of his genius he embraced the most difficult of problems and at least suggested the most brilliant of answers. It is only of late that he has been known as an author. His manuscripts, surviving in the fragmentary form of notes, have gradually been explored and edited, and now his* NOTEBOOKS *are available to those who wish to see how he conversed with himself in words rather than by line and color. Here as elsewhere he reveals a tireless and beautiful mind to which nothing in nature is alien. His reports of experiments, his generalized observations, his apothegms, even the turns of his phrases are those of a secret master. The* NOTEBOOKS *of Leonardo are not the least monument he erected to himself without the thought that it would some day be standing in the marketplace.*

## (MR. PAUL RADIN, GUEST)

*Cairns:* It is customary to put Leonardo forward as a universal man, and it is certainly true that he went into many fields. He explored mathematics and geology, art, anatomy, aviation, mechanics, music and many other departments of knowledge. There was hardly a field of interest at his time that he did not explore, and to which he did not make contributions. Mr. Tate, do you think we are apt to get more from such a man, or would you say that we are likely to receive more from a man who studies just one aspect of nature?

*Tate:* There are two points involved in such a question. We have first to define an aspect of nature, and then see what it is that we expect to get from any field of study. Take Leonardo's own practice. He was a painter and he was also a student of anatomy. For him—for all artists—the two fields are connected: he used his knowledge of anatomy in his painting. But I do not believe the two fields are equal or on the same level. For example, the painter encompasses, it seems to me, a great deal more than the anatomist—the artist more than a scientist pursuing any one field.

*Cairns:* Are you assuming that art and science can be separated?

*Tate:* Separated in a sense. They certainly are connected, insofar as the artist has to rely upon the common sense of scientific knowledge. I can illustrate that, I believe, with another point. Take Dante's universe. The ancient mathematicians could express it mathematically, but we needed Dante to show the experience of the human race within that universe. In that sense, by the way, it seems to me that Dante is far more the universal man than Leonardo.

*Van Doren:* Dante was a scientist too, was he not? Science means knowing, and for Dante knowledge was a very important thing. He assumed, as any good poet would assume, that knowledge is necessary to poetry. But the relation between the thing known and the poem written is a subtle relation, one that you cannot state by saying merely that a man is a poet and a scientist. A good poet's science becomes a part of his poetry.

*Tate:* Exactly, and they are not separable. We might put it this way: While you can abstract the science from the poetry, you cannot abstract or separate the poetry from the science.

*Cairns:* I would not agree with that. In Leonardo's case there is a fusion of science and art; he was not a scientist who became an artist, nor an artist who became a scientist. There is a single word that covers both aspects of his life and his consideration of them: he was a naturalist.

*Van Doren:* Would it not be true to say that for him his painting and his scientific investigations were both forms of the same exploration? He was always curious about the world.

*Tate:* Don't you believe that the fact that Leonardo did not succeed in bringing all the results of his investigations together into any great design would indicate that his vision was not actually universal? Probably he did it in painting; that is, the fusion of anatomy and the art of painting represents what you are talking about better than anything else. But he did not use his other knowledge that way.

*Radin:* That would assume that Leonardo really believed that you must have a unified vision of the world. It may very well be that Leonardo definitely saw the world, not as a unified thing but as one of very separate and only partially related facets.

*Cairns:* Do you find anything in the *Notebooks* to support that point? Would you not say rather that Leonardo was intensely interested in the universe, in the world as a totality, and that art was to him merely one method of exploring that universe, and that science was another method. It has always appeared to me that he regarded the universe, if I may speak abstractly, as continuous rather than discontinuous, if any man ever did. Yet he saw it whole.

*Van Doren:* He thought of it, if you like, as one thing. From the famous paragraph which is called a "hymn to force," the reader can form the impression that for Leonardo the universe was a living thing, a creature, an animal breathing and using its muscles. I was interested in what Mr. Radin said about Leonardo's vision of a world which cannot be easily known as a single thing, but can be known only in terms of facets that present themselves from time to time. If that is true—if Leonardo did see the world as something that can never be seen all at once—he may not deserve the epithet "universal" as a great painter like Rembrandt, a great scientist like Darwin, a great statesman like Julius Caesar deserves it. Those men, though in the beginning limited, or apparently limited, ended by seeming to cover the world and to unify experience.

*Tate:* There is still another question involved. Perhaps Leonardo is the modern, multiple man. He believed in "multiplicity," as Henry Adams would have expressed it. He was not concerned with the unified vision, and we inherit, I think, the Leonardo tradition, or the tradition of his age. We are still men of the Renaissance.

*Radin:* It seems to me to be only partially correct to say that Leonardo was a man of the Renaissance. We must remember that he emphatically rejected the return to Plato and that he stressed experiment and measurement, both of them traits not characteristic of the Renaissance.

*Van Doren:* I am glad to hear you mention Henry Adams, Mr. Tate, because Henry Adams writes hymns to force also, and they sound very much like Leonardo. Force for both men is something explosive and destructive; it tends to make the universe fly apart.

*Cairns:* We should seek a guiding thread for his scientific approach. The modern scientific mind, that is, the mind that has had the benefit of seventeenth-century science, is a product of two streams—legalism and naturalism. By legalism I mean the theory of order in the universe; that is to say, the notion that the universe operates in accordance with certain immutable laws.

*Van Doren:* You mean natural laws?

*Cairns:* The laws of nature. Their perception and formulation was the great contribution of seventeenth-century science. That influence is something that extended even to literature; Bunyan, for example, had it. He shared the world view of the seventeenth-century scientists. It is clear that he belongs in the school of Newton and the other seventeenth-century scientists as a legalist. In my opinion Leonardo anticipated the seventeenth-century scientists both as a legalist and as a naturalist. I find many instances throughout the *Notebooks* of a belief in the omnipresence of law throughout the universe.

*Tate:* Purely natural law. It is not the divine law of the medieval church. It is something else.

*Cairns:* Laws of this sort: Here is one of his statements: "Nature never breaks her own laws." Here is another statement: "Oh marvelous necessity, thou with supreme reason constrainest all efforts to be the direct result of their causes and by a supreme and irrevocable law every natural action obeys thee by the shortest possible process."

*Tate:* There is a very interesting quality in that statement, and you find it, I think, all through the *Notebooks.* Although Leonardo is talking about natural law, he expresses it in something like rhetoric. The vocabulary is not scientific and exact unless he is doing some precise piece of observation, or giving us a diagram. When he talks about science in general, it turns into a kind of pseudo-poetry; for example, his deification of force, which becomes, as Mr. Van Doren was saying, a personal and living thing. In other words, is he not on one side still a little medieval and religious? He has not made a clean break over into a strictly rational and scientific conception.

*Radin:* There was not any proper scientific vocabulary in existence then and we cannot hold him too responsible for expressing himself in what seems to us rhetoric and pseudo-poetry. Despite verbal inadequacies his was a strictly rational and scientific conception. As I see it, he knew the essential parts of the scientific practice of today: the observation of a phenomenon, artificial reproduction if possible, the discovery of some relationship between its various features, the measurement of these relationships and the deduction of a law.

*Tate:* I did not mean to hold him responsible, or to say that he was at fault. I thought it was an interesting fact that he was so placed historically that he spoke ambiguously.

*Cairns:* That is true, but at the same time I do not know anyone who was further on the modern side than Leonardo. Mr. Radin's point that Leonardo was without a proper scientific vocabulary undoubtedly accounts for the vagueness of many of his remarks. He suffered, moreover, from another disability: he lacked modern instruments. In estimating his work, we should always bear in mind that not until the seventeenth century were the microscope, telescope, thermometer, barometer, air pump and pendulum clock invented.

*Van Doren:* Mr. Cairns, I failed to understand something you said a minute ago, a distinction you were making between legalism and naturalism in scientific thought. Which of those things do you mean to say that Leonardo anticipated?

*Cairns:* Leonardo was the first man to represent or to embody to a really full degree both aspects. My point is that the modern scientific mind is the product of both of those streams; first, of naturalism in the sense that nature is the primary object of study; and secondly, of legalism. Bunyan, although he lived in the seventeenth century, represented only one aspect. He was a legalist and not a naturalist.

*Tate:* But in his conception of a world order, Bunyan is closer to the medieval conception of the divine order. It is very hard to separate Bunyan from that tradition. He is in a period in which the ideas can go in either direction.

*Cairns:* He lived in a period, of course, when the natural legalistic order was dominant in men's minds. All his contemporaries were thinking those thoughts.

*Tate:* But Bunyan's own education, which was almost wholly

Biblical, must have been such that he was not very conscious of the new discoveries in science.

*Cairns:* Probably not. But it was part of the climate of opinion of the time, and it would have been difficult for him to escape it.

*Van Doren:* Would Bunyan have been capable either of writing or of understanding this sentence of Leonardo? "A bird is an instrument working according to mathematical law." I should say that would be completely unintelligible to Bunyan, for whom a bird would be—well, what I should say a bird is.

*Cairns:* Bunyan would not have understood that sentence if he had ever heard it, and he certainly would not have written it; Bunyan would have thought of the bird in a religious sense. What Leonardo is doing in that sentence is making an assertion about a natural object, a bird, and he is also bringing in the element of legalism.

*Van Doren:* But your language itself is interesting. "To him a bird is a natural object." Why is it clear that a bird is a natural object? Why is the bird not one of God's creatures? That is another way of speaking of a bird, is it not?

*Radin:* That is what makes Leonardo definitely the naturalist. But this does not prevent his thinking of a bird as one of God's creatures. However, I should be inclined to disagree with Mr. Cairns that he had this other facet to his nature, I mean, legalism.

*Cairns:* Oh, my heavens! What do you do with these quotations I have just read you?

*Tate:* Are those quotations not tending to say . . .

*Cairns:* I ought to warn you I have many more quotations. I read only one or two.

*Van Doren:* Perhaps it does not make any difference how many quotations you have. They would all be sentences the subject of which was nature. Nature does this or that. Nature has this or that. Nature is this or that. Nature is a lady.

*Cairns:* Have you been peeking into my quotations? Because what you say is true. Let me read just one sentence from Leonardo on the bird, not on the bird precisely; but it is a general statement of his attitude toward the bird considered as any object in nature.

*Van Doren:* It does not happen to be a nightingale, does it?

*Cairns:* No, it does not.

*Tate:* It would be too complicated if it were a nightingale. What would Leonardo do with the song?

*Cairns:* He would provide for the song as subject to physical laws. He might even have anticipated the phonograph. He says, "Human ingenuity can never devise anything more simple and more beautiful or more to the purpose than nature does." When he looks at the bird, that represents the premise from which he starts.

*Van Doren:* To me, a bird is a wonderful thing. So is it to him, but this sentence seems to say that the bird is wonderful to him because it knows so much mathematics. You see, the bird without any effort at all solves almost insoluble mathematical problems. It beats its wings with a certain amount of force and at a certain rate of speed.

*Tate:* Was he really interested in the bird? Was he not rather interested in bird-power? Like horse-power.

*Van Doren:* I should say he was interested in the mathematics of the bird.

*Tate:* But in the bird-power too.

*Van Doren:* Which is not the same thing as the bird.

*Cairns:* I should like to explore a little bit more why Mr. Radin thinks Leonardo was not a legalist. I derived such a strong impression to that effect from my reading of the *Notebooks.* Let me give you, Mr. Radin, one further sentence which seems to me to go to the heart of Leonardo's scientific theory, insofar as you can say he worked out a general scientific theory, as to which I have considerable doubt. He makes this statement: "My intention is to give first place to experience and then by means of reason to demonstrate why the experience was as it was. This is the true rule according to which the investigators of natural phenomena must proceed." Now I can shorten that. What he is saying there is that experience is the point of departure and mathematical form is the point of arrival, which seems to me solidly to embrace legalism.

*Radin:* My objection is to the term "legalistic."

*Cairns:* I do not want to quarrel over a word, particularly when it is not even mine.

*Radin:* It seems to have certain implications that I do not think fit into this particular context. I, for one, always think the term legalism implies something mechanically rigid and static.

*Cairns:* It is a customary word in the history of science. All I mean is the conception of the universe as subject to general laws.

*Radin:* Clearly Leonardo was definitely interested in that, and he would have had no interest in his observations unless he could at the end of them have deduced certain laws. If you mean that, I certainly would agree with you, but that is part, of course, of the naturalist.

*Cairns:* You don't think they can be separated?

*Radin:* I do not think so.

*Van Doren:* I do not see the separation clearly.

*Cairns:* Don't you agree that you can study the natural object without attempting to generalize your observations? That is to say, the natural object can be studied by itself—as by a painter; but in that study there is no necessary implication about an order of nature.

*Tate:* By legalism in the seventeenth century, Mr. Cairns, do you mean the unique development of the science of physics? That was the special form that the development of science took at that time. If we take the physical view of the universe, we can think of it in terms of a very strict mechanical order, governed by "law," but certainly beyond an interest in mechanics. Leonardo probably was not much interested in the general science of physics. Or do you think he was?

*Cairns:* He did not arrive, of course, at a general physics, as Newton did.

*Radin:* He was a practical man, was he not?

*Cairns:* He was a wonderful inventor. And the real question is: How much more was he than an inventor?

*Tate:* I should judge that he was much more than that. He was a great artisan, let us put it.

*Van Doren:* He was a man who had a great natural curiosity as to how things worked. His tendency when he saw anything was to want to take it apart. When he saw a human being he wanted to cut him in two, so he could see his blood vessels and his nerves. He once said that he would like to saw the whole earth in two, so that he could see it in cross section.

*Cairns:* That is the naturalistic element that I had in mind. It has nothing to do with an order of nature or general laws.

*Radin:* I would agree with you then, if you meant that he liked to analyze and take apart. But that was generally for a purpose: namely, to put together again.

*Van Doren:* You throw light, then, upon the meaning of your term. I am still interested in the epithet "universal" which has been applied to Leonardo. I take it that we are faced with a legend about him, and Leonardo surely is one of the most interesting of men. But I agree with Mr. Tate that the method of Leonardo, the method which consists in adding always one more field to the number of fields already explored, will leave the student in the end somehow behind nature, behind the world. It will keep regularly ahead of him.

*Tate:* Perhaps the legend of Leonardo is largely due to our sympathy with his diffusion of interest. He had an interest in mechanics, an interest in anatomy, an interest in hydraulics. Well, in those scattered interests he becomes a symbol of our modern state of mind. It is merely an aggregation of interests and not a unity of purpose or a unity of vision.

*Van Doren:* You can say that he studied twenty-five things, but of course there are twenty-five million things to study; there is no end to the number of things. Whereas if you do happen to be fortunate enough to believe that there is one thing to study, perhaps you can study that with something like completeness, before you die.

*Cairns:* That may satisfy you personally as an individual, but

I do not see that there is any guarantee it will lead to a full comprehension of the world unless the world is continuous.

*Tate:* I think a full comprehension of the world is possible only to a man who sees it all his life from one point of view. Comprehensiveness is not the same thing as a statistical completeness. For example, if you look at the world from Leonardo's point of view, you must conclude that before you can have a unity of conception, you have to get the complete aggregation of all the scientific facts; and that is clearly impossible.

*Van Doren:* We are speaking of science. Perhaps we should say knowledge. Shakespeare knew the world. When you have finished reading his plays you have no sense that you are ignorant of the world. You know much more about it, indeed, than you did before.

*Cairns:* You know human beings but not nature.

*Van Doren:* Not nature? I doubt that. I have the sense, as I read Shakespeare, that I know nature too.

*Radin:* But not in certain formulations of interest to the scientist and just as complete and fundamental as those of the poet.

*Van Doren:* I am not talking about knowing formulations of nature. I am talking about knowing nature, which is a very different thing.

*Radin:* Well, if you can make valid formulations of nature, you know nature.

*Cairns:* Does Shakespeare add anything to our knowledge of the ultimate substance of the world? What is the nature of matter as Shakespeare sees it?

*Van Doren:* Does science add anything?

*Tate:* Science is always pushed on from one position to another.

*Cairns:* But science is closer. At least science attempts to answer such questions and Shakespeare does not even attempt to do that.

*Tate:* Maybe Shakespeare knows better than to attempt it.

*Van Doren:* That is quite right. In the long run, the poet knows more about the world than the scientist does, because he keeps his eye on the world. The poet is not interested in statements that can be made *about* the world. He is interested *in* the world.

*Tate:* May we say, Mr. Van Doren, that one thing that the poet knows is the scientist himself?

*Van Doren:* Yes.

*Tate:* And the scientist does not know the poet.

*Van Doren:* That may be.

*Radin:* I doubt that very much. I suspect he may know the poet better than the poet knows himself, or the poet the scientist.

*Cairns:* Mr. Tate and Mr. Van Doren are using "world" in a different sense. Mr. Radin and I are talking about the world of matter; they are talking about the world of human beings.

*Van Doren:* At any rate, we have in Leonardo a man who, whenever he drew a bird, and in my opinion he was the great draftsman of history, drew a bird which is a bird, which has the life of a bird as well as the looks of one. When he is a scientist he talks in that curious language which makes it possible for him to say that a bird is an instrument working according to mathematical law. I maintain that that is one of the most fantastic statements which can be made. Mr. Tate once complained that most people these days could not look at a horse and see simply a horse. They see it as a beast of burden, as something which ought to be saved from its misery, as a quadruped, as almost anything except what it is.

*Tate:* What Leonardo says about the mechanics of a bird is probably true, but suppose we look at the bird from the point of view of the ornithologist. He is not interested in mathematics. He is classifying birds according to shape, color, their phylogenetic habits and so on. But when you put all those different scientific pictures together, do you ever get the real bird?

*Cairns:* Perhaps Mr. Van Doren can help settle this matter of the bird. Leonardo, when he wanted to draw a bird as an artist, drew it. There is no greater European draftsman than Leonardo. Let me ask: What chapter in the *Notebooks* is that sentence in? What question is Leonardo trying to answer? What is the title of the chapter containing that sentence?

*Van Doren:* It is the first sentence of the chapter called "The Flying Machine." He is interested in adapting such knowledge as he can get of the mechanics of bird flight to the making of a machine with which a man can fly.

*Radin:* That is quite true.

*Cairns:* We can understand Leonardo's intention in that sentence when he approaches the bird from that point of view.

*Tate:* He is interested in the flying aspect of the bird.

*Van Doren:* These *Notebooks* are not a treatise, and it is unjust to Leonardo to give the impression that he thought so.

*Cairns:* It is not only unjust to Leonardo, but it is also hard on the reader. There is an old saying that all Leonardists in the end go mad.

*Van Doren:* All I want to say is that a reading of these remarkable notes does not leave me with a sense that Leonardo knows the whole world in anything like the way in which the legend makes him out to know it. He knows a great many things about the world, if you like. It is my belief that he did not know the world, and there are gaps even in his cursory knowledge which are astonishing. For instance, music seems to him contemptible and mean because it is an art of repetition. He thinks there is something unworthy about repetition.

*Tate:* Then as to poetry, his conception of it is extremely naive. For example, he says that if you put an image of God before a person he is much more moved than he is moved by the word God written on a piece of paper. Well, that is by no means a fair comparison of sculpture or painting with poetry. A poem is not isolated words.

*Cairns:* The explanation might be that the book is heavily weighted on the side of physics. It is largely natural science as Leonardo understood it.

*Tate:* Practical physics, let us say. It is not speculative physics, is it?

*Cairns:* No. It is largly technology. Occasionally you run across a sentence such as "Truth is the only daughter of time," which has a poetic element in it.

*Van Doren:* Here is one sign to me that he is not the effective mind he might have become. There is frequently in him, if not always, an element of the fantastic. He did not submit himself to that discipline which any art, if a man marries the art, makes him submit to, correcting each work that he does so that the next work becomes better. He tends to fray, to spread out, and is oftentimes childish.

*Cairns:* You mean he tends to the extraordinary and the extravagant in his speculation?

*Van Doren:* He tends to be extravagant, even trivial.

*Cairns:* You were not making the point that he had a naturalistic interest in ugliness as such?

*Van Doren:* No, although ugliness interested him as it interests anybody.

*Cairns:* As a painter, he was particularly interested in it.

*Van Doren:* There is a paragraph in the section of this book called "Philosophy" which I consider highly characteristic of Leonardo, for it expresses that man in him who saw the world as a creature. "Behold now the hope and desire of going back to one's own country or returning to primal chaos, like that of the moth to the light, of the man who with perpetual longing always looks forward with joy to each new spring and each new summer, and to the new months and the new years, deeming that the things he longs for are too slow in coming; and who does not perceive that he is longing for his own destruction. But this longing is in its quintessence the spirit of the elements, which finding itself imprisoned within the life of the human body desires continually to return to its source. And I would have you to know that this same longing is in its quintessence inherent in nature, and that man is a type of the world."

# HISTORY

(c. 55-120)

# TACITUS

# *History*

*TACITUS is a moralist as much as he is a historian. He lived in what he felt to be degenerate times—from the reign of Nero through that of Trajan—and his history of imperial Rome is, among other things, an indictment of cruelty and corruption. In common with others he looked back to the days of the Republic as to a healthier world now irrecoverably lost; but in his book on the Germans he envied the simplicity of life among contemporary barbarians—future enemies of Rome whose virtues it would be well to emulate. His history is in its later books the work of an eye-witness, or at any rate of one who lived through the years recorded. The worst years for him were the last three of Domitian's reign, when purges were depleting Rome of its best along with its worst citizens. So many judicial murders sickened him, confirming him in his despair of the imperial process. His* HISTORIES *and his* ANNALS *are therefore tragic and gloomy books, relieved only here and there by gleams of admiration for some isolated good man in a depraved world. His style, which has not made for popularity because of its closeness and its occasional obscurity, is nevertheless one of the great prose styles of all time, being concise, epigrammatic and deeply colored by his own personality; a careful reading of Tacitus is richly rewarding, for few more interesting or powerful men have ever written.*

*Cairns:* In his short study of the Germans, Tacitus claimed to observe certain unique characteristics in those people. Perhaps present-day Germans exhibit some of those characteristics. Tacitus pointed out that the Germans of his time were mystical. That is a point which might be made of contemporary Germans. He observed also that they did not adopt any habits of luxury. Perhaps the same claim might be made now. Tacitus also pointed out that the Germans of his day never engaged in any business, public or private, unless they were well armed. Some people might think that this is still characteristic of the Germans.

*Van Doren:* Tacitus also said that the economic system of the old Germans was entirely a system of barter; as everyone knows, the economic system recommended by the Germans of this day is a system of barter.

*Tate:* Didn't Tacitus say that gold and silver were withheld from the Germans—"is it by the favor or the wrath of heaven?"

*Van Doren:* My instinct would be to say of the Germans today, though I do not know them at first hand, that they are not easygoing, as on the whole Tacitus represents his Germans to have been. His Germans he refers to once as lovers of slumber—lovers of inertia. Paradoxically, he adds that they were haters of quiet. Our Germans may be haters of quiet; they do not seem to be lovers of slumber. I myself am always skeptical of generalizations made about peoples, I must confess. The Germans surely enough are not the only mystical people on earth—if they are mystical now.

*Cairns:* With that I agree heartily. When I come back from Europe people ask me if the people in England or Italy are sad or happy. I don't know. As I walk along the streets of European cities I see all kinds of expressions on the faces of the people. I could not say whether they were happy or not.

*Tate:* About this "mysticism" that Tacitus attributes to the ancient Germans, that is probably a rather loose expression. What he means is that they had a kind of pantheistic religion; their mythology was not as highly developed as the classical mythology; and they had mysterious rites which he had heard about and did not understand. Probably he lumped all this together in a kind of romantic mysticism.

*Van Doren:* So did the ancient Britons with their druids, and so did the Gauls.

*Tate:* Precisely. And in other ways these primitive Germans are very much like primitive peoples in any northern climate.

*Cairns:* I would not limit it to northern climes. In many ways the Germans were like the Ancient Romans. For one thing, neither possessed images of their gods. In fact, the early historians generally made the point that primitive people had no temples and no images. It was a characteristic, for example, that Herodotus observed of the Persians. Furthermore, Tacitus was appealing directly to the sensibilities of the Romans when he referred "to that secret power which they behold with the eye of adoration alone." The Romans were well aware of the effect of deep woods in propagating profound religious feeling.

*Van Doren:* The reason for my skepticism about generalizations concerning peoples is that one never knows whom to take as authority on peoples. You all remember, a few years ago, how many books were being written to tell us what the Russians were then like. Those books varied according to the expectation the visitor to Russia had before he got there. He found on the whole the Russia that he expected to find. And the same thing was true of European literature concerning America in the eighteenth and nineteenth centuries.

*Tate:* De Tocqueville's book on American democracy is very much like that; it is read with great interest today, but it is certainly not an accurate version of America at that time.

*Van Doren:* De Tocqueville found the democracy he wanted to find, and Matthew Arnold found the democracy *he* wanted to find too.

*Tate:* And so did Dickens.

*Van Doren:* So did Dickens, yes. Those two did not want to find an attractive democracy, and they did not find it.

*Cairns:* There is a historical principle that covers what we have been discussing—the so-called principle of transference. It is well illustrated by Chapter IV of the *Germania.* The principle asserts that certain characteristics and customs are believed to be typical of all primitive peoples, and that the ancient historians thought that those characteristics could therefore be predicated of any half-civilized people without any evidence. Chapter IV, for example, refers to the Germans as a race pure, unmixed and stamped with a distinct character; hence a family likeness pervades the whole, though their numbers are so great: Eyes stern and blue; ruddy hair; large bodies, powerful in sudden exertions but impatient of toil and labor, least of all capable of sustaining thirst and heat. Substantially those phrases have been used by historians prior to Tacitus to describe the Persians, Scythians and Thracians. Pliny describes the natives of Ceylon as having some of those characteristics.

*Tate:* But does not this linking together of general characteristics come of lack of intimate knowledge? If he had seen all the different tribes of northern Europe at that time, he would have distinguished much more minutely.

*Cairns:* Perhaps he would have, but it is doubtful that Tacitus even saw the Germans.

*Tate:* No, of course, he did not. For example, when he gives the reader an impression of the way Germany looked, the topography, the climate, I am inclined to be very suspicious of Tacitus because he is looking at Germany from the point of view of the semi-tropical climate of Italy. There are the "gloom in the forests" and the "cheerless scene," and the Germans are bound to be the way they are because they live in that kind of climate. Here Tacitus reads almost like a nineteenth-century historian.

*Cairns:* He observes that the Germans have no interest in gold, and that they do not distinguish their silverware from their earthenware. That is a characteristic that has been assumed without evidence of many primitive people prior to the rise of a critical ethnography.

*Van Doren:* Insofar as Tacitus has negative findings to report—that the Germans were not effete, that they were not overrun with vices of all sorts—insofar as he found them, in other words, to be simple and relatively noble, he did not have to go there for evidence at all, because there was already a literature in existence concerning unknown simple, half-civilized peoples, and that literature continues. We have it today; in the way the late D. H. Lawrence, for instance, wrote about the Indians of Mexico and New Mexico. There is always a sentiment for the discovery of those virtues in an uncivilized people which are lacking in the race for whom an author writes. Now Tacitus, it seems to me, very clearly deserves the legend which says that he was writing his *Germania* as much as anything else for home consumption. That is, he wanted the Romans of his own time to reflect upon the greater simplicity and the greater virtue of the barbarians to the north.

*Cairns:* There is certainly an element of truth in that view of Tacitus; although, of course, it is earnestly combated by modern students of Tacitus. It must be said for Tacitus, however, that he describes the vices of the Germans quite as much as their virtues. He admired the simple virtues of the old Roman Republic. I think the characteristics he most admired in the Germans were their simple and strict marriage customs: life-long fidelity to one mate. He is careful, however, to condemn the drunkenness, gambling and laziness.

*Tate:* There was no complacency in Tacitus's point of view; he was not saying that we, as Romans, are greatly superior to these barbarians. But don't you think that the famous Tacitean irony comes out in this little history of Germany? The irony cuts both ways. While he is saying these people are barbarians, he is holding them up to the Romans as models of a virtue which the Romans have lost.

*Van Doren:* And Tacitus as a historian, if we consider the whole scope of his work (because the *Germania* after all is a fairly slight item among his works), is moral—a man deeply concerned with the vices and the virtues of the Romans whom he knew. Indeed he once said frankly that he considered the materials of history to be its records of nobility and turpitude.

*Tate:* What do you think about that as a method for a historian? In reading the account of Tiberius, I was immensely struck with the way you are carried along, almost as you are carried along by an expert novelist. He never lets the character of Tiberius get very far away. He brings in innumerable characters, so many in fact that it is almost impossible to keep them in order. Every prominent character of Rome in the reign of Tiberius is brought in in that way. What is the secret of that method? It seems to me that he has established a certain point of view toward human nature and stuck to it with great consistency throughout. In other words, he has no "theory" about the way history ought to be written.

*Cairns:* I disagree with that view. He does definitely state a theory.

*Tate:* I know he states a theory in the course of the *Annals,* in the discussion of Tiberius, as a matter of fact, but I do not think it accounts for his effectiveness.

*Cairns:* No, I do not think it does, either. He says: "This I conceive to be the principal use of annals, that instances of virtue may be recorded; and that by the dread of future infamy and the censures of posterity, men may be deterred from depravity in words or deed." That is a simple-minded theory of history and was scarcely exemplified in practice by Tacitus. He was a much more sophisticated man and, I might add, historian.

*Tate:* Do you think anybody would get that simple message from the *Annals?* I do not think so. It is more complicated than that. He has a sense of the complications of human nature.

*Cairns:* Before we leave the subject of the *Germania,* I want to see if I fully understand Mr. Van Doren. Are you saying that he held a moral mirror up to the Romans, or are you saying that he is writing a description of Germany to enlighten the Romans as a modern traveler might write a book about Tibet for us? Or did Tacitus have some combination of purposes in view?

*Van Doren*: I should say that his first impulse was to write a book describing those Germans whom many Romans at the time were thinking about because wars were being fought up there and legions were occupying that border. But his interest as he went along—always a moral interest, and I mean by moral no more than human and serious—expressed itself in the way I have suggested; he made the comparison, which would be inevitable for him, between the manners of his people and the manners of those people.

*Tate:* Was it a conscious purpose at the beginning? Was it not rather an overtone in the account of the Germans?

*Van Doren:* I dare say it was, but it is a thing that everyone has found there, and properly found there, just as it is proper to find in many of the books about America which I spoke of a minute ago, in the eighteenth and nineteenth centuries, an implied rebuke to the manners of Europe, which were supposed to be less simple and less virtuous than ours.

*Cairns:* I think his method of describing the Germans carries through into his other histories. That is to say, he is a fair and conscientious historian; he first gives the favorable qualities of the Germans; he then gives the unfavorable qualities of the Germans. When he discusses Tiberius, while he is prejudiced toward Tiberius throughout the whole course of his portrait, he does include enough facts so that an impartial historian could put aside that emotional feeling and actually construct a portrait of Tiberius different in its total effect from the one presented by Tacitus, but still based upon Tacitus's.

*Van Doren:* But it is impossible for any reader of Tacitus to put aside Tacitus's emotions, which are surely very powerful. Mr. Tate a minute ago asked me what I thought of Tacitus's method as a historian—what I thought of his literary method, because he is surely a literary historian. My answer is frankly that I like that kind of history much the best. For me, the more history is literature, the more it is like fiction, the better.

*Cairns:* Tacitus was a literary artist who portrayed human character with the skill of a novelist; he also developed a unique literary style. The *Annals,* which opens with the reign of Tiberius, is his masterpiece. The *Annals* has been compared to a tragedy in two acts: the first act ending with the death of Tiberius; the second with the death of Nero.

*Tate:* In a work like this you actually get history in terms of immediate human experience, in terms of the characters. If you have a theory of history which is based upon an analogy to science, that is, if you say things are determined by this or determined by that, economic and social forces and so on, you are very likely not to have the history written, because in the long run mere method does not write anything: a human being must write history.

*Van Doren:* Tacitus never forgets that Rome was full of the most amazing human beings. The real power of this book is the power which is in any great story-teller. I should say that Tacitus was a historian by accident; he was first of all a story-teller. The privilege of any great story-teller is to give us people.

*Tate:* Mr. Cairns, you were just reading Tacitus's description of his special historical interest; that is, he was interested in holding up models of virtue and vice. It seems to me that in any great writer the secondary interest, or the secondary purpose, is often the more important of the two.

*Cairns:* I agree. Tacitus's moral reflections are at times amusing for their naïveté. I do not think that he followed his own historical theory. He was too great a historian for that.

*Tate:* For example, he does not succeed in making Tiberius a complete example of vice. Tiberius has a great many very fine qualities to his credit.

*Cairns:* That was the point I was trying to make. That although he does write this portrait of Tiberius with a pen dipped in malice, he gives you enough facts to counteract it, if your inclinations run in the other direction.

*Van Doren:* I should not agree with you there, Mr. Cairns. What counteracts a sense of prejudice in Tacitus is the more important quality which any great story-teller must have—a feeling that any human being has an integrity of his own. He had a sense of responsibility to character. I do not see Tacitus listing vices and virtues and coming to a decision about the preponderance between them, but I find him possessed by the personality of Tiberius, which he thinks he hates and which he does hate, to be sure, but the force of which, the intellectual force, he never misses.

*Tate:* There is another quality operating in his treatment of Tiberius. I should say that after we read the whole life of Tiberius, there is no possible way to explain how the Roman State could have endured twenty minutes under such a man, and yet the Roman State did endure.

*Cairns:* There are several explanations for that: Augustus had left a well-organized state which continued to function satisfactorily under many less able emperors. The reign of Tiberius was ably and peaceably administered by permanent officials who apparently were little affected by the terror, but, as a matter of fact, it has always seemed to me that Tiberius, except during the last years of his reign, was an able administrator.

*Tate:* It is significant that Tacitus is not specifically interested in that administrative organization as a modern historian would be. He never gives you an objective and elaborate description of it; he assumes it.

*Cairns:* His primary interest is Rome, and not the provinces, where the major effects of the bureaucratic administration would be displayed. Another facet of Tacitus is brought out when we compare him with Thucydides. He is a lawyer and he is interested in presenting Rome in the best light that he possibly can to the world. His arguments more often than not are lawyers' arguments; that is to say, he is trying to make the best of a bad case. Thucydides possesses a rigid impartiality.

*Tate:* It is, of course, not the Rome of his day; it is the Rome that has been and a Rome that may be later; in fact, the Rome that he knew under Nerva a little later on. But how do you compare him, Mr. Cairns, with Thucydides?

*Cairns:* Thucydides is more judicial, more impartial. Both men had elevated views of the function of history; Thucydides had a better control over his materials.

*Tate:* Do you think he is as interesting?

*Cairns:* Yes, I consider Thucydides is as interesting as Tacitus. However, Thucydides had a much greater subject than Tacitus had.

*Van Doren:* He has the greatest of all subjects—the death of Greece.

*Cairns:* And Tacitus has the death of Rome.

*Van Doren:* Tacitus recognizes that he has a limited subject, and that this limitation is tragic for him. He looks back with a certain nostalgia to the opportunity which the earlier Roman historians had of writing concerning the great days of the Republic, when events of vast importance were going forward and free men were developing their souls. He says in effect: Now, within the narrow limits of this dictatorship, all I can tell you about is intrigue, and that becomes monotonous and satiates me. Of course, the book itself is not monotonous.

*Cairns:* Tacitus felt that Livy, in writing the history of the Roman Republic, had the choice subject.

*Tate:* I have a passage here, just one brief sentence, which seems to me to contain a great deal of the secret of Tacitus's power as a historian. He is describing the decline of Tiberius, just before his death, and he attributes to Tiberius, even at the end, one of his characteristic vices, and yet he states this vice in such a way as to make it almost a virtue. For example: "Tiberius now drew near his end; his strength declined; his spirit sunk; and everything failed except his dissimulation." Well, that power to hold out with his dissimulation to the end showed a certain sternness of character.

*Cairns:* Tiberius became very bitter in his old age. He left

Rome and built his famous villas on the lovely Island of Capri. When he learned of the treachery of his long-trusted prime minister, Sejanus, that was the final blow and he no longer trusted anyone. Sejanus had had Tiberius's only son secretly poisoned years before. However, Tacitus emphasizes that Tiberius's reign began with dissimulation. The first point Tacitus makes about Tiberius is that his system of dissimulation started immediately upon the death of Augustus. Instead of demanding the suffrages of the Senate for his nomination as prince of the Senate, according to Tacitus, he feigned reluctance and accepted office only after the most earnest entreaty by the Senate.

*Van Doren:* He feels a responsibility as a writer to the ruling passion of Tiberius.

*Cairns:* Tiberius is one of the most difficult characters in Roman history to understand. I do not think I have made the point clear that I made a minute or so ago, when I said that Tacitus gives enough facts so that his view can be corrected. For example, when he describes the reign of terror that occupied the last years of Tiberius's reign, he indulges in a good deal of rhetoric. He describes Tiberius as never satiated with trials and condemnations; that those trials and condemnations aroused an even greater blood-lust in him. He describes the universal panic and the fact that even the most highly placed people in the state became informers; that men were put to death for past deeds as well as for recent ones, for speaking as well as for acting, and so on. But in all that rhetoric there are facts imbedded, such as cases of pardon, of acquittal, that some escaped by giving information, others by adjournment of the court or by being merely ignored by the police authorities; some even received sentences less than death. With these additional facts before us, can we say that Tiberius is the monster Tacitus paints? At the very least, it seems apparent that the reign of terror was not as unrelentingly bloodthirsty as Tacitus wants us to believe.

*Van Doren:* I should say that his method of making you understand Tiberius is what you say it is, among other things. I did not want to say that Tacitus was not interested in facts. Of course, he had the same kind of interest in facts that a great novelist has in truth. But it is also worth while to point out the way he has of rendering Tiberius to you by saying things about him, by making distinctions—moral distinctions—such as this one: "The best men about him he feared as a private danger, the worst as a public scandal." Now, you have in this antithesis a statement that Tiberius was always afraid, not only that something would happen which would wreck his government, but also that something would happen which would put his own position in danger. Or Tacitus could say of Tiberius: "He feared liberty and detested flattery."

*Cairns:* But he also quotes Tiberius as saying: "In a free state both mind and tongue should be free"; and also on the credit side of the ledger, he points out that Tiberius resisted the tax-gatherers in the provinces. Tiberius forbade them to collect taxes in excess of what they should collect. Tiberius said to the collectors: "My sheep may be shorn but not flayed by you."

*Tate:* And typical too of the Roman tradition of early American politics, our own early statesmen said things like that. It seems to me that Tacitus sums up the complexity and the paradox of Tiberius's character, when he puts these words into the mouth of Arruntius: "In despotic power there's a charm that can poison the best understanding!" To a certain extent Tacitus succumbed to this charm in Tiberius, in spite of himself.

*Van Doren:* He could not help respecting a man who, although he had to live by flattery, yet detested it. Tiberius's superiority to the sycophants who surrounded him, and who were the most disgusting flatterers, I suppose, on the whole human record, is expressed by his contempt for them, even though he found them necessary to sustain his power.

*Cairns:* Tacitus appears to me to be as great an artist as Thucydides and the most powerful of the Roman historians. He has a special relevance today.

*Van Doren:* And he is also a source of great pleasure to the reader of today. He is not a new discovery exactly, but I had not read him for years, and it is now clear to me that he is one of the great writers of the world. Who else ever wrote a sentence like that very famous one from his biography of his father-in-law, Agricola? It is a Briton, to be sure, speaking of the Romans: "They make a desolation and they call it peace." Who could say, as Germanicus, one of the heroes of the *Annals,* is made to say when he arrives and finds that a mutiny has been put down with too much butchery: "This is not a cure, but a calamity."

*Cairns:* I deliberately made the remark about Tacitus's relevance, because I wanted to venture a historical generalization. It seems to me that Tacitus is read in an age of the Caesars, in troubled times. When the Crown was powerful in England, Tacitus was read as a statesman's manual by British politicians; but when Parliament became supreme, he passed out of fashion. Montaigne read him in the sixteenth century and that was an extremely troubled century. Montaigne said of him: "His services were adapted to a sick and disturbed state as ours is at present. You might often think he were describing us and criticizing us." He was, of course, read during the reign of terror of the French Revolution. Madame Roland read Tacitus while waiting to be guillotined. Camille Desmoulins during the Revolution compared the activities of the Jacobins unfavorably with the reign of terror in Tiberius's time. Desmoulins was immediately sent to the scaffold by the Jacobins.

*Van Doren:* Tacitus, remember, lamented the fact that he could not write in a time of liberty.

*Cairns:* And he pointed out that if it was thought the Romans were not going to have any more dictators, that view was much mistaken. "Think you," he said, "that the race of tyrants ended with Nero? The men who survived Tiberius reasoned in that manner; after the death of Caligula they said the same; whereas, in the meantime, there sprang up one still more hateful and barbarous."

*Tate:* Tacitus has many passages concerning the civil and political disorders of his time. In the *Agricola,* there is a passage describing the state of disorder, not under Tiberius, but later under Domitian, which is one of the most eloquent passages in

Tacitus's works. "We have it upon record that Arulenus Rusticus, for the panegyric of Poetus Thrasea, and Herennius Senecio, for that of Helvidius Priscus, were both capitally convicted. Nor was it enough that those excellent authors fell a sacrifice to the tyrant's power; persecution raged against their books, and, by an order of the Triumvirs in the forum and the place of popular convention, the monuments of genius perished in the flames. The policy of the times, no doubt, intended that in the same fire the voice of the Roman people should be stifled, the freedom of the senate destroyed, and the sentiments of the human heart suppressed forever. To complete the work, all sound philosophy was proscribed, every liberal art was driven into banishment and nothing fair and honorable was suffered to remain. Restrained by the terrors of a merciless inquisition from the commerce of hearing and speaking and by consequence, deprived of all exchange of sentiment, we should have resigned our memory with our other faculties, if to forget had been as easy as to submit in silence."

(1737-1794)

# EDWARD GIBBON

# *The Decline and Fall of the Roman Empire*

*G*IBBON *in his* AUTOBIOGRAPHY *describes the moment when he conceived the plan of his great history. "It was at Rome, on the fifteenth of October, 1764, as I sat musing amidst the ruins of the capital, while the barefooted friars were singing Vespers in the Temple of Jupiter, that the idea of writing the decline and fall of the city first started to my mind." The temple was a Roman ruin, but the friars who had succeeded its priests still flourished, and that symbol of time's passage was enough for Gibbon, who as he went forward with his work gave particular attention to the part played by Christianity in the decease of ancient Rome. His first audience, aware of this, was shocked by the tone he took—"Sapping a solemn creed," as Byron put it later, "with solemn sneer." Gibbon was a citizen of the Age of Reason, and irony pervades the pages in which he recites the excesses of the past. But he was equally superior to the excesses of* *the pagans, whether in Rome itself or in the Eastern capital. His* DECLINE AND FALL, *covering more than ten centuries of time and the whole of the then known world, has a sweep and a momentum so rare in literature as to be almost unique. And its imperturbable style, caustic at the same time that it is sonorous, rolls without pause from the first word to the last. Whether for its subject or for its form, the* DECLINE AND FALL *remains a book with which any educated person sooner or later becomes acquainted.*

*Cairns:* Gibbon appears to be the only historian of modern times who is still generally read after the lapse of a hundred years. What special qualities do you think he possessed, Mr. Tate, that caused him to survive?

*Tate:* That is very simple. It is the quality of being a very great writer, and I doubt that there's a living historian, writing in the English language, who happens to be a great writer at the same time. Gibbon seems not to have had what we call today the historical method. He has no philosophical theory of history.

*Van Doren:* Are you sure about that?

*Tate:* I mean the modern sense of the term. That is, he doesn't have a scientific approach to history; he's not interested in scientific cause and effect. He's interested in human personalities, the force of ideas and emotions; and the whole Roman Empire, from the beginning of its decline to what he considers its fall, in the Middle Ages, is for him a vastly complex human movement. And while he doesn't have a theory which explains those complexities, he has a great style controlled by an imagination which is able to encompass all that vast life.

*Van Doren:* There was another great writer of his own century, that is to say the eighteenth century in England, David Hume, who wrote a history which was considered great and which was popular for a long time, but it is not read now as Gibbon is. Could you guess why Hume's *History* has not survived with Gibbon?

*Tate:* You mean Hume's *History of England*?

*Van Doren:* Yes.

*Tate:* I should say it is neglected because the style is peculiarly dry. Hume in fact had very little imagination; he couldn't combine the complex forces of history and state them. He was narrowly political and analytical. I have a sentence here which shows, I think, beautifully Gibbon's richness and power of compression. I pick it at random. He is talking about Arabia and the rise of Mohammedanism: "In Arabia as well as in Greece, the perfection of language outstripped the refinement of manners, and her speech could diversify the four-score names of honey, the two hundred of serpent, the five hundred of lion, the thousand of a sword; and there were times when this copious dictionary was entrusted to the memory of an illiterate people." The complexity of perception, the things he compresses together, indicate great literary power.

*Cairns:* I agree with you when you say that his book has survived as literature. I think he combined history and literature in a way that few other historians have done—perhaps only Thucydides and Tacitus. Of course, throughout his history he included everything—literature, law, archaeology, battles, descriptions of cities. He dealt also with the central problem of European history on a scale that no one has attempted and which, I should guess, so great was the detail that had accumulated, no one could attempt a hundred years after him.

*Van Doren:* By the way, Mr. Cairns, wouldn't you agree with me that he is interested in what he calls causes? He oftentimes makes lists of causes for an event.

*Cairns:* I was just coming to that.

*Tate:* But not causes as modern historians understand them—not abstract economic causes, social forces . . .

*Van Doren:* That is quite true.

*Cairns:* It seems to me, to revert to the question about Hume, that histories pass out of fashion, that there is such a high mortality among histories, for two reasons: Either deficiency in knowledge—later ages add to the knowledge that the earlier historian possessed and the earlier history goes out of date because it is regarded as inaccurate (this is not true of Gibbon)—or (the second reason) because the historian's explanation of why things happened as they did becomes outmoded. Froude liked to explain things on the basis of the workings of the moral law. That view is no longer fashionable and, as a consequence, Froude is no longer read. What has saved Gibbon is that he rarely explains anything.

*Van Doren:* May I add a third reason for Gibbon's survival? Those two reasons are doubtless important ones, but he also is witty, and wit is something which is difficult to kill. As everyone knows, the book is delightful for its epigrams. They are not as dark and somber and tragic as those of Tacitus, who was his master in history and whom he praises as the most beautiful artist in the field.

*Cairns:* You would give him also the quality of irony which he claimed to have learned from Pascal, would you not?

*Van Doren:* I was assuming irony under the word "wit." But the following sentence, for instance, which is encountered at the beginning of the very second chapter, is the sort of thing I have in mind: "The various modes of worship which prevailed in the Roman world were all considered by the people as equally true, by the philosopher as equally false, and by the magistrate as equally useful." Gibbon was undoubtedly smiling to himself under his eighteenth-century wig as he wrote that. And I am reminded of Byron's famous line in *Childe Harold* in which he referred to Gibbon as "sapping a solemn creed with solemn sneer."

*Cairns:* But at the same time I have no doubt that you feel there is an element of truth in the quotation you read. Not only is it witty, but it is a generalization that holds true also for other notions at various times and places.

*Van Doren:* It is pretty hard for me to call a thing witty in which I don't find truth.

*Tate:* It has been often said that Gibbon, whether intentionally or not, delivers in this work an attack on Christianity, in fact upon all revealed religion.

*Van Doren:* I should say not merely Christianity. Some of the good Christians of the eighteenth century, and Byron was referring to them, were unhappy because they thought he had attacked their religion and their religion alone.

*Cairns:* His account of Christianity is one of the great things in the book. It is one of the best examples of the use of rational method in the study of religious history that we have. Not the least interesting thing about it is the ineffectiveness of the replies it has provoked.

*Tate:* It is interesting that in his treatment of Mohammedanism, a religion which doesn't affect the particular culture in which Gibbon lived, he can be extremely tolerant; that is, Gibbon with Mohammedanism is at liberty to strip away all the theology and reduce it to a simple moral code; and he admires greatly, at a distance of course, certain virtues of the ancient Arabians.

*Van Doren:* Yes, but I never heard of a Mohammedan being pleased by this book.

*Tate:* Oh, no, not at all.

*Cairns:* As a matter of fact, the Mohammedans have a right not to be pleased. The sources available to Gibbon for that part of his study were extremely limited. It is one of the few sections of the book which stands today in need of extensive revision.

*Van Doren:* A Mohammedan would regret the trimming away of the so-called excesses of his religion just as much as a Christian would regret it.

*Cairns:* But don't you think that Gibbon's view of Mohammedanism is the typical view of the eighteenth century?

*Van Doren:* Toward all religions.

*Cairns:* Yes, not only is this book a history of Rome, but it seems to me also to be a history of the eighteenth century. That is to say, as Buckle once said, "There will always be a connection between the way in which men contemplate the past and the way in which they contemplate the present."

*Tate:* Isn't it provincial to that extent—provincial in time?

*Cairns:* Yes, but I know no better book to take us inside of the eighteenth century than Gibbon's *Decline and Fall.*

*Van Doren:* Mr. Cairns, you are familiar enough with Mr. Tate's own books to know that the charge of provincialism is scarcely a charge to him. Perhaps the highest praise that Mr. Tate can bestow upon any culture is that it is provincial. Am I right, Mr. Tate?

*Cairns:* Don't commit yourself, Mr. Tate.

*Tate:* I would have to qualify Mr. Van Doren's statement a little.

*Cairns:* I didn't want Mr. Tate to commit himself because I wanted to ask him if he did not think that modern history, so-called scientific history, is not provincial in an opprobrious sense.

*Tate:* Yes, in the opprobrious sense it is, and I think that Gibbon's brand of provincialism is greatly to be preferred, because it is humane, comprehensive and civilized. Many modern historians pursue what they call "historical method"—some abstract theory from the viewpoint of which, even if the theory were valid, it would be impossible for anybody to write as a civilized man.

*Van Doren:* I took it for granted, Mr. Tate, when I said that you have gone on record as liking provincialism, that you were liking it in the best sense of the term—provincialism meaning for you, if I may paraphrase you, nothing perhaps much more than a unity of view.

*Tate:* Unity and confidence of judgment.

*Van Doren:* Confidence in the right to make certain assumptions.

*Cairns:* The modern historian is provincial in that sense also.

*Van Doren:* Not in his moral assumptions. I think moral assumptions are very important to Mr. Tate.

*Cairns:* They are not present, I should say, in the modern historian; or rather, moral assumptions are present in the provincial sense in the opprobrious use of that term. They have a unity of view in the sense that it seems to me most of them suffer from the delusion that history can be scientific or objective.

*Van Doren:* And of course the man who praises himself as scientific in almost any field these days is likely to conceal within his writing here and there assumptions which he is not aware of, metaphors which he doesn't know he is using.

*Tate:* But which are not strictly scientific; they're only metaphors derived from real sciences.

*Van Doren:* Gibbon, however, always seems to know what he is saying.

*Tate:* Now look at the metaphor implicit in the title of this great book: *The Decline and Fall.* There's no pretense of scientific validity whatever.

*Cairns:* Why do you think he writes the history of Rome at that period—why does he begin with the decline of Rome?

*Van Doren:* If he is going to write a history of the Roman Empire, why doesn't he write the book which some people actually call, through error, "Gibbon's Rise and Fall of the Roman Empire"?

*Tate:* It's a difficult question. If we could answer it, we'd get at the source of Gibbon's historical interest—the thing that motivated the twenty years' study that he put into this work.

*Van Doren:* I have always assumed that his interest in the decline of Rome, rather than in its prime, was an interest in the great age of darkness which in his mind stretched between the great and philosophic days of Greece and Rome and the great and philosophic days of the eighteenth century. For him, I dare say, the whole region in between was something like a dark valley, a depression.

*Cairns:* Yes, it was. And he took his history and his philosophy seriously in spite of his wit. He once said that history was for the philosophic mind what gaming was to the Marquis de Dangeau. He saw in it a system, connections, a sequence, while others discerned only the caprices of fortune.

*Tate:* This question has often occurred to me in reading Gibbon: Could Gibbon have written the history of a civilization at its height? I'm inclined to think that he couldn't. He was not interested in that. His bias is very powerful against the Middle Ages, against the civilization which we ordinarily call Christendom. He couldn't even see it. He was interested in showing that a great civilization had been undermined by the barbarians and by this new religion. But I am inclined to think that he couldn't have handled even the great age of Rome. He had to take a negative point of view.

*Van Doren:* But think of the great histories—aren't they histories of decline? Tacitus is the contemporary historian of a decline. Thucydides is the historian of the death of Greece. Prescott in *The Conquest of Mexico* is more interested, I should say, in the death of ancient American civilization than he is in the triumph of the Spaniards.

*Tate:* Well, could we generalize and say that the historical consciousness arises . . .

*Van Doren:* Out of a sense of loss.

*Tate:* Out of a sense of loss. The historian goes back to recover and reconstruct. It seems to me that is one reason why Gibbon is a great historian. His procedure is very much like that of the poet. The poet has very much the same mode of imagination. He does not explain, he re-creates.

*Van Doren:* Would you mind qualifying the word "poet" by adding the word "tragic"?

*Tate:* History is tragedy?

*Van Doren:* A historian is a tragic poet.

*Cairns:* I think we may be misrepresenting Gibbon to some extent. He begins with the period A.D. 96 to 180, with the period of the five good emperors: Nerva, Trajan, Hadrian, Antoninus Pius and the philosopher king, Marcus Aurelius. Gibbon thought that the period from 96 to 180 A.D. was the period in which the human race was most happy and prosperous. It is true, I think, that he shared the eighteenth-century view that there had been four great periods in history: The classical age of Greece, the Augustan age, the Renaissance and the Age of Louis XIV. But at the beginning of his history he put his finger on what seemed to him the highest point of the Roman Empire. It was the period which he most admired of all periods in history. Liberty and government were apparently reconciled; from Britain to the Euphrates the Pax Romana ruled; education was general and there was a polite society.

*Tate:* I suppose we've got to grant him that. Perhaps my criticism of him is based on a modern revision of that conception of the ancient world; that is, we would be inclined to think of the Periclean age as the great age.

*Van Doren:* The age of the Roman republic.

*Tate:* Exactly.

*Cairns:* That reminds me of the theory of a contemporary historian who may be read a hundred years from now just as Gibbon is being read after a hundred years. I am thinking of Arnold Toynbee and his *Study of History*. He thought that Gibbon began at the wrong point, that the Roman Empire did not begin to decline at this period; that the age of the Antonines was merely an autumn summer. Toynbee, as Hegel did before him, puts together the Roman civilization and the Greek civilization, which we are inclined to separate and treat more or less as distinct cultures; but Toynbee in his own volumes regards them as one culture which he terms the Hellenic Society. He thinks that Thucydides described the fall of the Roman Empire; that the Hellenic Society, the Greco-Roman age, committed suicide at the time of the Atheno-Peloponnesian War in 431 B.C.; and that Gibbon's own history was merely a history of an Indian summer. He believes that the historian-coroner, in reporting upon how the members of the Hellenic Society perpetrated their monstrous crime, would probably lay equal emphasis upon inter-state and inter-class war.

*Tate:* Spengler puts Greece and Rome together in one "classical mind."

*Van Doren:* And of course Gibbon also can think of a culture there which is spread over both Greece and Rome. But I am interested in a phrase he uses somewhere—I have forgotten just where in this vast book—in which he refers to the Roman Empire as a polite and powerful Empire. The conjunction of those two adjectives is very amusing—polite and powerful.

*Cairns:* That again is eighteenth century.

*Van Doren:* It is eighteenth century, but also he is referring to something he really loved, the Rome which had got through the civil wars of Julius Caesar, Pompey, and all the rest, the Rome which had got through those civil wars and was peaceful and polite and grand and luxurious for a couple of centuries. It was an attractive age for him. I think it was a kind of age he would like to think was being inaugurated in his own time.

*Tate:* You feel that in his discussion of ancient polytheism. It seems to me that his criticism of the scrambled-up religions of Rome at that period is rather perfunctory, even insincere because in the long run he rather likes polytheism; it's mild, tolerant, ceremonious. He says there was not much religious conviction in it, but it was a powerful social unifier.

*Van Doren:* And to the magistrate it was useful.

*Tate:* Now what would Gibbon have felt perhaps about Greece just before the great age of Pericles? He might have felt that the Greeks took religion a little too seriously.

*Van Doren:* It is pretty clear to me that although he comes out for toleration of religion and indeed for what he calls religious indifference, he really would prefer an age which was nothing but "philosophic."

*Cairns:* He was a humanist, wouldn't you say? The last of the humanists? His philosophy, however, is not the philosophy of Voltaire, for example. It is much more a matter of form than substance.

*Van Doren:* He would prefer an age that had no religion at all.

*Tate:* Do you recall the passage which I imagine not even Gibbon had the boldness to expand? He refers to a legend which says that Tiberius thought of making Christ one of the gods in the Roman Pantheon, and he speculates in a brief sentence upon what would have happened to the world if Tiberius had succeeded. That would have neutralized Christianity completely; it would have destroyed it.

*Van Doren:* It would have taken away all the energy that it had because it was being persecuted.

*Cairns:* We ought to remember that no one before Gibbon had given such a wide and penetrating account of the rise of Christianity as a historic event. That problem is a narrow one and Gibbon treated it strictly on the historic plane. It was a bold undertaking because he was attempting to show that the methods of the historian could be applied in illuminating fashion to the development of Christianity. His own personal attitude toward religion, apart from his attitude as a historian, I suppose was some form of the eighteenth-century liberal outlook.

*Van Doren:* His only criticism of Socrates, whom of course he adores, is that Socrates had one little vein of superstition in him; that is to say he had a daemon. You remember the daemon that comes into the *Apology*. Gibbon would really like to look forward to a world—maybe he thought it was going to be in the twentieth century—in which religion would be nothing except a study for historians, in which the whole earth would be full of people walking about gracefully and with dignity, talking philosophy.

*Tate:* Reason as he understood it.

*Van Doren:* Yes, reason.

*Tate:* Which wasn't very profoundly rational. It was mild, tolerant and . . .

*Van Doren:* Negative. A reasonable man didn't do this, didn't do that; he didn't commit any madness. I take this book to be, among other things, a great panorama of mad actions by the Crusaders, by the Mohammedans, by Genghis Khan, by the Christians, by the perverted emperors of Rome. You find humanity in this book to be something of a menagerie, howling in the great trough between two ages of enlightenment.

*Cairns:* I think we get that impression because he views history as a panorama, he sees events as tableaux, one succeeding the other. He doesn't become passionate about any event; he has an insatiable curiosity, but he has no indignation and he rarely attempts to evaluate.

*Tate:* Don't you think, Mr. Cairns, to go back to the point with which we started off, that the pictorial method largely explains his power and continuing interest?

*Cairns:* Yes, he takes large segments of his subject and presents them serially, one after another. He is descriptive and he isn't analytical.

*Tate:* Exactly.

*Cairns:* And I think that what he describes in his book he has completely visualized. That is one source of his strength. I don't know any historian who is more concrete and who has a greater interest in details; when he describes a Persian banquet he tells you the number of courses. He goes into the nature of Greek fire; he describes cities. He was never in Constantinople, but his description of Constantinople is exceedingly accurate. His chapters on Roman law have been printed separately as a text for use in the German universities.

*Van Doren:* And of course the picture he leaves in your mind of Imperial Rome is very gorgeous and very completely furnished.

*Tate:* The description of the fire in the reign of Nero is certainly one of the great passages in historical writing. It has great economy and precision.

*Van Doren:* We also have a sense as we read him that he is never describing anything under the illusion that it is different from what it was. For instance, he didn't like to criticize his master Tacitus, but he implies a criticism of Tacitus's book on the Germans when he denies that Tacitus's description of them gives you a picture of a perfect people. He says: "They passed their lives in a state of ignorance and poverty, which it has pleased some declaimers to dignify with the appellation of virtuous simplicity." You see, Gibbon hated barbarism in any form, whether it was rich or poor, whether it was remote or near. The Germans for him were barbarous, they were "wretchedly destitute" of art, and he didn't fall into Tacitus's error—if Tacitus did err—of idealizing these people because of what they lacked.

*Cairns:* I do not think Gibbon idealized anything. Whether he was for it or against it he merely described it.

*Van Doren:* His tendency perhaps was to take anything down just a little bit.

*Cairns:* And he enjoyed it particularly if it were a little eccentric.

*Van Doren:* Yes, his attempt was to reduce this whole thousand years of human life to a certain level, which was for him of course the right level, the eighteenth-century level.

*Cairns:* The point has been made that Gibbon did not admire the barbarians. We have also said that the book really lacks a philosophy in the sense that modern histories have a philosophy, namely, a coherent theory of why things happen, why Rome fell, for example. Perhaps, however, Gibbon had a notion of why Rome fell. If you read the book carefully he puts forward five or six notions. The one that it is generally agreed he really believed in, was that Rome fell because of the triumph of barbarism and religion. Whether Gibbon believed that or not I don't know. He also attributed the fall of Rome to other things; to the long peace and uniformity of government; people became soft, their minds were reduced to the same level, genius could not appear and the military spirit was weakened.

*Van Doren:* It almost sounds like an inconsistency, doesn't it? Perhaps it isn't, because Gibbon is rarely inconsistent. We ourselves said that he admired the long reign of politeness and power with which he begins, and yet he more than insinuates, he states, that Rome had too long a peace. She softened and became effeminate.

*Cairns:* Yes, and there was too much luxury. And he also said, and this is in his own words—"the stupendous fabric yielded to the pressure of its own weight." It is important to ask this question: Is his theory of the fall of Rome such that it could be applied to any other Empire?

*Van Doren:* "Its own weight"—Gibbon is the sort of man who would expect nothing to last forever.

*Cairns:* I believe he went further and even hoped that nothing would last forever—now that the age of the Five Good Emperors was over. The study of history did not fill him with elation. He thought that the history of empires was the history of human misery; history, he believed, was little more than the register of the crimes, follies and misfortunes of mankind.

*Van Doren:* Any historian, I dare say, is impressed by the

melancholy thought that nothing lasts. And by the thought also that after a long, very painful period of progress some new invention, some apparently trivial change in the arts of mankind can overturn everything. He has this remark at the end of the sixty-fifth chapter, referring to the invention of gunpowder: "If we contrast the rapid progress of this mischievous discovery with the slow and laborious advances of reason, science and the arts of peace, a philosopher, according to his temper, will laugh or weep at the folly of mankind." Gibbon is more likely to laugh, I take it.

*Cairns:* He was a man who apparently had a streak of optimism in him because in 1781 he said that "the Balance of Power"—he is speaking of contemporary Europe—"will continue to fluctuate, and the prosperity of our own or the neighboring kingdoms may be alternately exalted or depressed; but these partial events cannot essentially injure our general state of happiness, the system of arts and laws and manners, which so advantageously distinguish above the rest of Mankind the Europeans and their colonists." You will remember at that time England was at war with the American Colonies, France, Spain, Holland, and things didn't look so well. By 1783 it was all straightened out and Britannia again ruled the waves.

*Van Doren:* The question was asked at the beginning of our discussion why it was that Gibbon chose to write concerning the decline and fall of the Roman Empire rather than of its prime. He himself in his autobiography has written two very beautiful and famous passages describing the inception of the work and its completion. They give his answer to the question—quite simply, perhaps too simply. "It was at Rome on the 15th of October, 1764, as I sat musing amidst the ruins of the capital, while the barefooted friars were singing Vespers in the Temple of Jupiter, that the idea of writing the decline and fall of the city first started to my mind." Then later: "I have presumed to mark the moment of conception, I shall now commemorate the hour of my final deliverance. It was on the day, or rather night, of the 27th of June, 1787, between the hours of eleven and twelve, that I wrote the last lines of the last page in a summer house in my garden. After laying down my pen I took several turns in a berceau, or covered walk of acacias which commands the prospect of the country, the lake and the mountains. I will not dissemble the first emotions of joy on recovery of my freedom and perhaps the establishment of my fame. But my pride was soon humbled and a sober melancholy was spread over my mind by the idea that I had taken an everlasting leave of an old and agreeable companion, and that whatsoever might be the future fate of my history, the life of the historian must be short and precarious."

(1770-1831)

# HEGEL

# *Philosophy of History*

*"ONE man has understood me," said the German philosopher Hegel, "and even he has not." Hegel is acknowledged to be one of the most difficult of authors, whether his subject is logic or religion, art or history. But his* PHILOSOPHY OF HISTORY, *made up from lectures given at the University of Berlin, is relatively easy reading, and for this reason among others it has been the most popular of his works. Another reason is the interest which the modern world has taken in generalizations of history; for a "philosophy" of history can be nothing more than a generalization or simplification of the too many things we know about the past. It is an attempt to state the broad tendencies in human time and to suggest the direction we now are taking whether we know it or not. Hegel, who of course helped to create such an interest, anticipates much that has been said by his successors, notably Spengler in Germany. For him the state is a person, and its rela-*

*tions with other states or persons, together with the relation of them all to the "world-spirit," is the story which history tells. The world-spirit expresses itself now through one people and now through another, according as liberty travels its rounds. The Oriental, the Classical and the Germanic peoples have had their turns at ascendancy; and the implication is that history now approaches its end with Germany at the helm. Limited as Hegel's view may be, by comparison to others it is broad; nor should it be forgotten that he was among the first to attack so formidable a problem.*

(MR. BERTRAND RUSSELL, GUEST)

*Cairns:* Mr. Russell, I have a letter here from you in which you state: "Hegel's *Philosophy of History* is important as a source of much evil, but (I think) of no good." Would you like to amplify that statement? It was the last sentence in your letter, and it was left hanging in the air. It whetted my appetite.

*Russell:* I am quite willing to amplify that statement. I think Hegel's *Philosophy of History* is a very important book indeed, judged by the effects it has had, and a totally unimportant book judged by any truth that it may contain.

*Tate:* Mr. Russell, don't you think it may contain a few incidental truths here and there?

*Russell:* It is a long book and it is difficult for a man to avoid saying something true when he uses so many words.

*Van Doren:* I like your distinction between influential books and true books. Rousseau's *Confessions* is often said to be an important book because it is influential. I assume it cannot be called important because it is true.

*Russell:* We do not know much about Rousseau's *Confessions,* whether they are true or false.

*Cairns:* Would you like to be a little more specific about Hegel?

*Russell:* I should be glad to be more specific about Hegel. I think Hegel's *Philosophy of History* is important, partly because it presented a pattern in history—a scheme, a system—according to which historical events were supposed to have developed, which of course people like. It is a simple formula and they think "now we understand it all"; if it is false, they do not notice it.

*Cairns:* That is an objection to all philosophies of history so far devised. The safest course, it has always seemed to me, is to reject the system and ascertain if the philosophical position of the writer contributes anything illuminating to the discussion of particular historical points. Nothing short of omniscience can devise a system that will embrace all the world.

*Tate:* But didn't Hegel, himself, say that he actually understood it all?

*Russell: He* understood it all. Oh, yes, of course, he understood it all.

*Van Doren:* As if he knew all history.

*Russell:* He, of course, happened to have read it all; so he knew.

*Tate:* You say his formula is simple. Could it be stated briefly?

*Russell:* Everything proceeds by thesis, antithesis and synthesis, and what moves it is the self-development of the Idea, and the Idea is what Hegel happened to believe. The whole course of the universe is making it just such as Hegel thought it was. That is the formula.

*Tate:* Don't you think one of the marvelous things in Hegel's system is that it applies both at the top and at the bottom? That is, he has a speciously convincing psychological argument, almost like Descartes', that consciousness has two aspects. First, it knows something, then the next problem is what it knows. It knows itself. When Spirit, or Idea, is triumphant, then the condition is reached where we become pure spirituality, and everybody will be merged in the state.

*Cairns:* Hegel claims that the great virtue of the system is that it accounts for everything in the universe. It is all-embracing, and it assigns to everything in the universe the place that is absolutely proper for it.

*Russell:* It is bound to; he thought the universe as a whole was the only reality, and if it did not account for the universe, it did not account for anything at all, because he thought you could not pick the universe to bits.

*Cairns:* Do you object to his primary aims? They are first to write a universal history and secondly to write history in terms of ideas representing periods.

*Russell:* I object to the second point. I do not mind a man writing universal history, if he has time; but I do object to the notion that there is a simple scheme or thread running through it all.

*Tate:* Most of us would probably disagree with a great deal that Gibbon says, but you would not object to that kind of comprehensive history, would you?

*Russell:* No, I don't.

*Cairns:* Would you mind elaborating a little your objection to writing history in terms of abstract ideas?

*Russell:* Such a system must be false. Let us say, if you think so, that it is what Hegel calls rational; of course, there are abstract ideas that can be distilled out of the facts, but they must be taken out of the facts and it is not a rational development.

*Tate:* Didn't Hegel try to distill the facts out of the ideas?

*Van Doren:* And it was easy for him to do that because any facts that he found he could use. He could choose among the infinite facts there are.

*Cairns:* I understand Mr. Russell's point to be that he objects to Hegel's system, or rather Hegel's basic notion that historical sequences follow the order of logical categories.

*Russell:* I object to that.

*Cairns:* I have no disagreement with you on that point. Such a notion is bound to lead to absurdities, as in Hegel's deification of Prussia. The order of logical categories, at least in Hegel's system, is finite, but since historical development is not finite, one of the two must yield. In Hegel's hands it was history that yielded. The question now, however, is not whether Hegel's system is true, but the nature of the objections which can be brought against historians for writing history in terms of abstract ideas.

*Russell:* Take Hegel's disciple, Marx. You can get Marx out of Hegel by just a few transformations. Where Hegel talks of nations, Marx talks of classes. Where Hegel talks about the Idea, Marx talks about methods of production. With those two changes the two are practically identical.

*Cairns:* But you are not going to attribute the sins of the disciple to the master?

*Russell:* I say they are the same sins. I do not say that Hegel is responsible, but I say that the same sin is there in both cases, of thinking there is a simple formula.

*Tate:* Won't you describe the relation of Marx to Hegel, Mr. Russell?

*Russell:* It was just the relation of a Hegelian of the left. Hegel started two movements in philosophy, the one of extreme conservatism and the other of extreme revolution. The one represented by the conservative Hegelians and the other by Marx and his followers. But there is not nearly as much difference between Marx and Hegel as there seems to be.

*Van Doren:* Couldn't the same objection be raised against both historians, insofar as Marx and Hegel were historians? For them, history writes itself. There is an idea, there is a spirit; the idea and the spirit express themselves in the things that have actually happened. The aim, as Hegel somewhere says, is equivalent to the result. In other words, whatever we see has happened in the world must have happened. For my part, I can see no point in either of them calling himself a historian, properly speaking; history is too easy for them to write. Anything that happened had to happen.

*Tate:* It seems to me that Hegel's conception of freedom is a complete paradox and is unreal. If history is the determinism of thesis, antithesis and synthesis, then freedom has no real meaning at all; it is nothing but a fiction.

*Van Doren:* History is completely determined.

*Tate:* Yes, an intellectual determinism, a logical determinism of history.

*Russell:* Certainly there is, but Hegel uses freedom in a very peculiar sense. Freedom means the right to obey the police, and it means nothing else at all in the works of Hegel.

*Van Doren:* I wonder if you don't want to substitute one word there. This might be fairer to Hegel: Freedom is the desire to obey. Not the right to obey, but the desire.

*Cairns:* I think he would say it is a duty to obey because the happy life, as he defined it, was one lived in accordance with duty.

*Van Doren:* I do not think so. When he describes a happy people, an effective people such as the Athenians, he says that a single Athenian's instinct was to love Athens and to obey its laws; and he represents the English people of the eighteenth century and the early nineteenth century as very happy at being Englishmen. There is nothing else they want to be. Their desires coincide, as he says, doubtless in a pretty highfalutin way, with their destiny. There is nonsense in the background of that, but there is something real in the foreground.

*Cairns:* I do not think Mr. Russell would make your point a ground of criticism of Hegel, if there is any evidence in support of the position that you just outlined. As I understand it, Mr. Russell, you think that the course of history cannot be determined speculatively.

*Russell:* I do.

*Cairns:* At the same time, you also think that the course of history is subject to laws; but that they cannot be determined because of their complexity.

*Russell:* I think the course of history is subject to laws and is probably for a sufficiently wise person deterministic; but nobody is wise enough. It is far too complicated and nobody can work it out; and the person who says he has done so is a charlatan.

*Van Doren:* Back to the subject of freedom for a while. Freedom probably does not mean freedom to do nothing, does it? Freedom is surely freedom to do something.

*Tate:* I think Hegel bases his most plausible argument on that very point, that there is no such thing as perfect freedom, or pure freedom.

*Cairns:* At one end he puts despotism and at the other end anarchy.

*Tate:* Hegel has a real insight there, even if it is a very common one and not at all profound. There is no such thing as unchecked freedom. But the trouble with Hegel is that he proceeds then to take that insight and contradict it with his logical determinism.

*Russell:* There is a different point here that we have not yet raised. That is Hegel's worship of the state, which I think is a far worse thing than any of the points we have mentioned. He says that the state is the perfect embodiment of spirit, that it is the divine idea as it exists on earth.

*Cairns:* I do not know what that means; it sounds like nonsense. Would you like to explain it to us?

*Russell:* It seems to me, of course, nonsense; but what Hegel means by it is that the state is the element of unity in the community, and the element of unity in the world is what he calls God; therefore, the state is analogous to God. He has first misused the word "God"; then he misuses the word "state," and so he comes to the conclusion that the state is what is divine.

*Tate:* Is he perfectly straightforward when he maintains that this vast unity of the state is based fundamentally upon a prior moral unity in the individual? I am not quite convinced by that, because I don't think he is much interested in unity in the individual.

*Van Doren:* He is interesting here. He seems to say that a man who is fortunate enough to be born into a state and not into a tribe such as the Scythians, for instance, or the Thracians—a man who is fortunate enough to be born in Athens is indeed fortunate because he has something to obey, something he is delighted to obey and honor.

*Russell:* But I think it is the community and not the state. Let me give an illustration. Hegel says: All spiritual reality that a human being possesses, he possesses through the state. Now let us apply that to St. Paul, who said he was a Roman citizen. Is anybody going to say that all the spiritual reality of St. Paul came from the Roman State? The thing is preposterous.

*Cairns:* I am not sure it is as simple as that. Hegel gives this illustration to explain his notion of freedom. He says it is realized by acting within the system and not in opposition to it. He gives a biological analogy, as I recall it; if you want to realize your full capacities as a human being, you must do so within the limitations of your human organism. If you oppose it, you do not realize your aspirations and you destroy your organism.

*Russell:* But there are many organisms besides the state. Take the church; or suppose you were a man of science and belonged to a learned body.

*Cairns:* That is true; and the political question is: Which institution has the right to demand the greatest degree of loyalty?

*Tate:* What did Socrates do about this very problem when he was condemned? Did he not accept the verdict of Athens and refuse to escape? He rejected the chance to evade the sentence of death. Now, why did he do that? Was it the community or the state that commanded his loyalty even to the point of death?

*Cairns:* My recollection is that Socrates said it was the state.

*Russell:* There it was, I think, the state; but then his loyalty was extremely limited. He made it perfectly clear that he would not stop talking, not for all the states in the world. He said there was only one way he could be made to stop talking; that was to make him drink the hemlock. However much they ordered him not to talk, he would talk. He makes that quite clear.

*Van Doren:* Of course, he could not have talked in any other country than Greece. Your instance of St. Paul was interesting, but say a contemporary of St. Paul lived in Vladivostok with all St. Paul's qualities, his brains and his heart. Now, you deny that St. Paul's achievement can be attributed to the existence of the Roman state. I think it might be so attributed, because a citizen of Vladivostok with those same qualities could have got nowhere.

*Russell:* I did not say his achievement; I said his spiritual reality—which is Hegel's phrase. Now, the spiritual reality of the man in Vladivostok may be the same.

*Cairns:* Some sentences have been quoted from Hegel that certainly cannot stand analysis. But have we been entirely fair to Hegel? He says explicitly that he is opposed to despotism; that the monarch or the ruler must act for the best interests of the people; that the monarch must encourage the utmost liberty among his people so that he will have an informed public opinion to guide him in his decisions. The monarch must encourage the liberty of the press to the utmost, that is to say, to the limit of abuse. This means that the ruler must submit to vilification on the part of the press as the price of greatness.

*Russell:* I think you are really overestimating what he says about the liberty of the press. You are not allowing for the fact that he always uses words in a Pickwickian sense.

*Cairns:* He does indeed.

*Russell:* He says there should be liberty of the press but not to the point of making the government ridiculous. It must stop short of that. And he sees a whole lot of limitations about that.

*Cairns:* But he also does say that the ruler must endure vilification.

*Russell:* He says this of the despot, for instance: The ruler should not be a despot. A despot is an absolute monarch ruling over a country which is not Prussia. That is the definition of a despot.

*Cairns:* Is that fair? Let us apply his own dialectic to that problem. What is the thesis? Despotism—is it not? The antithesis is democracy and aristocracy, and the synthesis is monarchy. He must, therefore, on his own logic reject despotism wherever it is; and he did so, it seems to me, in his *Philosophy of History.*

*Russell:* Take again, Mr. Cairns, what you said about public opinion. He is very clear that public opinion is not always right and that it must not always be submitted to; there may be a certain expression of it; but the ruler should not think it is right.

*Cairns:* He is certainly clear that public opinion should not always be submitted to. I do not think you would insist that a ruler should be bound by public opinion in all cases.

*Russell:* Absolutely bound. I do not know what else there is that is better, because while public opinion is very likely to be wrong, so is the ruler.

*Cairns:* That is right. But you must allow for the case where the ruler may have private sources of information not open to public opinion.

*Van Doren:* Private wisdom?

*Cairns:* No, I won't say private wisdom. No ruler's private wisdom is necessarily greater than that of public opinion. But I insist we must provide for the case of greater factual knowledge on the part of the ruler.

*Tate:* May I ask a question about another phase of this same point? In what respect does Hegel's despotism as thesis, aristocracy and democracy as antithesis, and monarchy as the synthesis of the two differ from the kind of compromise that Aristotle contemplated? I think it is the Aristotelian "commonwealth" that is a compromise between oligarchy and raw democracy. Now, doesn't Aristotle have some notion there of the Hegelian "synthesis"?

*Cairns:* It has always seemed to me that Hegel's theory was quite similar to some of Aristotle's thought.

*Russell:* I agree. I think it is very similar; but I do not think the better of it on that acccount.

*Cairns:* Are you implying that Aristotle is as wicked a man as Hegel?

*Russell:* Yes.

*All together:* Oh, you are?

*Tate:* Mr. Russell, before we began this conversation you said that Plato was very wicked. You would have neither of them, then?

*Russell:* I think that philosophy has suffered four misfortunes in the world's history: Plato, Aristotle, Kant and Hegel. If they were eliminated, philosophy would have done very well.

*Cairns:* Who would be left, Mr. Russell? We will exclude present company.

*Russell:* There would be very many people left. There would be Locke, Berkeley, Hume, Leibnitz and Spinoza.

*Tate:* A very bad tradition, Mr. Russell.

*Van Doren:* What about this man as a historian? I was interested in a certain conversion of terms that he seemed to make. Here is this sentence: "History in general is, therefore, the development of Spirit in time, as nature is the development of the

Idea in space." He makes a distinction between time and space which may remind us of Lessing in his *Laocöon.*

*Cairns:* I think it goes back to a point we were discussing before. In history the Idea unfolds its various phases in time and the dominant phase at any epoch is embodied in a dominant people. The succession of these phases, in Hegel's theory, constitutes world history.

*Van Doren:* Perhaps it is a modern—I wonder if it is an especially modern—notion that a philosopher can turn his attention from space relations which are either metaphysical or physical, scientific or rational, to those relations which are in time? Here is a philosopher trying suddenly to develop a new language—altogether a temporal language instead of a spatial one.

*Cairns:* He devised his own language to a large extent. While he viewed history as a temporal sequence, he did not thereby neglect spatial elements.

*Van Doren:* I wonder if you can see things arranged in time as clearly as you can see them arranged in space?

*Russell:* I think you can, yes. Of course, it did not suit him so well arranged in space because he wanted a dialectic process, so that the one-dimensional series was more suitable for his purposes.

*Van Doren:* But dialectic originally considered was not anything that took place in time, was it?

*Russell:* No, it was purely logical, but it was a one-dimensional series.

*Van Doren:* Something anterior in logic is not necessarily earlier, is it?

*Russell:* Not necessarily, but for Hegel it was.

*Van Doren:* Hegel literalized the anterior and posterior relation into before and after.

*Cairns:* If he proceeded in space, he would have to exclude America from the development of his system, as he did anyway.

*Van Doren:* Exclude what?

*Cairns:* America.

*Van Doren:* I thought you said a "miracle."

*Tate:* It is the same thing.

*Russell:* He did not exclude America. He said America was some day going to be very important; there would be a great war, he said, between North America and South America; that was when America was going to be important.

*Cairns:* He said America at that time, and he was speaking or writing in the 1820's, was not worth discussing because it was an echo of Europe, which may have been true in the 1820's.

*Tate:* Now, this question of time and space: I should like to ask about Spengler's relation to Hegel. It seems to me that Spengler's leading notion is the flow of time; it eliminates space altogether; the Faustian or modern culture is the great culture, and space is annihilated. Do you think he derives from Hegel?

*Russell:* A little, I think, yes.

*Tate:* His notion of the destiny, destiny of the world historical figure and of a culture, seems to me to come from Hegel.

*Russell:* Yes, the whole notion of the pattern in history. Of course, there is one spatial element in Hegel's *Philosophy of History*—he thinks that the absolute idea is always moving westward.

*Tate:* That is a geographical notion.

*Cairns:* Do you think it is unreasonable to think of the universe as Hegel did, both of nature and mind, as a process, a development, a history?

*Russell:* It is unreasonable to think of it as the development of an idea; because, while possibly it may be, it certainly is not a development of my ideas or your ideas or Hegel's ideas. Hegel assumes that he is as wise as the Creator of the universe when he says it is his ideas that are developing.

*Van Doren:* He tells us equally little whether we ask him what the Idea is or whether we ask him how he knows what it is. In either case, he has no answer to give us. If we do not believe this book, he cannot convince us.

*Russell:* I always think a man's inconsistencies are the key to his passions. Hegel thought that unity was the important thing and that the whole was always more real than its part, and so forth. He should, therefore, have emphasized mankind rather than separate nations or separate states. In fact, he makes the state supreme. He says no state has any duty whatever in relation to any other state. War is, therefore, a thing not to be deplored but is good. That is inconsistent with his metaphysic and shows therefore that he had a passion in favor of war.

*Van Doren:* The significant events for him have been military events.

*Russell:* He says men are warriors. He says, "War has the higher significance, that through it the moral health of peoples is preserved in their indifference toward the stabilizing of finite determination." He says war is the condition in which we take seriously the vanity of temporal goods and things.

*Tate:* Don't you think probably in the long run he would contemplate a world state, a Pax Germanica?

*Cairns:* No, he expressly repudiated the idea of a universal peace.

*Tate:* Would that not logically develop if the Idea is going to be completely realized?

*Russell:* That is just the point. It should have followed from his premises.

*Van Doren:* Is there anything for a philosopher to worry about in the notion some people have—Tacitus had it, William James had it too—that peace can be degenerating and softening? If we could imagine peace stretching ahead of us now for 10,000 years, is it possible to imagine what human beings would then be like? What would they be doing, what would they be interested in? Would they be bored to death? Is this a problem to be solved? The existence of such questions is the reason philosophers have advanced for worrying about the notion of universal peace.

*Russell:* Yes, they have; but I always regard that as a mark of brutality. I think that if you have brutal instincts, you like killing people. War is the only occasion when you can do it without being hanged. That is the sole reason why anybody likes war; anybody who praises war praises it from beastliness.

*Tate:* Isn't it possible to admit that while we dislike war, there may be no way to eliminate it from history?

*Russell:* Not from past history, but from future history you could eliminate it by the very method that Hegel so dislikes. Kant had proposed a league of nations and Hegel says we must not have that, because war is ennobling.

*Cairns:* That is one aspect of Hegel's general position on the question of the validity of judgments passed on nations. Hegel said that the world's spirit was the final tribunal and judge of the nations (exclusive of Hegel) and that no international state or court which passes judgment upon the peoples is possible; that the judgment of the nations is found in the fate which awaits them in the process of world history.

*Tate:* Hegel, as we were saying, is a complex man. Mr. Russell said that his character could be revealed in his contradictions. Here is a minor passage which I find very revealing. It reveals both his vanity and his wit, but I do not know whether he reveals the vanity consciously. We must decide for ourselves.

"What pedagogue has not demonstrated of Alexander the Great, of Julius Caesar, that they were instigated by such passions and were consequently immoral men, whence the conclusion immediately follows that he, the pedagogue, is a better man than they, because he has not such passions, a proof of which lies in the fact that he does not conquer Asia, vanquish Darius and Porus, but while he enjoys life himself, lets others enjoy it too. These psychologists are particularly fond of contemplating those peculiarities of great historical figures which appertain to them as private persons. Man must eat and drink, he sustains relations to friends and acquaintances. He has passing impulses and ebullitions of temper. 'No man is a hero to his valet' is a well-known proverb; I have added—and Goethe repeated it ten years later —'but not because the former is no hero, but because the latter is a valet.' "

# A SELECTED BIBLIOGRAPHY


ARISTOTLE, *Politics*
*The Basic Works of Aristotle,* Edited by Richard McKeon, Random House, New York. $4.00

MACHIAVELLI, *The Prince*
*The Prince and The Discourses of Machiavelli,* Edited by Max Lerner, Modern Library, New York. 95 cents

PLATO, *Symposium*
*The Dialogues of Plato,* Two Volumes, The Jowett Translation, Random House, New York. $5.00

ARISTOTLE, *Ethics*
*The Basic Works of Aristotle,* Edited by Richard McKeon, Random House, New York. $4.00

MONTAIGNE, *Essays*
*The Essays of Montaigne,* The Florio Translation, Modern Library, New York. $1.25

PASCAL, *Pensées*
Translated by W. F. Trotter, Everyman's Library, New York. 90 cents.

ROUSSEAU, *Confessions*
*The Confessions of Jean Jacques Rousseau,* Everyman's Library, New York. 90 cents

MILL, *Autobiography*
World's Classics, Oxford University Press, New York. 80 cents

## *Selected Bibliography*


ADAMS, *The Education of Henry Adams*
Modern Library, New York. 95 cents

DEFOE, *Moll Flanders*
Modern Library, New York. 95 cents

TOLSTOY, *War and Peace*
Modern Library, New York. $1.25

PROUST, *Swann's Way*
Modern Library, New York. 95 cents

AESCHYLUS, *Prometheus Bound*
*The Complete Greek Drama,* Two Volumes, Edited by Whitney J. Oates and Eugene O'Neill, Jr., Random House, New York. $5.00

SHAKESPEARE, *Antony and Cleopatra*
The Macmillan Company, New York. $1.25

LESSING, *Laocoön*
Everyman's Library, New York. 90 cents

COLERIDGE, *Biographia Literaria*
*The Selected Poetry and Prose of Samuel Taylor Coleridge,* Random House, New York. $3.50

ARNOLD, *Essays in Criticism,* First and Second Series
The Macmillan Company, New York. $1.20 each

LUCRETIUS, *On the Nature of Things*
*The Stoic and Epicurean Philosophers,* The Complete Extant Writings of Epicurus, Epictetus, Lucretius and Marcus Aurelius, Edited by Whitney J. Oates, Random House, New York. $3.00

DANTE, *The Divine Comedy*
The Carlyle-Wicksteed prose translation, Modern Library, New York. 95 cents

MILTON, *Paradise Lost*
*The Complete Poetry and Selected Prose of John Milton,* Random House, New York. $3.50

BUNYAN, *The Pilgrim's Progress*
Houghton Mifflin Company, Boston, Mass. 60 cents

LEONARDO DA VINCI, *Notebooks*
Reynal and Hitchock, Inc., New York. $5.00

TACITUS, *History*
Books I and II, The Macmillan Company, New York. $1.40

GIBBON, *The Decline and Fall of the Roman Empire*
Two Volumes, Modern Library, New York. $1.25 each

HEGEL, *Philosophy of History*
*Hegel Selections,* Edited by Jacob Lowenberg, Modern Students' Library, Charles Scribner's Sons, New York. $1.25. *Lectures on the Philosophy of History,* Translated by J. Sibree, George Bell and Sons, Limited, London.

# INDEX

# Index

# Index

# Index

WITHDRAWN
JUN 25 2024
DAVID O. McKAY LIBRARY
BYU-IDAHO